# Political Philosophy

# Political Philosophy
## From Plato to Mao

Martin Cohen

Pluto Press
LONDON • STERLING, VIRGINIA

First published 2001 by Pluto Press
345 Archway Road, London N6 5AA
and 22883 Quicksilver Drive,
Sterling, VA 20166–2012, USA

www.plutobooks.com

British Library Cataloguing in Publication Data
A catalogue record for this book is available from
the British Library

Library of Congress Cataloging in Publication Data
applied for

ISBN 0 7453 1604 2 hardback
ISBN 0 7453 1603 4 paperback

10  09  08  07  06  05  04  03  02  01
10  9   8   7   6   5   4   3   2   1

Designed and produced for Pluto Press by
Chase Publishing Services, Fortescue, Sidmouth EX10 9QG
Typeset from disk by Stanford DTP Services, Northampton
Printed in the European Union by Antony Rowe, Chippenham, England

To Lisa

# Acknowledgements

I should like to thank: Tessa Holloway of the Centre for Nietzsche Studies in Minehead; Professor Brenda Almond of Tom Paine's old stamping ground, Lewes in Sussex and of course, the Professor of the Centre for Confusion Studies, Qingdao, to whom the book is dedicated but who in no way can be held politically accountable for its insufficiently Maoist tone.

Dr Harvis of the Filing, Archiving and Typesetting Service in Bristol, (where the slave ships set out from) was invaluable in doing the 'backroom-donkey work', whatever that is; and then I do want to thank Wod, Lou and Anna Cohen, and the Professors Smith-Cohen, for their support over what has been a long winding project, and for 'taking an interest' – indeed, putting some interest back in too. 'Umble thanks are due to all those who have suffered over early manuscripts – even late ones too, Anthony!

And I also very much want to thank my good friends at the Centre for Information Technology and Education, in rain-swept Plymouth, and in particular its leader-cum-guru, Dr Jon Coupland. Without whom, as philosophers say, this book might not have been able to find its true form.

# 'How To' Guide

In places, this book can be hard going. That is because it is not, in fact, one book, but at least a dozen separate books. In here is not so much a 'digest' of some of the great works of political philosophy as a synthesis, not just the best bits, as it were, but all the ideas and arguments.

And that can make a book heavy going. It is written with a minimum of jargon, with none of the tedious interruptions by machine-gun referencing and footnoting that in the past 50 years has become an almost inescapable part of academic writing, and that helps. But nonetheless, the reader should be encouraged and forgiven for taking it slowly. Not, as Wittgenstein used to say about his arguments, 'because they are meant to be read slowly', but because, as a rich feast of ideas and concepts, there is much to savour and enjoy.

One thing that increasingly astonished me, at any rate, in the course of researching this book, is how little research anyone else seems to have done with their own commentaries. It is nothing short of eye-opening (read appalling) to return to a primary source and see how errors multiply over the years, as secondary source is piled upon secondary source in a kind of academic Chinese whispers. Not only is Machiavelli today generally hopelessly misrepresented, but Plato, Locke, Hobbes, Mill, and of course, Nietzsche. This last, in his favour! Then there are writers like Weber, Durkheim and Hegel, who left themselves open to misunderstanding and abuse by subsequent writers by producing books that are too long and too impenetrable. For that reason, I have tried to keep chapters in the present work strictly within that very short limit known as 'the attention span', cruelly but justly dictated by interest value.

There are, for example, the contents of the whole of the *political* sections of the *Republic* (which is not of course solely a political work); of the *Leviathian*; of both *The Prince* and the *Discourses* (which again, is not solely a political work, being much of it history, especially military history, and bad history at that). In the later portion of the book, the style changes of necessity and rather than pick over the entrails of the ultimately rather unimportant works of Comte, Weber and Durkheim, nor yet Gentile and Mussolini, I have opted instead to provide a rather more conventional account of their 'ideas', albeit one with as much direct quotation and close paraphrase as is compatible with revealing their arguments. Always, as the guide, aiming to do so in an interesting, accessible and not-too-lengthy way. (For the same reason, occasionally some of the direct quotation is re-translated, for style or for flow.) Hegel does not, it is true, fit into the category of political philosopher very comfortably, nor yet Nietzsche. They probably would not be grateful for the categorisation of their views as given here. But the reader can decide whether I have made the case – or not.

And that is a crucial element in this book, as in all books. The written word appears dispassionate, authoritative, definitive. Yet any writer is only expressing one perspective, drawn from necessarily incomplete and unreliable evidence. The reader can not only disagree with much in this book, but should do so. Otherwise they are not doing their civic duty!

# Introduction

This is the story of political society. It's not an evolutionary story, although some would have us think so. It's not the story of techno-logical advance, far less of economic progress. It's the story of a few, powerful ideas, which have been around for millennia, but reappear in different guises. It's a story told in the language of political philosophy, in the words of just a handful of writers.

This branch of philosophy is concerned with practical questions: about the organisation of social life, about the make-up of the government, the role and rights of the citizens, the duties and limitations of the state. But it is not to be unduly concerned with details, the nuts and bolts of particular ways of governing (although many of the great philosophers often did like to dabble in these). What characterises political and social philosophy is an awareness and a commitment to answering – or at least facing up to – certain great questions:

What is happiness? (Human flourishing?)
What is justice?
What is freedom?

Only secondly can we ask:

How can happiness be maximised?
How can justice and equality best be achieved?
How can human rights be respected?

The origins of the word 'political' itself come, like so many others, from Ancient Greece: *politikos*, pertaining to the running of the city, or *polis*. In this sense, political philosophy is concerned with the very practical matters of administration. For that reason, Plato's *Republic* discusses not only such obscure matters as the nature of goodness, but also the merits and demerits of various constitutional systems. Machiavelli writes not only of successful duplicity, but also of storming castles and military tactics, and Mill concerns himself not only with liberty, but with corn prices. But despite this second purpose, 'political philosophy' remains a much wider and deeper subject, concerned with fundamental questions about equality, needs and interests, welfare, and human nature. This is the reason why politics is important – it is part of us. As Durkheim later put it, through social rules and conventions, we define and create ourselves.

And, of the philosophers selected, each offers a particular response to one or other of the key questions. Plato outlines, in his *Republic*, a solution (although many today will not rush to accept it) to the question of 'justice'; Hobbes offers a particular view as to the nature of freedom – that it involves a sublimation of individual power into the collective whole; whilst Locke sets out the strongest argument for 'inalienable' human rights.

This book, then, aims to serve as a kind of grand tour of the landscape of political science, not to mention economics, philosophy and sociology. On this journey (and yes, like many of the political philosophers, I intend to take this already weary metaphor and really hammer it into the ground) our map will be the timelines section preceding each chapter, locating each theory in its technical and social context. Similarly, short biographical notes on each philosopher are incorporated into the chapters, encouraging the reader to see them as individuals reflecting their particular circumstances and time. The selection is idiosyncratic, even controversial, and certainly skewed towards the western realities of the writers it attempts to describe, but it aims not so much to impose any value judgements on history, as to reflect some of the hopes and ideas that (no doubt) inspired these political theorists.

At the end of each chapter, the various strands which have been teased apart in the process of both analysing the philosophers and occasionally too, even demolishing them, are drawn together in an equally idiosyncratic and controversial section – the key ideas. At the same time, throughout, I have tried also to reflect the breadth of each philosopher's vision of human society, rather than impose on them a straitjacket of critical analysis. That process, although alluded to in the concluding parts of each chapter, is left ultimately for the reader to do.

On the way, we travel necessarily fast, clutching a comprehensive itinerary amounting almost to a history of civilisation. Starting in Greece with the *Republic*, we move across the Tyrrhenian Sea to Machiavelli's Italy, north to the splintered war-torn England of Hobbes's *Leviathan* and Locke's civil rights, on through France,

Germany and Russia, eventually to end up in the twentieth century with the world's most widely read political pamphlet of all time: Chairman Mao's little Red Book. But on the journey we are more than mere political tourists, collecting snapshots. When we pause, it is to thoroughly explore and closely examine these great works, taking out the magnifying glass and investigating in detail, so as not only to recognise their main characteristics, but also to understand how they were constructed – and why.

For the concerns, subject matter and even the methods of the philosophers depend on their epoch, and reflect both the ethical and 'epistemological' assumptions of their contemporaries. In medieval Europe, for instance, the greatest political issue of the day was the battle for ultimate authority between church and state, a struggle eventually resolved in favour of the secular. In the sixteenth, seventeenth and eighteenth centuries, the primary issue became that of how the state should use this power, whether as absolutism or within the constraints of a limiting constitutional framework. By the nineteenth century, with increasing industrialisation, the emphasis had changed again to debates over social issues, a process carried forward into the last hundred years with a new language of human rights and international relations.

The ancient oracle at Delphi is said to have advised seekers after wisdom, Socrates amongst them, that the key task was to 'know thyself'. Later, indeed, Pope said that the proper study of man was man. Now, apart from the obvious lack of political correctness in such a statement, there is another, more important ambiguity. Is it 'man', as an individual or 'man' as a collective noun – that 'great Leviathan', society itself – to be studied? In an age of rampant political and social individualism, yet also a time when the lives of individuals are only possible through an increasingly complex web of collective efforts, it is more important than ever to return to the fundamentals of political and social philosophy.

# Prologue:
# The Story of Human Society

Human beings have been around a long time – at least 2 million years, depending on how you classify being 'human' – but human society itself is comparatively new. Indeed, between about 1 million and 12,000 years ago, it seems to have scarcely existed, and what collective life there was changed very little.

It is only since the end of the last Ice Age that social life begins to evolve, in the various partially desirable, partially successful and also, all too often, partially dreadful forms that we have come to know. Most political science claims an historical authenticity, and so we should also take a long perspective, and start by briefly recalling the first chapter of the story of human society.

For these 50,000 generations, 'society' consisted only of family-sized groups scattered around Africa, southern Asia and the Mediterranean area. There were probably no more than a million human beings in the world. That's ten Wembley Stadiums full. There were no rules, no traditions, no laws and no social structures.

Over the last million years or so, that is just in a blink of the evo-lutionary eye, something occurred which changed the fate of the human species for good. (Or perhaps, for worse.) *Homo sapiens*, to a greater extent than any of the other (more agile!) animals, began to use tools. The significance of this subtle but profound process is not immediately obvious, but using tools, the physiologists say, is associated with developing a sense of left and right handedness. As the left and right hemispheres begin to develop differently in the human brain, so do speech centres.

After the ice finally retreated, about 12,000 years ago, the pace of change accelerated. These were technological, rather than biological or evolutionary changes. With improved climate and growing conditions, perhaps along with changes in animal life; farming and the first static communities appeared like so many unexpected mushrooms on the fertile plains and in the ancient woods, along with new social demands. From being a roving hunter-gatherer, *Homo sapiens* became a creature with a highly developed sense of property.

The earliest 'societies' were groups of perhaps a hundred families, living in simple buildings grouped around a central, communal hall used for social and spiritual meetings. (Psychologists say we can only relate on a one-to-one basis within groups of less than 500 people.) These societies seem also to have been female in character, worshipping not only fertility in nature, but fertility in the human form. Some of the oldest stone statuettes represent pregnant women. In these societies, the grandmother was head of the community, and the mother head of the family. There are still large communities, notably in Southern China, today following this ancient model.

Sometimes too there was a kind of totem pole in the centre of the settlements, with carvings on it representing both spiritual and political values and codes. These poles are an early form of 'writing'. But the earliest surviving examples of two-dimensional writing (around 6,000 years old) are fragments of neolithic pottery, bearing marks believed to be the 'names' of important families or clans. These inscriptions were the first 'ideograms' of the Sino-Tibetan language, which by slow stages evolved into the 50,000-symbol written language of China today. Although actually the earliest pictures, cave paintings, are equally a form of writing, and so perhaps are another , even older, influence on the evolution of language.

Fortune telling played a large role, both in the cave paintings and other early forms of inscription and indeed in social organisation. The practice of making symbolic marks on pieces of bone, which are then burnt in a fire, with the results inspected for clues as to the intentions of the Gods, has left evidence of some of the first words. Short phrases relating to hunting, religious ceremonies, and wars have also been discerned, all carved into the oracular bones by ancient diviners. And it is no coincidence that the first published political theory, and probably the oldest book in the world – the *I Ching* – developed by the Emperor Fu-Hsi in China's first dynasty nearly 5,000 years ago, is a mix containing not only divination but also practical wisdom. As much as any overtly political work, it was a guide for those in power. All decisions and situations are represented there in the form of 64 'hexagrams' made up several smaller 'trigrams', in turn made up of 'strong' or 'yielding' lines. Over the centuries, sages such as King Wen and Confucius wrote full commentaries on the lines, all intended to guide 'the superior man'.

Other fragments and scraps of the first written records, perhaps maps or stock records, etched on tablets of clay some 5,000 years ago by the Sumerians of Mesopotamia, reflect a separate linguistic tradition. These ancient people may well have had a sophisticated culture and considerable technical skill, as the Pyramids and remains of ancient towns like Kish, Lagash and Uruk suggest. Indeed, some anthropologists believe they had both telescopes and theodolites. But these early words are evidence not only of the mental tools of writing and number, but of the key social tool of property, the tool identified not just by Marx, but also by Plato, Locke and Rousseau, as the key to understanding social life.

Sumerian writing developed rapidly and soon offered representations far more powerful than just the amounts of sheep and goats or other 'things', albeit still always in the cumbersome form of one 'sign' for each idea. But the next major event in the story of the influence of writing only comes around 1000 BC, as the Phoenicians and the Greeks developed the first alphabets.

The Phoenicians were also amongst the first people to set sail and begin to systematically develop trade (as opposed to just plunder). And it was around this time that they discovered in Spain a valuable source of the attractive and useful metal, silver. The silver was not the most significant factor, in social terms, however. Rather the fact that they immediately began to fortify the trade routes to prevent others from joining in. These military outposts developed into towns, such as Carthage in North Africa, which, in due course, became social and indeed cultural centres in their own right. When the Greeks followed suit 250 years or so later, developing a string of colonies along the coast of the Aegean, a new Mediterranean society evolved, with a common written language and a sophisticated political culture.

But these Greek city states were small and frequently fought wars with each other (and the rest of the Mediterranean). They would have had little long-term influence had it not been, paradoxically, for the military success of one of their enemies. The Roman Empire, with its unprecedentedly well-organised and efficient armies and navies, enabled many of the Greek political and social innovations to be adopted, adapted and, above all, spread.

So it was through the Romans that the Greeks would set the style of the new world. Even if it was still based on what was only an Iron Age economy, dependent on slavery for the production of goods, it was enough to support the corresponding, new intellectual and political elites, with their polished cultural and intellectual structures. Athens, in particular, lucky enough to find its own rich vein of silver at the mines of Laurion, was able to grow to become a city of an unprecedented 35,000 people, making it then by far the world's largest city. Even after building the all-important warships, Athens still had money to spare, which the city wisely spent on making itself the most beautiful in the world. And Athens spawned more than just magnificent buildings. It produced a sophisticated and politically active citizenry who delighted in poetry, music, theatre and, of course, philosophy. It is these intangible investments by the ancient Greeks that left a legacy of thought, first amongst them the writings of Plato, which has yet to be exhausted.

But if Athens was exceptional in supporting some tens of thousands of inhabitants, Rome went several steps further. By the reign of the Emperor Augustus, it was home to hundreds of thousands of citizens, all supported (in a system to make conservatives today quail) for free by the Imperial government. One of the main responsibilities of the paternalistic Roman state, along with the provision of public entertainments, was the safe delivery of bread to the people. Grain was brought from the fertile Nile delta in Egypt in specially built freighters, and was stored in huge warehouses in the capital, ready to be baked and distributed. And in later years, the government added in free cooking oil and meat as well. But, it is for the provision of free mass entertainment that Ancient Rome is most notorious. This was on an equally massive scale to the supply of food. The Colosseum alone catered for 50,000 spectators under a cunningly designed canvas roof there to keep the hot Roman sun off them. Ultimately, though, even such remarkable engineering feats were insufficient to keep disaster at bay. With such an enormous population located in such cramped conditions, their city was too far ahead of its time, too big for its physical well-being – and too underemployed for its mental well-being. It slowly succumbed to both corruption and disease. Yet, for all that, Rome was the first truly 'cosmopolitan' society – of a type which is easily recognisable today, even across the ages.

After its destruction by the northern barbarian hordes, Europe declined and produced little of consequence for the next thousand years. It became locked instead into a petty and credulous mindset where the human spirit was ruled by a mixture of fear and force – the force of armies and the fear of damnation. (This is why our chronology of political thought jumps so abruptly from the Greeks to the Renaissance.) Not until after the year 1500, did the 'rise of science' (perhaps together again with a period of benign climatic warming) begin to provide the conditions for the great thinkers of the Enlightenment to renew social progress. This is the backdrop for the writings of Niccolò Machiavelli and Thomas Hobbes.

Towards the end of the seventeenth century, economic, social and political life begins to change dramatically. Indeed, our selection includes three British philosophers; but this is not just parochialism – it reflects the peculiar historical facts of the time. In particular, London became the biggest city in the world. By the mid-1700s, its population had grown to nearly 700,000, outstripping its rival, Paris, by nearly a quarter of a million people. This growth, like Athens' 2,000 years earlier, reflected England's success as a centre for trade with its associated, and much fought over, inflows of wealth, particularly from the new growth industry of banking. This is the time and context of Adam Smith's *Wealth of Nations*. Not that the wealth did the Londoners much good. At this time, *three-quarters* of children born in the capital did not live to see the age of five. The inventions of the Industrial Revolution – the spinning jenny in the 1760s, the first waterwheel-powered cotton mills and the steam engine itself – brought in their wake both poverty and prosperity to the new industrial cities.

The last years of the eighteenth century, with Thomas Paine discussing the implications of the writings of John Locke in quiet, half-timbered Lewes, saw the old political systems beginning to break up across the globe. In both America and France, new Republics would displace monarchies. Of these, it is the American revolution that proved the most successful, politically. The care the Patriots took to ensure that their new government was soundly based on fundamental principles of 'liberty' and 'opportunity' ensured that their revolution continued to have a profound effect both on the way people see the world and in the way they perceive their place in it, whatever its other failings.

When in 1787 George Washington amended the British constitutional example to form that 'tripartite' system of three separate sources of authority: executive president, upper and lower houses of 'parliament' passing laws, and an independent system of justice, charged with its duty to watch all the time on behalf of the citizens for infringements of their liberty, a system was created that would not only prove both long-lasting and stable, but which would set a pattern other countries would follow.

On the other hand, the French government, left impoverished by its support for the American Revolution, was less successful in its attempts at finding a new constitution; a situation worsened by the pressing need to do so in order to raise new taxes.

So, on 14 July 1789, the mob stormed the Bastille and set in motion a chain of events that would culminate in the metronome drop of the guillotine, each beat marking out the progress of the purges of class enemies. First to the scaffold were the Royal family and the aristocracy (inherited power), followed by the clergy (divine power, in the form of priests and nuns both), finally finishing up (as it usually does) with the political 'reformists'. France thus pioneered a new form of socialist anarchy which would continue for several years until its antithesis, the military dictatorship, arrived led by a young officer by the name of Napoleon Bonaparte. But his military prowess was no cure, for he had no solution to the social illness.

After the fall of the Napoleonic Empire, Europe staggered through another tumultuous period of political and social revolution. Between 1815 and 1848, the year in which the *Communist Manifesto* claimed that the history of all previous society was the history of class struggle, the French alone got through three kings, whilst in Germany, Italy and Austria, rioters took to the streets demanding new political rights and new governing institutions. All over Europe the call was for social justice, demands aggravated both by the sight of the wealth of the new capitalists and by a new nationalist awareness, often envious of the economic strength of a booming Britain, with its liberal constitutional model. Not that even then everyone liked the model. One observer wrote, of the new English industrial towns:

> The cottages are old, dirty and of the smallest sort, the streets uneven, fallen into ruts and in part without drains or pavement; masses of refuse, offal and sickening filth lie among standing pools in all directions; the atmosphere is poisoned by the effluvia from these, and laden and darkened by the smoke of a dozen tall factory chimneys...

The writer was the son of a rich German mill owner, sent to Manchester, who had become concerned at the condition of the mill workers in his charge. He was to become better known later to the world as the co-author of the *Communist Manifesto* – Friedrich Engels.

The *Communist Manifesto* marked a particular moment in time – a time when it seemed that society was rapidly moving towards the resolution of its final crisis, a time when it seemed that the new industries, which perpetually lurched between overproduction and glut, underproduction and recession, must yield to a new socialist order.

Yet the moment passed. Capitalism proved more adept at resolving its contradictions than Marx and Engels had expected, and the workers they urged to unite proved less conscious of their collective interests than the two revolutionaries thought they ought to have been. Instead of political change bringing about a radical redistribution of wealth and power, reform in the modern states simply created ever more complex mechanisms designed to protect and placate individuals and enable the new industrial cities of more than a million inhabitants to continue to function and develop.

And develop they did. The first working internal combustion engine (using gas) came in 1859; at the end of the century the engine was successfully adapted to run on petrol and oil, and Benz and Daimler then applied the technology to the task of making a 'horseless carriage'. And the invention of the motor car, symbol though it would become of modern society, was only the tangible aspect of a more fundamental technological breakthrough – the new production methods and 'white-collar' skills of 'Fordism' itself. Henry Ford's dream of a mass-produced car for the new class of consumers had introduced two new 'tools' to the art of making things: 'time and motion' studies and the 'production line'. The first model-Ts were towed around the Detroit works by two men with a rope, each car taking twelve hours to assemble, for an output of 100 vehicles a day. By the end of the first year, with the assembly line completed, production time was down to just an hour and a half, and the factory was turning out 5,000 cars a week.

For the United States especially, with Europe still distracted by the legacy of the futile nationalism of the First World War, the 1920s was the decade of consumer durables – not just cars, but radios, electrical appliances for the home, and new leisure products: jazz music, dances, the movies and, for the first time, organised consumer credit. In 1929 President Hoover even announced that the end of poverty was in sight, and promised a new era of prosperity for all. The announcement was made only just in time, for a year later came the poverty and mass unemployment of the Slump and the Great Depression.

Expansion, it turned out, had been fed on a diet rich in loans and expected future profits – a spiral of credit both within countries and between them. When things began to go wrong, as they inevitably did, the end was swift. By 1932, production had halved in America. The motor car market plummeted to a paltry one-tenth of its 1929 level. One in four workers lost their job. As no one could afford to buy anything, prices fell, and in doing so, made yet more businesses collapse. When F.D. Roosevelt was elected, he inherited an economy that had effectively imploded. Even his dramatic 'interventionist' emergency economics could barely stem the decline. Nevertheless, the 'New Deal' seemed to offer hope, indeed, the only hope, and his combination of public works and organised poor relief enabled the political structures of the world's largest democracy to struggle on in search of better times. In Europe, similar economic problems spawned instead a new creed, fascism, which began taking hold in Italy, in Spain – and in Germany.

Fascism is a political throwback, a powerful but ultimately self-defeating creed, simply because, like communism, it fails to respect human beings as ends in themselves, treating them instead only as a means to an end. Perhaps more importantly, from the point of view of the impersonal forces of history, it also fails to respect economic realities, and the reality of human nature.

Only in China would one totalitarian model, a new form of communism, arise which for a while would manage to combine both of these things. Maoism, although often regarded as just another Marxist demon to be exorcised, particularly by the western transnational companies that dallied so disastrously with Japanese nationalism, should more accurately be understood as a doctrine in its own right. Maoism was the necessary embodiment of peasant power, in a society which had never before accorded this colossal force any recognition. In South America and Africa, the land is, likewise, still the social key.

Under Chairman Mao (as in conventional notions of legal justice), the *welfare of the people* was to be the measure of the success of the system. For 20 years, at least until the Cultural Revolution, on this criterion, it succeeded. But today it seems likely that although Maoism, and to some extent Russian communism, can raise people above subsistence, neither form can for long hold back from the economic reforms stipulated by the likes of Adam Smith, reforms which have resulted in such prodigious gains in efficiency and productivity – and ultimately wealth – for the nations that have embraced them.

For that reason, the end of the twentieth century has seen a convergence of all societies around a capitalist model that was foreseen much earlier.

# Timeline: From Prehistory to Plato

ABOUT 6000–7000 YEARS AGO
Neolithic pottery fragments provide first clues as to early writing and social life.

ABOUT 3400 BC
Construction of Stonehenge begun in Ancient Britain, actually originally made of wood.

ABOUT 3000 BC
Menes, King of Upper Egyptian region, conquers the Nile Delta and becomes Pharaoh in a world previously grouped only by tribes or cities, of the first nation state. Egypt, at this time, was made up essentially of villages. The first written records on papyrus date from this period.

2500 BC
The first pyramid constructed. Not smooth but stepped like a ziggurat, to conduct the Pharaoh Zoser into the next world.

1700 BC
In China, an early use for writing is for fortune telling by burning bones with names and symbols scratched on them. In the Middle East, another early use is for issuing laws to the general public, greatly increasing the efficiency and effectiveness of the law-making process. The 'Eye for an Eye' code is published by Hammurabi setting out precise penalties for all types of wrongdoing.

ABOUT 1500 BC
The first writing systems using alphabets, that is with symbols for combinations of consonants and vowels, are developed in the Middle East.

ABOUT 750 BC
The first true alphabet, with separate signs for consonants and vowels developed by the Greeks, who, together with the Lydians become the first people to use coins. (The first banknotes have to wait until the middle of the seventeenth century, AD 1658, when they are issued in Stockholm.)

ABOUT 500 BC

In China, Confucius teaches the five virtues of humanity, courtesy, honesty, moral wisdom and steadfastness.

ABOUT 420 BC

Another early use for writing is for the cataloguing of doctrine, which yields powerful religious works. The *Ramayana* becomes main work of Hinduism. The first five books of the Christian Bible, the Hebrew *Torah*, traditionally ascribed to Moses, are written at this time.

399 BC

Socrates, Plato's teacher and inspiration, is executed by the first Athenian democracy, for heretical views.

# 1   Plato's Utopia

*It has been said that all subsequent philosophy is merely a footnote to Plato, and this is certainly true of political philosophy. Plato's Republic sketches out the fundamentals of political theory. The origins of society, it suggests, are in practical self-interest. But although the pursuit of wealth motivates all, it must not motivate the rulers – the Guardians. Plato sees two main threats to society, either external – requiring a military response, or internal – requiring a political response. Internal threats are minimised by ensuring the ruling class are there solely on merit, and receive no rewards other than satisfaction from performing their duty and achieving a well-ordered society.*

The origins of human society may be, as they say, obscured in the mists of antiquity but they certainly lie outside Europe, probably with the ancient African cultures. The first theorising that left written records only seems to have been about 5,000 years ago. But these early cultures and records are by no means primitive. In China, the great sages, Confucius and Lao Tzu were teaching the virtues of the well-ordered, harmonious, society, whilst in the south west coastal strip of what is now modern Turkey, the trading ports that would later grow up into the city states of Asia Minor were founded, and with them an unparalleled period of innovation in art, literature, architecture, politics – and philosophy .

It was here, in the fifth century BC, that Democritus described the shadows cast by the mountains on the moon, and realised that the pool of celestial light in the night sky – the Milky Way – was in fact made up of thousands upon thousands of stars. And it was here too that Democritus observed that 'one should think it of greater moment than anything else that the affairs of state are conducted well', neither being 'contentious beyond what is proper' nor 'allotting strength to oneself beyond the common good'. For a state which is conducted well 'is the best means to success: everything depends on this, and if this is preserved, everything is preserved and if this is destroyed everything is destroyed'.

It was whilst Democritus was devising a theory of atoms in Mesopotamia that Socrates, in Athens, was holding the philosophical discussions that, through the *Republic*, and many other writings of Plato, have come not merely to influence but to determine much of western culture, education and society. Socrates' position in European thought, it has been said, is like that of a religious leader, who, although he himself wrote nothing, has had the kind of influence normally reserved only for messiahs, spread through the accounts of his followers, of whom Plato is only the most immediate and direct. And the style of Plato's political philosophy is also religious in tone, set out in the form of dialogues in the *Republic*. Socrates is portrayed there as the wise one, extolling the need to come to know the 'Good', or to be precise 'the Form of the Good'. This some see as indistinguishable from 'God', and it certainly has many similarities.

Plato was born about 40 years after Socrates, and knew him only in his last years. He grew up during the Peloponnesian wars, which ended in 401 BC with the defeat of Athens, followed by a putsch by a small group of aristocrats which, after only eight months, degenerated into a tyranny counting in due course among its victims Socrates himself, on charges of 'impiety' and 'corrupting the young'.

Plato writes as a member of a highly distinguished family, who had both the means and the inclination to be a member of the governing elite. That he never did govern, in fact, having to content himself with setting out his blueprint for society in the *Republic*, was due, he felt, to his inability to find others with whom to share the burden of government. Like the British Prime Minister, Margaret Thatcher, who is reported to have once said that she needed just six men, good and true, to govern the United Kingdom, but could never find them all at the same time, Plato found human capital to be the critical factor lacking, and decided instead that education was the key to society. Rulers, in particular, would need special training, if there were ever to be enough of them.

On the other hand, as well as Socrates himself, there were many others around to influence Plato in the design of his 'republic'. As well as Democritus, there was Parmenides advising that 'truth must be eternal and unchanging', and Heraclitus, who conversely concluded (it is said after standing in the river) that 'all is flux'. The two views being reconciled and reflected in a tradition in which the earthly, visible world was seen as being illusory and impermanent, whilst the world of the intellect and truth was eternal and timeless.

For Plato, it followed, the ideal state would be designed not to continually adapt and evolve, but rather to have a fixed and unalterable structure controlling and directing changes.

The *Republic* then is a serious bid to sketch out the ideal society, an effort which partly reflects Plato's frustration at being unable to play a significant political role in his own society. Its main recommendation, coming from a philosopher, is that philosophers should be in charge of governments. The rule of philosophers had already been tried in other city states, and it was common practice to employ a sage to draw up laws. Plato would certainly have agreed with Marx, in believing that the point is not only to understand the world – but to change it.

His writings are in the form of conversations, or dialogues, between historical characters, the most important of whom is Socrates. The title is misleading – the *Republic* is really about any form of political organisation that a community the size of a Greek city could take. Similarly, Plato's preoccupation with 'justice' – *dikaiosyne* in the Greek – is not so much with the administration of the law, with seeing that criminals get their just deserts, but with the right way to behave. It is justice in a moral not a legal sense, and is closely linked to the idea of wisdom. Justice is to Plato the 'correct ordering' of the organism.

So Plato starts by making the equation, strange to modern eyes, of justice in the workings of the state with justice observed in the behaviour of the human individual. Indeed, Plato believes that because it is easier to see justice at work in the larger organism, we should look at the ordering of society in order to find the answer to the question of how to live ourselves.

> We think of justice as a quality that may exist in a whole community as well as in an individual, and the community is the bigger of the two. Possibly, then, we may find justice there in larger proportions, easier to make out...

In this way, Plato's politics is based on the philosophical and ethical question, 'What should I do?' His concern at the deterioration of morals in Greek society is the wellspring of the *Republic*, and strengthens his conviction that there can be no escape from injustice and the many ills of society until it is guided by those who have come to a knowledge of the 'Good'.

Plato, like Marx, is actually a materialist in this, saying that a state comes into existence because no individual is self-sufficient. We all have many needs – for food and shelter, for heat and tools, for roads and paths, and for protection from attack. We call on one another's help to satisfy our various requests and when we have collected a number of others together to live in one place, helping and supporting each other, we call that settlement a state, he says. It is here that we find the origin of society, in the free exchange of goods and services between people. But this coming together of people is not a social contract, nor even an enlightened act. For 'one man gives a share of his produce to another, if he does, or accepts a share of the others produce, thinking it is better for himself to do so'. Economic need and self-interest comes first; this is the defining feature of Plato's society.

> Let us build our imaginary state from the beginning. Apparently, it will owe its existence to our needs, the first and greatest need being the provision of food to keep us alive. Next we shall want a house; and thirdly, such things as clothing.

How can the state supply this? Plato suggests through the division of labour. 'We shall need at least one man to be a farmer, another a builder, and a third a weaver.' In fact, as Socrates and his audience then apparently realise, at least two more will be useful: namely a shoemaker and someone to provide for 'personal' wants, the like of which are not specified. This 'minimum state' works best when each member of it is making only the things for which he or she is best suited (Plato is very egalitarian, giving women the same employment opportunities as men, because, after all, the only important part of human beings, the soul, is neither male nor female). And that means specialisation. 'The work goes easier and is better done when everyone is set free from all other occupations to do, at the right time, the one thing for which they are naturally fitted.'

As Socrates goes on to say, at least according to Plato's dialogues, in fact, a bigger organisation encompassing carpenters and blacksmiths, shepherds and weavers, builders and masons, is more efficient and successful still. Indeed, Socrates even suggests a middle class of sorts, composed of shopkeepers and bankers, managing and selling goods. After all, as his companion puts it, perhaps rather unkindly: 'In well-ordered communities there are generally men not strong enough to be of use in any other occupation.' These middle classes stay in the market place, whilst the farmers are out farming and the craftsmen crafting, to take money from those who wish to buy, and to purchase goods from those who wish to sell.

Both Plato and his pupil Aristotle, who would later categorise, rather obsessively, the natural world into the various species and genera that we use today, saw social life as a means to enable individuals with particular skills to achieve their proper 'function': the businessman to produce wealth, the doctor, health and the soldier, victory. The ruler's art of 'politics' is in turn fulfilled when the state is in balance and human happiness and the 'Good' is maximised. When, on the other hand, a ruler believes the nation should concentrate on generating wealth to the detriment of this, or tries to pursue power and military adventure, then the political art is perverted.

It has to be remembered here, as elsewhere, that in the *Republic* there is always that slight, but vital, distinction to be drawn between the views of its main character, Socrates, and its author, Plato. For the historical Socrates, the only sort of happiness that counts is that which comes through wisdom. Specifically, the realisation that the only thing worthwhile is knowledge of the 'Good'. It could quite easily be suffering that brings about this discovery and illumination. However, for Plato himself, the 'Good' is a slightly broader notion, rooted in the social and political context, although still not solely the materialist concept it is often taken for today.

Let us begin, then, with a picture of our citizens' manner of life, with the provision that we have made for them. They will be producing corn and wine, and making clothes and shoes. When they have built their houses, they will mostly work without their coats or shoes in summer, and in winter be well shod and clothed. For their food, they will prepare flour and barley-meal for kneading and baking, and set out a grand spread of loaves and cakes on rushes or fresh leaves. They will lie on beds of myrtle-boughs and bryony and make merry with their children, drinking their wine after the feast with garlands on their heads and singing the praises of the gods. So they will live pleasantly together and a prudent fear of poverty or war will keep them from begetting children beyond their means.

If we recognise the material impulse, Plato argues that we must also recognise that, 'in time, the desire for a life of idle luxury will inevitably lead to conflict', and the land which was once large enough to support the original inhabitants will now be too small. 'If we are to have enough pasture and plough land, we shall have to cut off a slice of our neighbour's territory; and if they too are not content with necessities, but give themselves up to getting unlimited wealth, they will want a slice of ours.'

This will mean a considerable addition to the community – a whole army – 'to go out to battle with any invader, in defence of all this property and of the citizens we have been describing'. For as Plato records in another dialogue, the *Phaedo*, 'All wars are made for the sake of getting money.'

By now the state has become unable to manage itself. Who will run the new society? Who will be in charge? A small group of philosophers known as the 'Guardians' are Plato's (self-serving) choice. The Guardians are indeed appointed primarily to protect the state, and are specialists in the arts of war, but are also skilled in the arts of ruling, and in management. They must be 'gentle to their own people yet dangerous to others', like a well-trained guard dog. Dogs, says Plato, extending the metaphor (presumably humorously), are philosophic creatures. They distinguish friend from enemy by the simple test of deciding whether they know the person or not. The dog, like the philosopher, likes only that which he knows.

In Plato's republic, the bringing up of the 'guard dogs' is the key to sound government. The young are selected for aptitude, and brought up in a tightly controlled environment by older Guardians. It is a community of Spartan simplicity, free of the distractions of family ties and bonds. Goods are held in common, unlike the situation for lowly industrious classes of the republic, who are allowed to accumulate private property. But the Guardians will step in to prevent extremes of either great wealth or great poverty from occurring, as such extremes set rich against poor, disturbing the equilibrium of society. For unity is all important, and the Guardians must further protect it by ensuring that the state does not grow too large, and by preserving the principle of promotion only on merit – there must be no hereditary governing class. Generally the balance of the state is akin to the need for balance in the individual.

> When a man surrenders himself to music, allowing his soul to be flooded through the channels of his ears with those sweet and soft and mournful airs we spoke of, and gives up all his time to the delights of song and melody, then at first he tempers the high-

spirited part of his nature, like iron whose brittleness is softened to make it serviceable; but if he persists in subduing to such an incantation, he will end by melting away altogether.

He will have 'cut the sinews of his soul'. Likewise, if there is no attempt to cultivate the mind, but an overemphasis on training the body, it leads to a soul that is 'blind and deaf because the darkness that clouds perception is never cleared away' and the man becomes a dull beast 'in a stupor of ignorance without harmony or grace'. Balance, says Socrates, mirroring the conclusions of the Eastern philosophers and mystics, is the key for the individual, and equally, for the state.

In many ways, Plato is more progressive than he gets credit for. Plato believes that, at least in relation to education and philosophy, men and women are equal. He says that they must share the same education and practice the same occupations 'both in peace and war', and that they should be governed by 'those of their number who are best'. As in Athens, at the time, women lived in seclusion and took no part in politics or most of social life, Plato's suggestion that they should have equal opportunities to become Guardians was quite revolutionary. However, it made sense for Plato, as he believed the physical person was not important (as mentioned above), that it was the soul in which morality resided, and souls have no gender.

Of course, this might cause some practical problems, as the *Republic* notes in one of its regular whimsical asides.

'Possibly, if these proposals were carried out, they might be ridiculed as involving a good many breaches of custom.'

'Indeed, Socrates, they might.'

'The most ridiculous being the notion of women exercising naked along with the men in the wrestling schools; some of them elderly women too, like the old men who still have a passion for exercise when they are wrinkled and not very agreeable to look at ...'

Only relevant differences, such as the slighter build of women, should be allowed to influence their treatment.

However, far from being considered a progressive, Plato is sometimes accused of being an early advocate of totalitarianism, particularly censured for his approach to the arts and education, with children being brought up by the state rather than by parents.

Actually, the abolition of private property for the Guardians includes the breaking of parental bonds with children, as part of the general scheme. Offspring were instead to be reared collectively by everyone, using the guiding principles of eugenics to sort the good from the not-so-promising. By destroying family ties, Plato believed it would be possible to create a more united governing class, and avoid the dangers of rivalry and oligarchy. Inferior children would be demoted to the appropriate class. In the perfect state, women too would be 'held in common' producing the children for the state, and there would be no permanent marriage or pair-bonding. As for the upbringing of the children, his aim is primarily to get people to think for themselves, rather than to put thoughts into their heads. Education is too important to be left to parents in any case, and so all children would essentially be brought up by the state. But the child is not to be passive, but active in the learning process. It is not indoctrination, Plato imagines, as the teacher can only try to show the 'source of the light'. As Plato says at one point: 'A free man ought not to learn anything under duress. Compulsory physical exercise does no harm to the body, but compulsory learning never sticks in the mind.' And he advises: 'Don't use compulsion, but let your children's lessons take the appearance of play.'

However, Plato is insistent on the need to control the influences on developing minds, and does advocate strict censorship of poetry and literature.

> Our first business is to supervise the production of stories and choose only those we think suitable and reject the rest ... Nor shall any young audience be told that anyone who commits horrible crimes, or punishes his father unmercifully is doing nothing our of the ordinary but merely what the first and greatest of the gods have done before.

Because, as Socrates explains, 'Children cannot distinguish between what is allegory and what isn't' and opinions formed at that age are usually difficult to eradicate or change. It is therefore 'of the utmost importance' that the first stories they hear aim at producing 'the right moral effect'. In general:

... ugliness of form and disharmony are akin to bad art and bad character, and their opposites are akin to and represent good character and discipline ... Our artists and craftsmen must be capable of perceiving the real nature of what is beautiful, and then our young men, living as it were in a good climate, will benefit because all the works of art they see and hear influence them for the good, like the breezes from some healthy country, insensibly moulding them into sympathy and conformity with what is rational and right.

This is a striking passage, both for a message which is becoming more, not less, relevant with the creation of high-tech, densely populated societies, with weakened family structures and bonds, and stronger media and peer-group ones, and for its more sinister, totalitarian undertones.

It is not just bad theatre and poetry that corrupt. Indeed, Plato holds that 'wealth and poverty have a bad effect on the quality of work and on the workman himself'. Wealth produces 'luxury and idleness and a passion for novelty', whilst poverty produces 'meanness and bad workmanship and revolution into the bargain'. That is why the upbringing of the ruling class, the Guardians, has to be so closely prescribed and detailed.

All Guardians follow the same basic education, and undertake years of military training. At this point, some will become just 'auxiliaries', charged with defending the state, whilst a minority progress to studying philosophy and take on the burden of actually ruling.

The rest of the citizenry are also sorted into their correct, humbler but perhaps more lucrative, roles. Physicians look after physically sound citizens, physically unsound ones are left to die – although not actually killed). That is reserved for 'those who are incurably corrupt in mind'. This, all agree, is the 'best thing for them [!] as well as the community'.

In due course (Plato suggests at about the age of 50) the Guardians are ready for public office and taking up their burden of guiding the community. The lives of the Guardians must be as simple as possible, with their only pleasures being the pursuit of philosophy, although, perhaps, they can be allowed some pleasure from serving the community. Property, certainly, is forbidden. 'They shall eat together in messes and live together like soldiers in camp. They must be told that they have no need of moral and material gold and silver as they have in their hearts the heavenly gold and silver ... '

If this can be done, then Plato's republic, the justly ordered state, will exemplify the following virtues:

- wisdom – in the manner of its ruling;
- courage – in the manner of its defending;
- temperance – in the acceptance of all of the system of government.

Wisdom, we have seen, stems from the Guardians themselves. 'Courage' is passed over quickly by Plato, but assumed to be part of a professional army. But 'temperance' is more subtle, and comes about only by ensuring that there is a balance between the various parts of the state – the governing part or rulers, the administering part or executive, and the productive part or the working classes.

Critics of Plato have seen a parallel in modern times between Plato's political approach and that which, for over half a century, was being applied in the Soviet Union (Karl Popper, for example, has done so, of which more in the concluding chapters). This was 'neo-Platonism' in the key respects that there was a governing elite – the Communist Party – rigorous attention to education and moral influences, equality of the sexes and weakening of family ties, and, last but not least, a general disapproval of private property and wealth. However, the system failed to produce the wise and beneficent society that Plato imagined.

But Plato not only described the ideal state, where justice flourishes: he also tried to show how such a state could decline, examining the various forms of the degenerate state – unjust societies where evil permeates throughout. In these societies, the basest elements of human nature are allowed to predominate and warp the whole.

There is the 'timocratic state' (Greek *timé*: honour), where ambition has become the motivating force of the rulers. In Plato's republic, the danger is that of a divided ruling class of Guardians beginning to compete amongst each other. (Timocracy was often an element in the competition amongst the aristocracy in the Middle Ages in Europe, for example.)

Once civil strife is born, the two parties will begin to pull different ways: the breed of iron and brass towards moneymaking and the possession of house and land, silver and gold; while the other two, wanting no other wealth than the gold and silver in the composition of their souls, try to draw them towards virtue and the ancient ways. But the violence of their contention ends in a compromise: they agree to distribute land and houses for private ownership; they enslave their own people who formerly lived as free men under their guardianship and gave them maintenance; and holding them as serfs and menials, devote themselves to war and to keeping these subjects under watch and ward.

Plato specifically suggests that the usurpers will fear merit and tend towards authoritarianism. They will become greedy, avaricious and secretive, 'cultivating the body in preference to the mind and saving nothing for the spirit'.

In time, an elite emerges, defined by wealth. This is 'oligarchy', or rule of a clique.

As the rich rise in esteem, the virtuous sink... the competitive spirit of ambition in these people turns into mere passion for gain; they despise the poor and promote the rich, who win all the prizes and receive all the adulation.

Oligarchy, by making wealth the sole purpose of life and at the same time arranging that only a few have that wealth, sows the seeds of its own destruction in the masses' eventual demand for more. The resolution of this, says Plato, is democracy. Not that he thinks very much of it, considering it a close relation of anarchy.

'What is the character of this new regime? Obviously the way they govern themselves will throw light on the democratic type of man.'
'No doubt, Socrates.'
'First of all, they are free. Liberty and free speech are rife everywhere; anyone is allowed to do what he likes... every man will arrange his manner of life to suit his own pleasure.'

The kind of democracy the city states practised was significantly different from more recent versions. Decisions were not delegated to representatives, who would, we might like to suppose, have special expertise and training, but were decided upon at mass meetings of all citizens, that is citizens with no particular knowledge or claim to qualification.

So democracy was, in this sense, 'an agreeable form of anarchy with plenty of variety', liberty 'its noblest possession'. But, worse still, the democratic state was vulnerable to sinking into tyranny. This at least was Plato's objection to democracy, and it has a certain plausibility, even piquancy, being presented in the dialogues as coming from Socrates, who was one of that system's first victims. Because it is almost anarchic in form, it must gradually settle into three classes: the capitalists (not that Plato uses the term), gradually accumulating wealth; the common people, disinterested in politics but just working steadily away, and the sharks and demagogues, perpetually looking for a way to usurp the system for quick personal gain. Inevitably, one such will succeed and seize control, which he then can only maintain by despotism. Although, in

the early days he has a smile and a greeting for everyone he meets; disclaims any absolute power; makes large promises to his friends and to the public; sets about the relief of debtors and the distrib- ution of land to the people and to his supporters; and assumes a mild and gracious air...

It does not last for long. Soon he will be provoking wars and conflict as a means of ensuring power at home, and purging his followers as well as his enemies.

Plato's aversion to tyranny was shared by Aristotle, for 20 years one of his pupils in the Greek forums, and one of three candidates for Plato's post as Head of the Academy. However, like many job candidates since, he was to be disappointed – the job went to Plato's nephew, Speusippus. Aristotle left Athens after this, but writing later, in his description of the rule of the tyrant he seems to speak of a very modern age: '... the forbidding of common meals, clubs, education and anything of a like character... the adoption of every means for making every subject as much of a stranger as possible to every other'.

All citizens, Aristotle warned, would be constantly on view, and a secret police 'like the female spies employed at Syracuse, or the eaves- droppers sent by the tyrant Hiero to all social gatherings' would be employed to sow fear and distrust. For these are the essential and characteristic hallmarks of tyrants.

Aristotle was more of a scientist than Socrates and Plato, and had a resolutely practical – 'rational' – approach to most matters, which served well in the fields of logic, biology and so on, albeit less so in ethics and psychology. As part of his practical bent, he was naturally particularly concerned at the fractious nature of the Greek city states in his time (the fourth century BC) The states were small, but that did not stop them continually splitting into factions that fought amongst themselves. A whole book of Aristotle's political theory is devoted to this problem. But let us step back a moment to put Aristotle into perspective.

Aristotle was born 15 years after the execution of Socrates, in 384 BC, and, as we have seen, studied at the Academy in Athens under Plato until Plato died peacefully in 347 BC. After this, Aristotle went out of favour with the mathematicians of the academy, and left Greece for Asia Minor where he concentrated for the next five years on developing his philosophy and biology. He returned to Macedonia to be tutor to the future Alexander the Great, which might have been an opportunity for him to inculcate his political views, but if he did try to do so, there is little evidence of him succeeding. In any case Aristotle seems to have been largely oblivious to the social and geopolitical changes that were already making his *Politics* largely irrelevant.

For even whilst Aristotle was teaching about the *polis* in the Lyceum, Alexander was already planning an empire in which he would rule the whole of Greece and Persia, producing a new society in which both Greeks and barbarians would become, as Plutarch later put it, 'one flock on a common pasture' feeding under one law. For almost two millennia, the area was to see no more city states, but instead a succession of empires. The rule of Macedonia, of Rome, and of Charlemagne came and went. It would only be in the Middle Ages that Aristotle's ideas would be rediscovered by St Augustine and St Thomas Aquinas and, through the eventual marriage of the Catholic Church with the state, become at all influential.

Aristotle sees the origin of the state differently from Plato, stating explicitly that 'a State is not a sharing of a locality for the purpose of preventing mutual harm and promoting trade'. True to his being a keen biologist first, a metaphysician second, he believed the state should be understood as an organism with a purpose, in this case, to promote happiness, or *eudaimonia*. Of course, this is only a particular type of happiness, quintessentially that of philosophical contemplation, that the Greeks – or at least the philosophers! – valued most. But in this basic assumption, Aristotle's theory of human society is actually fundamentally different from Socrates' and Plato's.

mankind will have no respite from trouble until either real philosophers gain political power or politicians become by some miracle true philosophers.

This is the theme of the *Republic*.

## Key Ideas

Plato's version of the origins of political society is Marx's 'materialist conception of history'; his picture of self-interest governing economic relations is both Hobbes' social contract and Smith's hidden hand; there is liberalism in the strategy of mitigating the effects of either extreme wealth or extreme poverty; and there is even a type of utilitarianism at work in ascribing to the ruler the task of maximising happiness (and the 'Good').

But Plato's most important influence comes from the suggestion that the natural and most 'efficient' form of social organisation is one in which individuals and classes have different roles and specialisations. Plato justifies using this to create both an educational and a social hierarchy. That hierachy is the factor that, above all others, determines the practical reality of society.

- People come together naturally and start to specialise.
- The state is like an individual – with a head, a heart and a body. It is most successful when the parts can fulfil their different functions.

## Key Text

Plato's *Republic*

# Timeline: From the First Exams to the Renaissance Artists

ABOUT 300 BC
The ancient Indian philosopher Kautilya produces the *Arthasatra*, a ruthless political work sometimes compared to *The Prince*. Kautilya describes a system in which the King is just one amongst seven powers, all charged with the sacred duty of safeguarding the welfare of the people

ABOUT 150 BC
The Chinese use written examinations to select civil servants – but the process becomes tainted by the practice of training the applicants in the correct responses, a problem no examination system has yet overcome.

115 BC
High point of the Roman Empire – in 122 BC Emperor Hadrian builds Hadrian's Wall in Britain to defend the civilised areas from the Barbarians. In AD 212 citizenship is conferred on all free adults in the Empire.

AD 751
The first known printed book, a copy of the Buddhist *Diamond Sutra*.

AROUND AD 850
In Persia, the mathematician Al Khwarizmi develops the first 'algorithms' and early 'algebra' – both named after him. Later, in the Middle East, the physicist Alhazen (965–1039) lays the foundations for the studies of mirrors and lenses.

AROUND AD 1000
In North America, early cities like Cahokia, now under St Louis, exceed medieval London and Paris in size and sophistication.

1042
First known use of movable type recorded in China. It is not until 1454 that Gutenberg uses movable type and an adapted wine press to print religious indulgences for Europeans.

AROUND 1100
The rise of the city in the West, particularly in Italy and northern Europe. Settlements such as Venice, Paris, Bruges and London contain populations over 10,000.

1315–19
Two significant technological breakthroughs. The invention of the verge and pallet escapement enables mechanical clocks to be installed on church towers, dividing up the day for the general public. (The Chinese had been using water clocks since around AD 1000.) Also at this time, the first guns capable of killing someone (other than their owners) are developed.

1430
Joan of Arc, the simple shepherd girl whose 'vision' inspires the French resistance enough to enable them to defeat the English invaders at Orleans, is captured by her fellow countrymen – the Burgundians – who sell her to the English. They burn her at the stake a few years later.

1434
Cosimo di Medici becomes *de facto* ruler of Florence, and founds a dynasty that lasts until 1737, with the exception of a brief period when an 'anti-corruption' Friar, Savonarola, seizes power. This is the period of Italy's great 'Renaissance' of learning and culture.

1502–07
Leonardo da Vinci, as well as making a number of important discoveries and inventions, paints the Mona Lisa.

1508
And Michelangelo paints the Sistine Chapel.

1513
Machiavelli begins *The Prince*, the classic statement of the art of politics, published in 1532.

# 2 Niccolò Machiavelli and the Psychology of the State

*Ironically perhaps, for one writing of 'princes', Machiavelli is the first writer to move way from the paternalism of traditional society, towards something closer to our own notions of 'democracy'. In his writings, the masses, ignorant and vulgar though they may be, are better guardians of stability and liberty than individuals can ever become. And despite his reputation for cynicism, Machiavelli reminds us that injustice threatens the foundations of society from within, and urges that it always be combated – wherever it appears and whoever it affects.*

Sixteenth century Italy contained a number of elements that made it, like Greece centuries before, peculiarly fertile ground for all types of arts, philosophy and political thinking.

Out of the whole of Europe, it was the least feudal, the most wealthy and the most politically diverse land. Its culture was sophisticated, urbane and secular, its administrative structure made up of city states or 'communes' presided over by their own 'princes' and governing cliques. As a result, the country was a patchwork quilt of oligarchies, like that of Venice, and tyrannies, like that in Milan. But in some (although in rather fewer) a third system had taken root.

One such was Florence, the magnificent Italian city where Dante had written some centuries earlier not only of his vision of hell, the 'inferno', but of the politics of human society. Dante had asked the question why people should want to live peacefully and collectively together, when they could often gain more by either striking out alone, or by competing one against the other? And he answered it by supposing that social life was the best, indeed the only way, for them to develop their rational nature. But by the fifteenth century the ruling family in Florence, the Medicis, their name a byword for over-indulgence and corruption, had instead for a century promoted conflict between small traders and large powerful guilds as a means to gain and retain control. The opportunities for the people to develop their rationality had to wait until the Medicis were displaced by a Dominican friar, Savonarola, who took control of the city in the people's name.

Early auguries for the system were not promising, however. Concerned only with morality and not at all with politics, let alone with consolidating his own position, Savonarola neglected to prepare his defences, and when the poor began to tire of him, as in a democracy they will, the displaced rich were able to make a comeback. In 1498 the moral crusader (like Socrates, so many centuries before) was executed. His democratic experiment, however, lasted a bit longer – until 1512 when the Medici returned to power. And Savonarola left another unintended legacy: Niccolò Machiavelli, who worked for the new Florentine democracy as a middle-ranking civil servant, gaining experience of being involved with the real issues in government.

In fact, during the purge following the Medici's return, Niccolò Machiavelli was arrested, and then tortured, by the triumphant new administration. Only when finally acquitted was he allowed to retire peacefully and concentrate on writing up his political ideas. Two of the most notorious political works ever written, *The Prince* (*Il principo*) and the *Discourses* (*Discorsi sopra la prima deca di Tito Livio* – Discourses on the first Ten Books of Titus Livy) followed in due course.

## Works

The first of these is often said to have been an unsuccessful bid to regain favour and indeed is dedicated in glowing terms to 'Lorenzo the Magnificent', son of Piero de Medici (presumably a deliberate, punning association with the earlier, more famous, prince of the same name). Machiavelli introduces this first work with the words: 'It is customary for those who wish to gain the favour of a Prince to endeavour to do so by offering him gifts of those things which they hold most precious, or in which they know him to take especial delight. In this way Princes are often presented with horses, arms, cloth of gold, gems, and suchlike ornaments worthy of their grandeur.' What can Machiavelli, a retired (deposed) civil servant, offer? 'I have been unable to find among my possessions anything which I hold so dear or esteem so highly as that knowledge of the deeds of great men which I have acquired through a long experience of modern events and a constant study of the past', he confides, thus managing the difficult task of combining obsequiousness with pomposity.

Having set out his stall in this respectful manner, and set the style for his investigations, Machiavelli announces his intention to leave discussion of republican government to 'another place'. This is, in fact, the *Discourses*, which, although less celebrated, is his longer and more substantial work. It even contains some additional, liberal, ideas at odds with pleasing the Medici, but there is no essential contradiction between the works. Indeed, there is a great deal of duplication.

Machiavelli's most important and original points are usually considered these days to relate to the dry matter of the analysis of the conditions for republican government, but he also allows himself to spend much time and word space discussing military tactics. 'When an enemy is seen to be making a big mistake it should be assumed that it is but an artifice', he warns, before describing 'the rival merits of fortresses and cavalry', not to forget all the while utilising his main literary device of much self-serving name-dropping. Despite these other personal aims and interests, his analysis of government is still far more detailed than that of either Plato or Aristotle, and there is after all, no one (in the European context) to compare with him in the centuries in between.

And indeed his writings have stood the test of time too. If Machiavelli writes of, and for, a pre-industrial society, his notions are still – sometimes strikingly – relevant. In sixteenth-century Italy, society and power were split between three groups: the land and peasantry, industry (such as it was), and the bureaucracy, of which Machiavelli had been a member. All of which is a surprisingly timeless arrangement. Even Machiavelli's discussion of military adventures can be taken as a metaphor for the strategies and effects of economic competition today. Taken literally, Machiavelli may be 'off message', but taken more thoughtfully (reading between the lines, as all medieval texts need to be), his discussions are not so far from today's needs.

Unfortunately, Machiavelli has rarely been read thoughtfully – or even read at all – before being condemned. His reputation is far worse than he merits. Rather than being a 'doctor of the damned' recommending immoral behaviour whenever necessary or convenient, his name a synonym for what dictionaries today record as 'cunning, amoral and opportunist' behaviour, there is much in his writings to suggest a fundamentally good man trying to understand human society in its political form. But Machiavelli would probably, in any case, have taken his bad press philosophically. As he sardonically observes at one point: 'genuine virtue counts in difficult times, but when things are going well, it is rather to those whose popularity is due to wealth or parentage that men look'. And he had neither. Elsewhere, Machiavelli dismisses the apparently successful but unscrupulous activities of Agathocles the Sicilian, who rose by means of wickedness from 'the lowest and most abject position' to become King of Syracuse as worthless. Agathocles was in the habit of playing tricks, such as calling the people and senate to discuss something, and then giving a signal to his soldiers to have them murdered. The real Machiavelli's conclusion is that the Sicilian may have succeeded in achieving power, but not 'in gaining glory'; the apocryphal Machiavelli is imagined to praise him.

Perhaps Machiavelli's most controversial and unscrupulous claim is that if a prince must choose to be either feared or loved, it is better that he be feared, for 'love is held by a chain of obligation which [for] men, being selfish, is broken whenever it serves their purpose; but fear is maintained by a dread of punishment which never fails'. In this sense, he is Hobbes a century later, or even Mao Zedong in the twentieth century – Mao equally notorious for his aphorism, often quoted, that power comes out of the barrel of a gun. But, rather unlike Mao, Machiavelli's advice for princes includes the guidance that when:

> a Prince is obliged to take the life of any one, let him do so when there is a proper justification and manifest reason for it; but above all he must abstain from taking the property of others, for men forget more easily the death of their father than the loss of their patrimony.

As Machiavelli notes, 'the pretexts for seizing property are never wanting, and one who begins to live by rapine will always find some reason for taking the goods of others, whereas causes for taking life are more fleeting'.

Actually, much of Machiavelli's notoriety probably relates to his attacks on the Roman Church, the body that he blames for the political ruin of Italy, even though, on his deathbed, he asked for – and received – absolution (although this could of course have been just a ploy) At one point Machiavelli writes (pre-dating Nietzsche, for example, by some 400 years): 'Our religion has glorified humble and contemplative men, rather than men of action. It has assigned as man's highest good humility, abnegation, and contempt for mundane things...' The advice Machiavelli offers to would-be rulers in Renaissance Europe instead is that:

> it is as well to... seem merciful, faithful, humane, sincere, religious, and also to be so; but you must have the mind so disposed that when it is needful to be otherwise you may change to the opposite qualities... [and] do evil if constrained.

Here, Machiavelli heralds the tactics of the emerging secular societies in redefining their relationship with the moral authority of the Church, and is very clear: the prince has a 'higher' morality rather than no morality at all. This is not just a Machiavellian view – many societies depend on just such a contradiction, resorting to the claim that the end justifies the means, even if the means fall below the publicly held standards of morality. Even Plato allowed it in his 'noble lie' used to explain the different upbringing and roles of the citizens. Machiavelli is simply enunciating plainly what most governments prefer to keep secret and hidden. 'Everybody sees what you appear to be, few feel what you are', Machiavelli says of his prince's duplicity. Some centuries later, in the turmoil of the Second World War, the philosopher Bertrand Russell would comment 'such intellectual honesty about political dishonesty would hardly have been possible at any other time'.

'Doctor of the Damned' or not, one of Machiavelli's strongest and most consistent themes is warning against the perils of ignoring injustice, instead urging princes to '... consider how important it is for every republic and every prince to take account of such offences, not only when an injury is done to a whole people but also when it affects an individual'. Typical of this concern is his retelling of the story of the Greek noble, Pausanias, brutally raped by one of the King's other favourites, who is later promoted. The victim vents his anger against the King by killing him on the way to the Temple, even though this involves 'all manner of dangers' and entails Pausanias' own downfall. The story purports to demonstrate too that it is not in the prince's interests to allow the injustice.

'As we have remarked several times,' Machiavelli continues, warming to his theme, 'in every large city there inevitably occur unfortunate incidents which call for the physician, and the more important the incidents the wiser should be the physician one looks for.' In Rome, for instance, some incidents occurred which were 'both curious and unexpected'. On one occasion all the ladies of the city had conspired to kill their husbands. Quite a number of the unpopular husbands were found actually to have been poisoned, and many more to have poison waiting for them! Indeed, when ancient Rome was threatened by other conspiracies, such as that in the Bucchanals during the Macedonian war, it was only (Machiavelli thinks) the resolution of the city's rulers in pronouncing sentence of death 'on a whole legion at a time' that saved the day. Equally praiseworthy is the effectiveness of the practice of decimating an army – selecting by lottery one in ten of a mutinous force and executing them.

> For when a great number of people have done wrong, and it is not clear who is responsible, it is impossible to punish them all, since there are so many of them; and to punish some, and leave others unpunished would be unfair... the unpunished would take heart and do wrong at some other time – but by killing the tenth part, chosen by lot, when all are guilty, he who is punished bewails his lot, and he who is not punished is afraid to do wrong lest on some other occasion the lot should not spare him.

Advice like this leads even sympathetic commentators like Bernard Crick to say that Machiavelli would not have recognised the merits of the famous words inscribed on the Old Bailey in London: 'Let justice be done though the heavens fall.' But in another sense, Machiavelli is insisting precisely that justice must be done. Machiavelli may be immoral, but surely history is wrong to condemn him as simply amoral.

But Machiavelli's writings are primarily an historical and contemporary political analysis of how power is won, maintained and lost. Italy in the fifteenth century had many examples to offer – mainly to do with misrule. Authority, even for the Papacy, rested on corruption in elections, and the use of violence and deceit to manipulate opinion. Machiavelli looks through history for examples of certain incidents, and notes the consequences, good or bad, for the ruler. He then forms a hypothesis which is tested and either confirmed or disproved. It is in this context that Machiavelli sets out the means to achieve certain ends, irrespective of any virtue or merit in those ambitions. His own ends, were, in fact, quite worthy.

Together, these 'historical experiments' make up the test bed for Machiavelli's theory of society. And the first finding is that the origins of societies in general, and cities in particular, are defensive.

In the beginning of the world, when its inhabitants were few, they lived for a time scattered like the beasts. Then, with the multiplication of their offspring, they drew together and, in order the better to be able to defend themselves, began to look about for a man stronger and more courageous than the rest, made him their head and obeyed him.

The Venetians are an example of this – the city resulted from numerous peoples seeking refuge from the daily wars of Italy after the decline. Eventually, 'without any particular person or prince to give them a constitution, they began to live as a community under laws which seemed appropriate for their maintenance'.

What sort of communities? What kinds of laws? Machiavelli, following Aristotle, says that there are six types of government, of which 'three are bad and three are good in themselves but easily become corrupt'. The good forms are *Principato, Ottimati e Popolare* – Principality, Aristocracy and Democracy – and the corresponding bad ones are Tyranny, Oligarchy and Anarchy. States are perpetually degenerating and regenerating through the various forms, although fortunately, Machiavelli thinks, a state in one of the inferior forms will normally fall under the political control of one better organised.

The rewards for a prince in getting the system of government right are considerable, 'in short, the world triumphant, its prince glorious and respected by all, the people fond of him and secure under his rule'. But similarly, under a bad leader, we find 'princes frequently killed by assassins, civil wars and foreign wars constantly occurring, Italy in *travail* and ever a prey to fresh misfortunes, its cities demolished and pillaged'. We witness 'Rome burnt, its Capitol demolished by its own citizens, ancient temples lying desolate, religious rites grown corrupt, adultery rampant... the sea covered with exiles and the rocks stained with blood'. Truly, it is out of fear and self-interest that citizens seek the good in government.

For Machiavelli, the state follows a cycle of growth, maturity and then decay, in contrast to the happy notion, increasingly prevalent today where people tend to imagine that some sort of virtuous evolution in politics is working towards a permanent near-perfect system. This doctrine of 'perfectibility' has been endorsed (through the centuries) by thinkers of different political persuasions. Hegel suggested liberal democracy would prove to be the 'end of history', whilst Marx adapted him to try to demonstrate that Utopia could be attained through socialism and communism. (We shall return to this myth.) But for Machiavelli, since all forms of government are unsatisfactory (the good ones because their life is so short, the bad ones because of their 'inherent malignity'), a mixture is best. In consequence, prudent legislators must choose a form of government that contains all the elements – principality, aristocracy and democracy – so as to minimise the faults , and so that each can 'keep watch over the other'. In this, Machiavelli anticipates the doctrine of the division of powers, to be found most explicitly implemented in the American Constitution, where Prince (President), Oligarchy (Senate) and People (Congress) all keep watch over one another.

Machiavelli adds that it is necessary, as those who governed Florence in the fifteenth century were said to have found, to 'reconstitute the government every five years', because by this time:

> men begin to change their habits and break the laws, and, unless something happens which recalls to their minds the penalty involved and reawakens fear in them, there will soon be so many delinquents that it will be impossible to punish them without danger.

This is an early perspective on the otherwise recent convention for democracies to hold five-yearly elections. But as to the election event itself, Machiavelli has no romantic expectations. He suggests sadly that, asked to choose a candidate, the populace 'relies on common gossip and on their reputation when it has otherwise no knowledge of them based on noteworthy deeds; or else on some preconceived opinion it has formed of them'. This is unfortunate as, 'though men make mistakes about things in general, they do not make mistakes about particulars'.

At the same time, he notes that Aristotle, too, recommended that 'principality, aristocracy and democracy' should all coexist in one state. The success of ancient Rome, for Machiavelli, was in harnessing this synergy, achieving the Greek ideal of active, virtuous citizens, in a united state under sound laws. In the *Discourses* he advises that the constitution should share power between the nobles and people as well as with the Princes, 'then these three powers will keep each other reciprocally in check'. The Roman constitution is held up as the ideal one, despite the 'squabbles between the populace and the senate', an inconvenience necessary to arrive at its 'greatness'. Remarks like this underline Machiavelli's determination to ignore the Christian tradition of Saint Thomas Aquinas and other medieval thinkers, drawing instead directly on the works of Aristotle and (indirectly) Plato.

Although there are six types of government, for Machiavelli there are only two types of state: republics and principalities (constitutional monarchies). Republics flourish when they respect customs and traditions; when town dominates country; when a large middle class exists; when popular power is institutionalised, and when there is plenty of civic spirit. On the other hand, adaptability to circumstance is the central virtue of republican government. 'A republic or a Prince should ostensibly do out of generosity what necessity constrains them to do'. Discord in a state (such as the mobs that characterised Rome) can actually strengthen the republic: '... every city should provide ways and means whereby the ambitions of the populace may find outlet, especially a city which proposes to avail itself of the populace in important undertakings'.

It is really only in times of crisis that a Prince is needed. Such times as when, for example, a ruthless individual cannot be stopped, or when the state lacks virtue and there is civic injustice, or when the republic has been fashioned from 'unsuitable material'. In general, though, 'where there is a Prince... what he does in his own interests usually harms the city, and what is done in the interests of the city harms him'.

Machiavelli is certainly cynical about human nature. The people don't seem to know their interests either. As he puts it: 'men are easily corrupted', passing 'from one ambition to another, and, having first striven against ill-treatment, inflict it next upon others'. The masses, in particular, are gullible. If

> proposals which have been laid before the populace look like sure things, even though concealed within them disaster lies hid, or when it looks like a bold thing, even though concealed within it lies the Republic's ruin, it will always be easy to persuade the masses to adopt such a proposal.

One section in the *Discourses* is headed with the warning: 'How frequently erroneous are the views men adopt in regard to matters of moment.'

Likewise, 'Human appetites are insatiable, for by nature we are so constituted that there is nothing we cannot long for, but by fortune we are such that of these things we can attain but few. The result is that the human mind is perpetually discontented, and of its possessions is apt to grow weary.' Machiavelli goes on:

This bears out what has been said above, namely, that men never do good unless necessity drives them to it; but when they are too free to choose and can do just as they please, confusion and disorder become everywhere rampant. Hence it is said that hunger and poverty make men industrious, and that laws make them good.

Machiavelli adds that he could 'discourse at length on the advantages of poverty over riches, and how poverty brings honour to cities, provinces and religious institutions, whereas the other thing has ruined them; if it had not already been done so often by others'. But Machiavelli is too pragmatic:

... in all human affairs one notices, if one examines them closely, that it is impossible to remove one inconvenience without another emerging. If then, you want to have a large population and to provide it with arms so as to establish a great empire, you have made your population such that you cannot now handle it as you please...

In all discussions one should consider 'which alternative involves fewer inconveniences and should adopt this as the better course; for one never finds any issue that it clear cut and not open to question'.

## Influence

A century later, in the chaos of revolutionary England, Thomas Hobbes would consider people's nature to be so bad that the only way anyone could be assured of safety and security would be to create a strong government capable of suppressing individuals. But Machiavelli is following the tradition of Plato and Aristotle who had believed in the fundamental goodness of the soul (if not of actual people!), and still sees everyone as having the ability to draw upon this source of natural wisdom. So for Machiavelli, as for Plato and

Aristotle, the role of the state is to help people to fulfil this potential. At the same time, all accept that the psychology of the rulers and the ruled varies depending on the prevailing political system and the structure of the state.

Prior to Machiavelli, medieval writers had based legitimacy on God, who expressed His will through the hierarchy of Pope, bishops and priests, or alternatively through the Emperor and the royal families of Europe. Machiavelli, in contrast, has no doubt that power is available to all and any who are skilful enough to seize it. Popular government is better than tyranny not for any overriding 'moral' reason, but by reason of its success in bringing about certain political goals: national independence, security, and a well-rounded constitution. This means sharing power between princes, nobles and people in proportion to their 'real' power. (For maximum stability, Machiavelli thinks, the people's share should be substantial.)

Machiavelli's interest in social life assumes that people are basically the same everywhere, whatever their society, but that their behaviour differs, as states encourage certain traits and not others. Man is primarily concerned to impose his will on others – or to impress them – and gain recognition. Aristotle, too, had described man as a political animal but, unlike Machiavelli's version, as one concerned to work within a community for the common weal. Machiavelli's citizen is only political in 'being a lover of power and reputation'. Thomas Hobbes and the nineteenth-century philosopher Nietzsche would later agree with that, and Nietzsche would go further, saying that the only function of most people is to give the 'heroes' or 'supermen' something to use to glorify themselves. Machiavelli is more generous – he values 'the mob', considers it vital for democracy. As we have seen, every city should provide 'ways and means whereby the ambitions of the populace may find an outlet, especially a city which proposes to avail itself of the populace in important undertakings'. However, because the populace, 'misled by the false appearance of advantage, often seeks its own ruin, and is easily moved by splendid hopes and rash promises...' we must remember that 'a crowd is useless without a head'. Nor is it enough to 'first use threats and then appeal for the requisite authority'!

Machiavelli concludes that, 'contrary to the common opinion', when the populace is in power and the state is well ordered, it will be 'stable, prudent and grateful', even more so than a wise prince. For even if 'princes are superior to populaces in drawing up laws, codes of civic life, statutes and new institutions, the populace is superior in sustaining what has been instituted...' He concludes:

> Government consists in nothing else but so controlling subjects that they shall neither be able to, nor have cause to, do you harm; which may be done either by making quite sure of them by depriving them of all means of doing you harm, or by treating them so well that it would be unreasonable for them to desire a change of fortune.

Even so, although the masses may be 'more knowing and more constant than is a Prince', Machiavelli's 'democracy' only extends, like that of the Greeks, to a minority of the richest countrymen, whose job it is to stop others seizing power, perhaps by exploiting the power of the mob. But, because the nobility desire to dominate and control, whereas the common people merely wish to avoid being dominated, 'the latter will be more keen on liberty'. And, although the many are incompetent to draw up a constitution, 'since diversity of opinion will prevent them from discovering how best to do it', once they realise it has been done, 'they will not agree to abandon it'.

Machiavelli is the first major European figure to praise freedom as a primary virtue, writing variously that 'those who set up a Tyranny are no less blameworthy than are the founders of a Republic or a Kingdom praiseworthy...' and that 'all towns and all countries that are in all respects free, profit by this enormously'. The year of Machiavelli's death, 1527, marks the time that the Emperor Charles V's armies reach and sack Rome, and marks the passing of the Renaissance period itself.

## Key Ideas

Machiavelli is often narrowly portrayed as simply promoting the use of force and duplicity, even though his intention was highly moral: to protect the state against internal and external threats and ultimately to promote the welfare of the citizens, not simply the interests of the prince.

In the *Discourses*, Machiavelli advocates 'civic virtue', putting the common good ahead of selfish interests, and identifies that curious feature of collective decision making – that the judgement of the masses may be sounder than that of even enlightened individuals.

- People are all a mixture, none much superior to any other, and no system is perfect either. As even a good Prince can become corrupt, so it is best to design the state with series of checks and balances.
- The state is only as good as its citizens – the rulers must be aware of the dangers of allowing civic spirit to wane.
- Although there are many routes to power, only a few of them are worth following.

**Key Text**

Machiavelli's *Discourses* (1531)

# Timeline: From the Age of Discovery to the English Revolution

### 1516
Thomas More publishes his account of a 'Utopia' in which poor people are not hanged for stealing bread, but merely made into slaves, and in which landlords are prevented from enclosing pastures.

### 1530
Copernicus circulates copies of his heretical theory that the Earth in fact revolves around the Sun. (He delays publishing for another 14 years until after his death.)

### 1570
The first 'Atlas of the World' is published by Ortelius in Antwerp. This is the period of discovery, epitomised by the travels of Columbus.

### 1572
Appearance of a nova in Cassiopeia shows that even the heavenly firmament is not entirely 'fixed'.

### 1628
In England, Parliament obtains the 'Petition of Right', the agreement of the monarch not to impose taxes without its agreement, or to arrest citizens without cause

### 1637
In the Netherlands, the price of tulip bulbs shoots up as fantastic prices are offered for rarer varieties of bulbs, leading to the first known example of a financial collapse. London's infamous financial crash – the South Sea Bubble – is 83 years after this.

### 1640
King Charles in England is obliged to recall his troublesome Parliament to ask for funds after the kingdom is invaded by the Scots. Two years later there is civil war between the Parliamentary forces and the King's, and in 1645 Cromwell's New Model Army

crushes the Royalist forces at Naseby. Charles flees to his former enemies, the Scots, but they sell him back to the Parliamentarians in 1647 for the very princely sum of £400,000. Two years later, Charles is executed. England becomes a 'Commonwealth' instead.

1651
Thomas Hobbes publishes the *Leviathan*

# 3 Hobbes' Wicked World

*Aristotle thought that people, being rational, would be naturally inclined to organise themselves voluntarily in societies. Thomas Hobbes, writing nearly 2,000 years later, thought that people, being rational, wouldn't.*

Thomas Hobbes has a more cynical and, he would say, realistic, view of human nature than the Greeks. Whilst he agrees that people have regard for their self-interest, there is little else Hobbes will accept from the Ancients. Where Aristotle and Plato imagined that (at least some) people were virtuous (and even Machiavelli at least believed it was worth appearing to be so), Hobbes considers that society is only a mixture of selfishness, violence and fear, topped with a healthy dollop of deceit, the last there to make things work more smoothly. Hobbes even has the temerity to describe this as the 'State of Nature', a shocking phrase calculated to arouse the wrath of the Church, directly conflicting with the rosy biblical image of Adam and Eve in the Garden of Eden before the Fall.

How had Hobbes come to such a negative view of society? After all, for most of the Middle Ages in Europe, virtually the only theorising on these matters had been that of the Catholic theologians in their monasteries and convents. In his commentaries on Aristotle, Saint Thomas Aquinas (1225–74) had built upon Aristotle's notion of rationality the necessity of a virtuous and divinely inspired social order, that none could challenge without challenging God. For precisely doing this (amongst other reasons) Hobbes was considered by many of his contemporaries to be, if not actually an atheist, certainly a heretic. Indeed, after the Great Plague of 1666, in which 60,000 Londoners died, and the Great Fire straight afterwards, a parliamentary committee was set up to investigate whether heresy might have contributed to the two disasters. The list of possible causes included Hobbes' writings.

But Thomas Hobbes was born in middle England into a Tudor society which was beginning to collapse into the acrimony of the English Civil War. Much has been made of this fact, as explaining

Hobbes' desire for one all-powerful authority, and perhaps it is too easy to explain away retrospectively Hobbes' unique contribution to the development of the western model of society. After all, the Greeks lived in circumstances in which governments were continually coming and going, and yet they produced theories favouring quite different aims. It might as reasonably be said by the psychological behaviourists that Hobbes' approach stems from emotional distress at being separated from his father, a vicar, who lost his job after quarrelling with another pastor at the church door. (This certainly would explain his own tendency to battle with the Church, yet not disown it.) After that event, the young Hobbes had to be brought up by his uncle, eventually becoming an accomplished scholar at Oxford.

Leaving university with a degree in scholastic logic and, it has been said, several more degrees of contempt for Aristotle in particular, and universities in general, Hobbes obtained a post as tutor to the Earl of Devonshire. He travelled widely with the Duke, moving in increasingly aristocratic circles and even meeting the celebrated Italian astronomer, Galileo, in 1636. Four years earlier, Galileo had published his famous *Dialogue*, setting out some of his conclusions from his observation of the heavens through the newly reinvented telescope, notably his discovery that the moons of Jupiter went around their mother planet and the suggestion that the planets too went around the Sun. Even for this carefully worded suggestion, Galileo was summoned to Rome by the Church, required to recant, and forbidden to make any further astronomical observations. After all, the Earth, the Cardinals reminded him, was the centre of the universe, and did not go round anything. Hobbes admired and to some extent modelled his own writings on Galileo's example. His political system is as radical an upturning of social life as anything the astronomers offered of the solar system.

Hobbes' books are a strange mixture of jurisprudence, religious enthusiasm and political iconoclasm. There is an undertone of guilt reminiscent of St Augustine a thousand years before. Augustine, who had, in his own writings, devoted many thousands of pages to alternately apologising and blaming himself for the wickedness of a soul that had led him, amongst other sins, to steal apples – and, as he solemnly recounts, worst of all, to enjoy it. Other aspects, however, particularly Hobbes' legal points, are innovative and frequently perceptive, even if occasionally dubious in the logic of their argument. Of it all, it is the political theory, the first significant one since Machiavelli's, that is most interesting and, historically, the most influential.

## Work

The starting point for Hobbes' theory of society is a mechanistic view of both the universe and of human life within it. 'Nature (the Art whereby God hath made and governs the World)', Hobbes writes, by way of introduction to the *Leviathan*:

> ... is by the *Art* of man, (as in many other things so in this also) imitated, [so] that it can make an Artificial Animal. For seeing life is but a motion of the limbs, the beginning whereof is in some principal part within; why may we not say, that all *Automata* (Engines that move themselves by springs and wheels as doth a watch) have an artificial life? For what is the *Heart*, but a *Spring*; and the *Nerves*, but so many *Strings*; and the *Joints*, but so many *Wheels*, giving motion to the whole Body, such as was intended by the artificer?

His view is that people are just machines, moved by what he terms 'appetites' and 'aversions'.

> These small beginnings of Motion within the body of Man, before they appear in walking, speaking, striking, and other visible actions are commonly called ENDEAVOUR. This Endeavour, when it is toward something, is called APPETITE or DESIRE; the later, being the general name, and the other often times restrained to signify the Desire of Food, namely Hunger and Thirst. And when the Endeavour is fromward something, it is generally called AVERSION.

It follows that automata, the clockwork mechanisms that were such a great feature of the period, appearing like outrageous children's toys on the church steeples of the richest towns, didn't actually look alive, they *were* alive – artificially alive. 'Life itself is but Motion, and can never be without Desire, nor without Fear, no more than without Sense.'

The motion of the automata are no more mindless than the motion of the animal or human being, and the human being is no more free to direct its impulses than the machine is. Some, but not many, of these 'motions' are innate, the rest are the result of experience. Everyone seeks to fulfil these appetites, varying only in degree and particular taste. Hobbes thinks the 'human machine' is programmed to direct its energies selfishly. He doubts if it is ever possible for human beings to act altruistically, and even apparently benevolent action is actually self-serving, perhaps an attempt to make them feel good about themselves. In human beings, the primary motion is towards power: '... in the first place, I put for a general inclination of all mankind, a perpetual and restless desire of Power after power, that ceaseth only in Death'.

This view is often associated with the writings of Nietzsche, sometimes with Hegel, but it is Hobbes who puts it so much more convincingly and elegantly 200 years earlier. This desire for power is the cause of human strife and conflict, the origin of the 'War of all upon all', as Hobbes puts it. It is only through an overarching authority that society can overcome this struggle for power over others, and this requires that people abandon their 'natural' rights in return for protection and stability. Hobbes begins the *Leviathan* thus:

> *Art* goes yet further, imitating that Rational and most excellent work of Nature, *Man*. For by Art is created that great LEVIATHAN called a COMMON-WEALTH, or STATE, which is but an Artificial Man; though of greater stature and strength than the Natural, for whose protection and defence it was intended...

The political nature of human society is uncovered by an examination of its earliest origins, in this case traced by Hobbes from the 'invention' of speech, when God teaches Adam the names of the creatures.

> The general use of discourse is to transfer our mental discourse into verbal; or the Train of our Thoughts, into a Train of Words; and that for two commodities; whereof one is, the Registering of the Consequences of our Thoughts; which being apt to slip out of our memory, and put us to a new labour, may again be recalled, by such words as they were marked by.

The other use is for communication – to teach, to 'make known to others our wills and purposes, that we may have the mutual help of one another'. But, immediately, alongside the opportunities for communication, speech makes possible new abuses. People can use words to try to deceive others – or themselves.

For the errors of Definitions multiply themselves, according as the reckoning proceeds; and lead men into absurdities which at last they see, cannot avoid, without reckoning anew from the beginning; in which lies the foundation of their errors. From whence it happens, that they which trust to books, do as they that cast up many little sums into a greater, without considering whether those little sums were rightly cast up or not; and at last finding the error visible, and not mistrusting their first grounds, know not which way to clear themselves; but spend time in fluttering over their books; as birds that entering by the chimney, and finding themselves enclosed in a chamber, flutter at the false light of a glass window, for want of wit to consider which way they came in.

Many of the ideas in the *Leviathan* have, however, been fluttered over by philosophers. Nietzsche misappropriated the 'will to power', John Rawls borrowed the idea of a social contract to explain moral decision making, and social determinism in general is today often echoed, for example in talk of 'the selfish gene' that is sometimes claimed to explain human behaviour.

Commentators later made much of Hobbes' lack of academic or indeed scientific rigour, perhaps reflecting the prejudices of his contemporaries who despised his lowly origin, but Hobbes ploughs his own furrow, himself mocking the philosophers. Yet perhaps the most striking aspect of Hobbes' political philosophy is that, at a time of elaborate respect for the various authorities of God, the Pope, the high-born or whoever, it is resolutely rational in its approach. And, in his theory of motions, Hobbes is reflecting the popular view of science in his time, impressed by Galileo's rediscoveries of the mountains on the Moon (Democritus had written too of them), the phases of Venus and the movements of the planets, as well as by biological discoveries such as that of the circulation of the blood by Harvey, all of which tended to challenge established opinion. His arguments are based on clearly set out grounds, his reasoning shown in clear step-by-step terms with no waffle or 'fluttering', and no appeal to mystic or traditional authorities. This is a conscious aim, too, for as he writes of the 'abstruse philosophy' of the Schoolmen:

When men write whole volumes of the stuff, are they not Mad, or intend to make others so?... So that this kind of Absurdity, may rightly be numbered amongst the many sorts of Madness; and all the time that guided by clear Thoughts of their worldly lust, they forbear disputing, or writing thus, but Lucid intervals. And thus much of the Virtues and Defects Intellectual.

Hobbes' emphasis on clarity and common sense leads him to his low opinion of Aristotle's methods, and much of the work of the Ancients. Whereas Aristotle, and indeed Machiavelli, are often to be found extrapolating conclusions from inadequate data whenever and whatever their 'natural light' inspires them to, Hobbes is much more cautious. Experience confirms nothing, universally, Hobbes writes in another of the many books he produced during his 91 years, pre-dating David Hume in his rejection of induction.

Actually, Hobbes is challenging his critics here on a point that Aristotle himself had demonstrated originally: that inductive reasoning – that is, drawing general conclusions from limited actual occurrences – is always, philosophically speaking, invalid. Or, as Bertrand Russell has put it, a chicken may have plenty of evidence for a theory, thinking the farmer is its friend (handfuls of grain each morning) and still be mistaken when it attempts to generalise. For one morning the unfortunate bird will emerge to find its 'friend', the farmer not scattering the grain, but wringing its neck.

Hobbes is anxious to avoid such an undignified fate for himself, particularly in Civil War England, and is careful in his approach. He breaks down (by analysis) social phenomena into their 'basic constituents', and only then synthesises these to produce a new theory.

It is this technique, as much as his theory of power as the motivating spring of mankind, that makes Hobbes a distinctly modern thinker. This shows itself, for example, in what he then makes of his first and most basic commitment, the idea that people have internal desires or motions, and are 'of necessity' seeking the power to fulfil them.

The Power *of a Man* (to take it Universally,) is his present means, to obtain some future apparent Good. And is either *Original*, or *Instrumental*. *Natural Power* is the eminence of the Faculties of Body, or Mind; as extraordinary Strength, Form, Prudence, Arts, Eloquence, Liberality, Nobility. *Instrumental* are those Powers, which acquired by these, or by fortune, are means and

Instruments to acquire more; as Riches, Reputation, Friends, and the secret working of God, which men call Good Luck. For the nature of Power, is in this point, like to Fame, increasing as it proceeds; or like the motion of heavy bodies, which the further they go, make still the more haste.

There are three things that follow directly from this compulsion, three 'principle causes of quarrel' as Hobbes puts it. The first is *competition*, for gain; the second is *diffidence*, and a compulsion for safety; whilst the final one is the compulsion for *glory*, and for reputation. Yet they all precipitate violence.

The first use Violence, to make themselves Masters of other men's persons, wives, children, and cattle; the second, to defend them; the third, for trifles, as a word, a smile, a different opinion, and any other sign of undervalue either direct in their Persons, or by reflection in their Kindred, their Friends, their Nation, their Profession, or their Name.

Of course, people see that they are at risk from their fellow beings, and live perpetually both in danger and in fear.

Hereby it is manifest, that during the time men live without a common power to keep them all in awe, they are in that condition which is called War; and such a War as is of every man, against every man. For WAR, consists not in Battle only, or in the act of fighting; but in... the disposition.

Every man becomes 'Enemy to every man', living without any security other than 'what their own strength, and their own invention shall furnish them with'. In such conditions, Hobbes observes, in a passage culminating in the *Leviathan*'s most notorious words:

... there is no place for Industry; because the fruit thereof is uncertain: and consequently no Culture of the Earth; no Navigation, nor use of the commodities that may be imported by Sea; no commodious Building; no instruments of moving, and removing such things as require much force; no Knowledge of the face of the Earth; no account of Time; no Arts; no Letters; no Society; and which is worst of all, continual fear, and danger of violent death; And the life of man, solitary, poor, nasty, brutish, and short.

To those of his contemporaries who dispute this nature for Man, perhaps asking why God should create such a race, Hobbes challenges them to go to sleep with their doors and money chests unlocked. Anyway, he says, he is not accusing man's nature so much as man's actions. 'The Desires, and other Passions of man, are in themselves no Sin.' Because, in the

> war of every man against every other man, this also is consequent; that nothing can be Unjust. The notions of Right and Wrong, Justice and Injustice have there no place. Where there is no common Power, there is no Law: where no Law, no Injustice.

Notions of 'justice' or 'fairness' and 'rights' are 'Qualities that relate to men in Society, not in Solitude'. Morality requires society. The solitary man is not moral. Only through society can 'the solitary man' achieve any relief from fear, any peace and security: 'Fear of oppression, disposes a man to anticipate, or to seek aid by society: for there is no other way by which a man can secure his life and liberty.'

Even an exceptionally strong or ruthless leader needs society, unable to escape from their essential equality with their fellows:

> Nature hath made men so equal, in the faculties of the body, and mind; as that though there be found one man sometimes manifestly stronger in body, or quicker in mind than another; yet when all is reckoned together, the difference between man and man is not so considerable.

Although many may believe the differences in intellect to be great, this is but a 'vain conceit'. 'For they see their own wit at hand, and other men's at a distance.'

For individuals are all mortal and all fallible. This fundamental equality makes it impossible for anyone to feel secure from others, except by creating the overriding power of the state. Partly because of this, the founders of commonwealths will have to implant in the masses the beliefs that the laws are divine, 'from the dictates of some God, or other spirit', or else that they themselves are 'of a higher nature than mere mortals'. Hobbes' 'covenant' (by which the ruled exchange their freedom for security) is just such a virtuous fiction:

he does not suppose it to have any actual historical parallel, merely offers it as a convenient rationalisation. Philosophers sometimes raise the objection that the entire social contract raises the question of how it itself can ever be started or got going, as no one is supposed, on Hobbes view, to act out of anything but immediate self-interest – a kind of 'bootstrap' problem. But such objections are inappropriate. Hobbes himself is making no historical claims, only offering fictions.

However, the laws of nature are real enough. The most fundamental of these laws is the right to protect your own life. Since the best way of doing this is for there to be peace, and not war, the reqirement is to seek peace.

> The Passions that incline men to Peace, are Fear of Death; Desire of such things as are necessary to commodious living; and a Hope by their industry to obtain them. And Reason suggests convenient Articles of Peace, upon which men may be drawn to agreement. These Articles, are they, which otherwise are called the Laws of Nature.

Transferring the right to use force to the sovereign authority, by the people, 'the mutual transferring of Right' is 'that which men call CONTRACT'. The general expression of the Laws of Nature is that of the biblical commandment, to do unto others only what you would have done unto yourself. And Hobbes draws another contrast with the views of Aristotle on 'political creatures':

> It is true, that certain living creatures, as Bees, and Ants, live sociably one with another... and yet have no other direction, than their particular judgments and appetites; nor speech, whereby one of them can signify to another, what he thinks expedient for the common benefit; and therefore some man may perhaps desire to know why Mankind cannot do the same.

The reason is that men like to compare themselves with each other – unlike the creatures, whose individual interest is more simply identical with the collective interest. Ants and bees do not differ over methods, merely accepting the system, far less do they try to trick each other. The only way, Hobbes continues, to reproduce such a virtuous system with people, is to confer all the power and strength upon one Man, or upon one assembly of men, that may reduce all their Wills, by plurality of voices, unto one Will... This is more than Consent, or Concord; it is a real Unity of them all, in one and the same Person, made by Covenant of every man with every man...

And this is 'that Great Leviathan', the Commonwealth, and it comes about when either one man 'by War subdueth his enemies to his will', or when 'men agree amongst themselves, to submit to some Man, or Assembly of men, voluntarily, on confidence to be protected by him against all others'.

Hobbes quotes the book of Job on the great power God gives the Leviathan: 'There is nothing on earth to be compared with him. He is made so as not to be afraid. He seeth every thing below him; and is *King of all the children of pride.*'

Much of the *Leviathan* is legalistic in tone, as befits a theory based on constructing order out of anarchy. Crucially, there are even restrictions on the all-powerful sovereign. And, 'no man... can be obliged by Covenant to accuse himself' much less to 'kill, wound, or maim himself'.

Covenants entered into out of fear are obligatory, just as, Hobbes says, with Machiavellian pragmatism, if someone has agreed to pay a ransom, then they must pay it. 'For it is a contract wherein one receives the benefit of life; the other is to receive money, or service for it.' If it were not so, then it would invalidate the supposed contract between the individual and the sovereign, for this is precisely that of one motivated by fear. However, there is one exception to this, and that is a covenant not to defend yourself from force. (To forgo the 'right to self-defence'). This is always void, for 'no man can transfer, or lay down his Right to save himself from Death, Wounds, and Imprisonment'. For the same reason, most sound systems of law do not compel an accused person to testify against their own interests – the citizen has what today we would value as 'the right to silence'.

Hobbes even defends the man who flees court, a position which seems to be based on a low opinion of judges rather than any philo-sophical consistency. 'The Lords of England were judges, and most difficult cases have been heard and determined by them; yet few of them were much versed in the study of the Laws...' It is especially important for judges, of all people, to acknowledge equal rights.

Nor can anyone be bound to kill another. Even a soldier may refuse to fight the enemy 'though his Sovereign have the right to punish his refusal with death'. This may seem to be inconsistent, but there, that's autocracy for you! At least, Hobbes is more generous than the generals of World War One to their shell-shocked conscripts, in saying: 'Allowance may be made of natural timorousness, not only to women... but also to men of feminine courage.'

Indeed, if a man is in danger of dying, 'Nature compels him to' break the law. On the other hand, Hobbes has no time for 'the poisonous doctrine' that 'every man is a judge of Good and Evil actions', and that listening to your conscience takes higher priority than following the law. Judges should have a sense of 'equity', contempt of riches, be dispassionate and capable of listening patiently and attentively. At the same time, Hobbes bases his law on what he supposes to be the reality of human psychology, even rejecting the commandment not to 'covet', saying that this makes a sin out of human nature.

Certain technical repercussions of a system of laws are considered, such as what happens when someone does not know of the law. Ignorance of the 'Law of Nature' is no excuse, for the law of nature is simply that one should not do to others what one would not like done to oneself. However, ignorance of a civil matter, perhaps like that of a traveller in a strange country, is an excuse. Ignorance of the sovereign is never allowable, for the sovereign is always the citizen's protection, nor is ignorance of the penalty. Ideally, children should be brought up to obey the law instinctively. On the other hand, no law made 'after a Fact done', can make something a crime.

In general, premeditated crime is worse than that arising 'from a sudden Passion' and crimes undermining the law are worse than those of no effect. Punishment must be sufficient to deter a rational criminal, whilst being essentially positive in its aims, a notion which includes, for example, the deterring of others.

Hobbes recommends a series of limitations on the power of the law to punish. Punishments should not constitute revenge, but only restitution, that is, righting wrongs. They should inflict no pain unless it can be offset against some future good – perhaps persuading others not to behave similarly. But, the punishment must be greater than the benefits of the crime, and any ill effects that by chance strike the wrongdoer are not to be offset against the eventual sentence, for these are not 'inflicted by the Authority of man'.

The final Cause. End or Design of men, (who naturally love Liberty, and Dominion over others,) in the introduction of that restraint upon themselves... is the foresight of their own preservation and of a more contented life thereby; that is to say, of getting themselves out from that miserable condition of War, which is necessarily consequent... to the natural Passions of men, when there is no visible Power to keep them in awe, and tie them by fear of punishment to the performance of their Covenants... Covenants without the Sword are but Words.

Yet the sword has great range and freedom in Hobbes' civil society. To begin with, any man who fails to consent to the decrees of the Leviathan may 'without injustice be destroyed by any man whatsoever' (with the exception of 'natural fools, small children and madmen, who do not understand the injunction in the first place'). At the same time, anyone with sovereign power cannot justly be punished, for whatever they do is by definition just. It is not even acceptable to question their actions, for that is to superimpose a new authority over the sovereign. 'It belongeth to him that hath the Sovereign Power, to be Judge.'

There is one exception possible, when the Sovereign 'licenses' another to exercise power 'to certain particular ends, by that Sovereign limited'. (When a colony is funded, the sovereign may need to license them to govern themselves.) Anyway, people are bad judges. 'For all men are by nature provided of notable multiplying glasses, (that is their passions and Self-love,) through which, every little payment appeareth a great grievance; but are destitute of those prospective glasses, (namely Moral and Civil Science,) to see afar off the miseries that hang over them, and cannot without such payments be avoided.'

So what are the details of Hobbesian commonwealths? There are three types. There is that of just one ruler, which is a monarchy; then there is that of an 'Assembly of All', which is a democracy; and lastly, there is that of an assembly of just part of society which is an 'Aristocracy'. Any other forms identified by the Greeks (that Aristotle again) are simply the same ones misnamed, because they are 'misliked'. Thus the Greeks dubbed an unpopular monarch a 'tyrant', a disliked aristocracy an 'oligarchy', and a rogue democracy, 'anarchy'. Hobbes has no time for such false distinctions. They only encourage 'sedition against the state'.

Of the various forms of government, Hobbes is not in principle opposed to assemblies, but monarchies, he thinks, are less likely to be subject to factionalism than assemblies, although there is one monarchic 'inconvenience' – that the crown may sometimes 'descend upon an infant'. Hobbes seems to have in mind when he writes of parliamentary government a body made up of unelected individuals serving for life, rather than representatives removable in the event of public dissatisfaction – the English House of Lords rather than the House of Commons.

What of social policy in the commonwealth? Hobbes thinks that those incapable of work should be helped and looked after, but those unwilling must be compelled. His egalitarianism extends to the distribution of 'Things that cannot be shared out': these must be held in common (or else distributed by lot).

State and church should be united – and then the Laws will be unambiguous. It is not possible for the sovereign to be accused of holding an heretical opinion, for the sovereign's opinion will be the highest and holiest. Most of the deliberate heresies are due to the 'vain and erroneous philosophies' of the Greeks, especially Aristotle, whom Hobbes cannot resist a final go at in the *Leviathan*.

> Their Logic which should be their method of reasoning, is nothing else but Captions of Words, and Inventions how to puzzle such as should go about to pose them... there is nothing so absurd that the old Philosophers... have not some of them maintained. And I believe that scarce anything can be more absurdly said than that which now is called Aristotle's *Metaphysics*; nor more repugnant to Government, than much of that he hath said in his Politics; nor more ignorantly, than a great part of his *Ethics*.

This contempt is due because the 'Heathen Philosophers' define good and evil by reference to the 'appetite of men', by which measure, Hobbes has already said, there is no law, and no distinction between right and wrong. Aristotle's next mistake was to have not men, but laws, governing. For who thinks that 'words and paper' hurt more than the hands and the swords of men? Finally, by extending the laws to cover thoughts the Greeks allow government to exceed the proper role of the institution.

After this outburst, Hobbes piously hopes that there is nothing too controversial in his views, and brings to an end his 'Discourse of Civil and Ecclesiastical Government, occasioned by the disorders of the present time...' with the respectful wish that it might some day in the future be adopted by a sovereign as a partial guide. 'I ground the Civil Right of Sovereigns, and both the Duty and Liberty of Subjects, upon the known natural Inclinations of Mankind, and upon the Article of the Law of Nature; of which no man... ought to be ignorant.'

However, as John Locke was to write a century later, for many people Hobbes' social contract is actually worse than the state of nature it is supposed to help them to rise above, because of the arbitrary powers it gives to the sovereign. Who, Locke asked, would sign a contract to escape from 'polecats and foxes', if the result was to be put 'at the mercy of lions'?

## Influence

Hobbes' influence is profound. For the first time individual rights are deduced and derived from a supposed 'fundamental right' to self-preservation. Together with the works of the Dutch lawyer and politician, Hugo Grotius, he both set the style and laid the foundations for future work in the areas of political theory, social ethics and international law.

## Key Ideas

Thomas Hobbes provides an antidote to the high-minded reasoning of the schoolmen and indeed the Ancients. Starting from a pragmatic assessment of human nature, he strengthens the case for a powerful political and social apparatus organising our lives. And with his interest in the methods of geometry and the natural sciences, he brings a new style of argument to political theorising that is both more persuasive and more effective. But from Hobbes we also obtain a reminder that social organisation, however committed to fairness and equality it may be intended to be, being motivated by a struggle between its members, is also inevitably both authoritarian and inegalitarian.

- People are motivated by selfishness. Left to their own devices they always come into conflict.
- Self-preservation is the highest law. Not even the state can overstep this mark.

**Key Text**

Hobbes' *Leviathan* (original text 1651)

# Timeline: From the English Dictatorship to the First Taxes

## 1653
The Commonwealth becomes a dictatorship as Cromwell seizes total power and calls himself 'Lord Protector'. When Cromwell dies, England restores the monarchy.

## 1667
Locke's *Essay Concerning Toleration* is published. The French army develop the use of hand grenades.

## 1689
The first 'civil government' in Britain, a constitutional monarchy.

## 1695
The first universal tax is unveiled in France, in England a tax is developed on windows, and, in 1698, in Russia, a tax on beards. By the 1720s there will be riots in France against the *'cinquantième'* or 2 per cent tax on incomes.

# 4  John Locke: The True End of Civil Government

*John Locke was born in a quiet Somerset village into a Puritan trading family, and into a rather less quiet period of civil war between Parliament and Royalists. His political theory starts, like Plato's, with a search for moral authority. And, like Plato, he makes human conscience beholden only to God for judgement on all matters, placing individual judgement firmly above that of both church and state, and limiting the latter's role to protecting property. 'All being equal and independent, no one ought to harm another in his life, health, liberty, or possessions', he proclaims.*

John Locke is a kind of 'lowest common denominator' of political philosophy, the intellectual forebear of much of today's political orthodoxy, a role that befits a thinker of a naturally orthodox turn of mind. In actual fact, as with Thomas Hobbes, the upheaval of the English Civil War is the background to his writings and it no doubt had its influence. But, notwithstanding this, Locke seemed to enjoy a placid enough childhood undisturbed by the activities of the rebellious parliamentarians, including amongst their number his father. Even the execution of King Charles in 1649, whilst he was a schoolboy, failed to radicalise him. Instead Locke rose steadily up through English society until well into middle age, particularly after rather fortuitously saving the Earl of Shaftesbury's life by performing a hazardous but successful operation on him. (At this time, of course, any successful operation had the nature of something of a miracle, requiring lavish rewards.)

Earl Shaftesbury went on to three notable political achievements: he led the opposition to Charles II, he founded the Whig Party, the forerunner of the Liberals, and he pushed Locke into politics. Unexpectedly, it was Locke who would eventually become one of the most acclaimed figures of his century, and one of the most influential political philosophers of all time.

The significance of the Civil War itself for Locke was that it represented a flare-up in the perennial dispute between the king and his parliament of aristocrats (and bishops), who were always seeking a greater role, particularly in the setting of tariffs and the levying of taxes as well as in the conduct of religious affairs. Matters, at this time, hinged on the relative influence of two factions in the country, the Independents who were politically moderate, but who sought a State Church and wished to abolish bishops, and the Presbyterians who insisted, on the contrary, that every congregation should be free to choose its own theology. Eventually the dispute was resolved on the battlefield by Cromwell's New Model Army in favour of the Independents. After this, the hopes of 'moderates' for a compromise with the king were dashed. Cromwell happily assumed the role of Napoleon the pig in *Animal Farm*, Orwell's classic allegorical novel (of a much later, communistic revolution), who having led the farmyard animals in revolution against their human master, ends up walking on two legs, eating and sleeping in the farmer's old house.

So, after a period of increasingly less democratic parliaments, England witnessed the rule of the 'Lord Protector', and with it her first and only republic, rapidly descend into a personal dictatorship. By the time of Cromwell's death, most English were relieved to have Charles' son return as, effectively, their first constitutional monarch, bound to Parliament by the principles of *habeas corpus* and the need to seek its approval for new taxes. And perhaps there was another, more subtle, legacy of the Civil War – a fear and dislike of over-powerful individuals, such as Oliver Cromwell.

John Locke fitted the times very well (Bertrand Russell even described him as the 'apostle of the Revolution of 1688'). His philosophy was actively adopted by contemporary politicians and thinkers; his influence was transmitted to eighteenth-century France through the medium of Voltaire's writings, and inspired the principles of the French revolution. And his views would spread still more widely, through the writings of Thomas Paine, eventually shaping the American revolution too.

Locke's political life begins around the time of the Black Death, when London was burning in the Great Fire, as the son of a Puritan trading family at last abandons the life of polite debate within academia or the church that had been beckoning. Apparently undergoing something of a 'Damascan' conversion, Locke decided to write what amounted to a work of sedition – which was a very dangerous thing to do in the seventeenth century. Of Locke's immediate circle, Earl Shaftesbury would flee for his life in 1682 to Holland, whilst poor Algernon Sidney, Lord William Russell and the

Earl of Essex would all be imprisoned for spreading the wrong sort of (politically controversial) views. Sidney and Russell eventually met their deaths on the scaffold, to the end insisting unheeded on their right to resist tyrants, whilst Essex cheated the hangman – but only by taking his own life whilst languishing in the Tower of London.

## Work

Fortunately for John Locke, such grim choices were never necessary. At the time of the crackdown that netted his friends, he himself was of such trifling political importance that he was allowed to slip away abroad largely unnoticed and completely unheeded. Not that his views were particularly radical even when noticed. Locke's political writing is mainly presented in academic style as a response to issues raised before him by writers such as Hugo Grotius, the Dutch lawyer and statesman with a special interest in ethics and international law, or by the English political theorist (pundit, we might say today), Sir Robert Filmer. Filmer's royalist tract, *Patriacha* (published 1680) earned the author a knighthood from Charles I. It also earned him a particular notoriety in the eyes of the parliamentarians who later vented their pent-up frustration during the war by ransacking his house not just once but ten times.

It is with an eye to Sir Robert's comfortable, traditionalist thesis that people are *naturally* born unfree and unequal, and rulers are equally naturally over them – directly descended from the First Man, Adam (who had been given dominion over all creation by God himself) – that John Locke begins his political writings. The *Essay Concerning the True, Original Extent and End of Civil Government* starts by declaring that:

> ... it is impossible that the rulers now on earth should make any benefit, or derive any the least shadow of authority, from that which is held to be the fountain of all power, Adam's private dominion and paternal jurisdiction, so that he that will not give just occasion to think that all government in the world is the product only of force and violence, and that men live together by no other rules but that of the beasts, where the strongest carries it, and so lay a foundation for perpetual disorder and mischief, tumult, sedition and rebellion...

At this time, the prevailing view, exemplified by Sir Robert, was that the state, through its officers, had the same sort of authority over the citizen as a father (in a patriarchal society) had over his children, or a squire over his servant, a lord over his slave – or a man over his wife. Locke takes them all on. He is always most outspoken and unusual in his firm advocacy of women's rights. Quoting in his support the Christian commandments of Exodus to honour both 'thy father and thy mother', Locke suggests that 'it might perhaps have kept men from running into those gross mistakes they have made' if they had remembered that there was another equal authority in the world. Even a monarchy should properly be understood as that of more than one person, for where there is a king, there needs must be a queen. And Locke points out that the hereditary principle itself is dubious and flawed as it would appear to allow only one true heir to Adam, with all the other supposed kings exposed as frauds. On the other hand, any weakening of the literal hereditary system, say one that simply allows power, like property, to be handed down from father to son, cannot provide the stability that the 'descent from God' principle does. Unlikely though this political debate may seem to modern eyes, the notion of 'direct descent' does hang on even now, for example in the Japanese royal family, in the 'political families' such as the Kennedys and the Bushes in America, and (at least until the end of the last century) in the British House of Lords. In the seventeenth century, it was widely accepted as the uncontroversial and literal truth.

To justify his position, Locke, like Hobbes (who published the *Leviathan* whilst Locke was preparing to study at Oxford), goes back to consideration of the 'state of nature'. Again like Hobbes, he imagines this as a situation of lawlessness, where all may do as they will, without 'asking leave, or depending on the will of any other man'. It is a state of equality, yet not total anarchy, for there is one rule – the 'sacred and unalterable law of self-preservation'. Thus far, then, thus unremarkable. But now Locke extracts a palatable dish from Hobbes' bitter brew.

The state of nature has a law of nature to govern it, which obliges everyone: and reason, which is that law, teaches all mankind, who will but consult it, that being all equal and independent, no one ought to harm another in his life, health, liberty or possessions.

The reason is that as we are all the work of the 'one omnipotent Maker', and 'furnished with like faculties, sharing all in one community of nature', there 'cannot be supposed any such subordination among us, that may authorise us to destroy one another, as if we were made for one another's uses, as the inferior ranks of creatures are for ours'. This 'State of Nature', as Locke notes, still existed then, and continues to do so today, in international relations, between states.

It follows that, in the state of nature, no one may interfere with another's liberties – 'we are born free, as we are born rational' – but if once one transgresses another's rights or property, then, be warned, everybody has a right to 'punish the transgressors of that law to such a degree, as may hinder its violation'. But this punishment must still be 'proportionate', only just in as much as it serves to undo the original harm, or to prevent future occurrences. For Locke's state of nature has two faces. It is a benign, cooperative existence originally, until an individual or group (like Cromwell and the Independents) seeks power over others. Then it becomes a state of war, with the individual entitled – nay obliged – to use any means to regain their freedom.

This freedom is the kernel of Locke's philosophy: 'The freedom ... of man and liberty of acting according to his own will, is grounded on his having reason which is able to instruct him in that law he is to govern himself by...'

It is freedom from 'absolute, arbitrary power', not necessarily freedom to do anything, but liberty to follow one's own will and volition, except where a rule, 'common to everyone of that society, and made by the legislative power erected in it', prohibits such action. To which extent his doctrine is an early kind of utilitarianism, the engine of a machine with the aim of increasing the sum of human happiness. Locke has in mind only the enlightened self-interest of individuals. But in the priority he gives to individual rights, Locke appeals to a moral conception which is beyond self-interest, and which lies at the heart of political liberalism.

This new morality starts with the institution of property. The earth, and 'all inferior creatures', belong to everyone in common – with one important exception. Each individual does own one thing, they have property in their own person. 'This nobody has any right to but himself', Locke adds, neglecting, it would seem, the issue of slavery and indeed his own investments in the Royal Africa slaving company, doing a profitable trade for him at the time. Consequently, 'the labour of his body, and the work of his hands', are rightly considered to belong to each individual. 'Whatever people produce through their own effort, using the commonly owned raw materials of nature, are also (properly) theirs.' This apparently socialist principle, anticipating Marx's Labour Theory of Value by some centuries, Locke amplifies further:

> ... for 'tis labour indeed that puts the difference of value on everything; and let anyone consider, what the difference is between an acre of land planted with tobacco, or sugar, sown with wheat or barley; and an acre of the same land lying in common, without any husbandry upon it.

But this, Locke appreciates, is jumping ahead in time from the true state of nature to agrarian society. In the beginning there was only hunting and gathering. Yet, even there, labour is the key.

> He that is nourished by acorns he picked up under an oak or the apples he gathered from the trees in the wood, has certainly appropriated them to himself. Nobody can deny but the nourishment is his. I ask then, when did they begin to be his? When he eat? Or when he boiled them? Or when he brought them home? Or when he picked them up? And 'tis plain, if the first gathering made them not his, nothing else could.

The labour of picking up the acorns makes them the gatherer's, as 'of private right'. Nor is it necessary to seek the approval of the whole of mankind for it.

Locke sails close to the wind here, as on other occasions, for the rights of 'non-landowners' to 'commons' in seventeenth-century England was a sensitive matter. Common ownership had already been taken rather further by the Diggers, active during the first part of Locke's life, with their 'alternative' communities. Commons, perhaps underused but, by definition, unenclosed areas available for grazing or, indeed, collecting acorns, were always being threatened by the aristocracy, who wished to appropriate the common land to themselves. But the English common lands gave rural labourers the ability to produce food for themselves directly, which they would otherwise have only been able to achieve as payment for their labour on their lord's estates. In the rest of Europe, where there was no equivalent tradition of common land, the suggestion that people had a 'right' to the products of their labour would have been even more scurrilous and revolutionary. Even so, all Locke has in mind is a limit on appropriation. No one should take 'more than they are able to make use of' before it spoils. Whatever is beyond this 'is more than his share, and belongs to others'. Of course, Locke hastens to add, gold and silver do not 'spoil', and therefore there is no harm in their accumulation.

Locke also assumes an effectively unlimited supply of property (as with the gold and silver), thereby avoiding the more problematic issues his theory raises.

> Nobody could think himself injured by the drinking of another man, though he took a good draught, who had a whole river of the same water left him to quench his thirst. And the case of the land and water, where there is enough of both, is perfectly the same.

Locke likes to advance, as an example of this, the unlimited acres of America, ignorant or uncaring of the effects of European 'property rights' on the native Americans with their long-established communal use and management of the land. Indeed, through most of the medieval period, settlements in the Americas were larger and more sophisticated than the European equivalents. But, most likely, Locke would have followed the prejudices of his time, even if he had considered there to be a conflict in ownership. Locke says that God gave the world to 'the industrious and rational', and the native Americans might well have been found wanting in his eyes – seen as lazy and neglectful of their natural inheritance, and consequently living in poverty.

Locke, of course, means well. He writes:

> I ask whether in the wild woods and uncultivated waste of America left to nature, without any improvement, tillage or husbandry, a thousand acres [will] yield the needy and wretched inhabitants as many conveniences of life as ten acres of equally fertile land do in Devonshire.

In the beginning the whole world was America, explains Locke, meaning that the world was an unexploited wilderness, before, through the efforts of people, there came farms and manufactures and buildings and cities. With these come trade, and money. But although property is the foundation of political society, Locke traces its origin back not to commerce, but to 'the conjugal union'. The first society was between man and wife, and later their children.

> Conjugal society is made by a voluntary compact between man and woman: and though it consists of right in one another's bodies, as is necessary to its chief end, procreation; yet it draws with it mutual support, and assistance, and a community of interest too, as necessary not only to unite their care, and affection, but also necessary to their common offspring, who have a right to be nourished and maintained by them, till they are able to... shift and provide for themselves.

This rule which, Locke notes, the infinitely wise Maker has set, is obeyed by all the 'inferior creatures' too, even though many of their offspring can fend for themselves almost as soon they are born. In the *Two Treatises*, Locke argues that where a person is unable to provide the basic means of sustenance for themselves, they have a right to the surplus goods of others, and, indeed, people have an obligation 'by charity' to offer them this. And the handover must be done without exacting an undue toll, for

> ... a man can no more make of another's necessity, to force him to become his vassal, by withholding that relief God requires him to afford to his brother, than he that has more strength can seize upon a weaker, master him to his obedience, and with a dagger at his throat offer him death or slavery.

Like Hobbes, Locke assumes a kind of 'social contract' between ruler and ruled, with an even weaker attempt at explanation than Hobbes made. He imagines that people join voluntarily together as one society, giving up their natural rights in the area of law-making or what he terms the 'executive power of the law of nature'. In the *Two Treatises*, as in other earlier writings, he is content to take these issues as fairly self-evident, and leave the details of 'natural law' unexplored, the better to press on with drawing his conclusions.

> Men being, as has been said, by nature, all free and equal and independent, no one can be put out of this estate, and subjected to the political power of another, without his own consent... when any number of men have, by the consent of every individual, made a community, they have thereby made that community one

body, with a power to act as one body, which is only by the will
and determination of the majority... to move... whither the greater
force carries it...

The American constitution is founded on the comforting
declaration that certain truths are 'self-evident': it is Locke who
provides much of the philosophical impetus for this dubious, if
happy, notion.

Society is thus authorised by each individual to 'make laws for
him as the public good of the society shall require'. The 'inconveniences' of anarchy ensure that this is a free decision quickly taken.
The state of nature now gives way to the laws made for the common
weal. This, Locke adds, demonstrates that absolute power, as for
instance recommended by Hobbes, and generally present in the
principle of monarchical rule, is not actually part of civil society,
indeed not part of civil government at all. Where there exists no
independent judge to ensure that justice is done, rulers and the ruled
remain in a state of nature. Indeed slightly worse. 'For he that thinks
absolute power purifies men's blood, and corrects the baseness of
human nature, need read but the history of this, or any other age to
be assured of the contrary.'

And so,

whoever has the legislative or supreme power of any commonwealth, is bound to govern by established standing laws,
promulgated and made known to the people, and not by
extemporary decrees; by indifferent and upright judges, who are
to decide controversies by these laws; and to employ the force of
community at home, only in the execution of such laws, or abroad
to prevent or redress foreign injuries, and secure the community
from inroads or invasion. And all this to be directed to no other
end, but the peace, safety, and public good of the people.

## Influence

Locke has no particular view about the form government should
take, as long as it is based on popular consent. It may be a republic,
but it could be an oligarchy and there might still be a monarch. But
whatever form the government takes, Locke says it does need to
include some 'separation of powers', and sets out fairly precisely the

distinction to be made between the law-making part of government – the legislature – and the action-taking part – the executive. The executive must have the power to appoint and dismiss the legislature, but it does not make the one superior to the other, rather there exists a 'fiduciary trust'.

Despite the fact that 'rigged justice' was very much a central issue of the 'Glorious Revolution', and after all Locke himself lived through the 'Cavalier Parliament' of 1661 to 1679 – which did little other than pass increasingly totalitarian and repressive laws (mainly against religious freedom) – it was left to Montesquieu (in his *Spirit of the Laws* some half a century later, 1748) to argue the need for the additional separation of judicial power characteristic of the American constitution. Before the Civil War, judges could be dismissed at will by the King. Afterwards, they were removable only with the consent of both houses of Parliament.

Locke argues too that because self-defence is the foundation of the law of nature, people must always be allowed to protect themselves from an unjust or tyrannical government. (Observers of the changes of 1989 and later in Eastern Europe have claimed that these were 'Lockean' revolutions, in that the people – a political community not just a class – withdrew their assent from their governments after years of waiting and biding their time.) Locke himself considers various objections to this final and most desperate liberty – the right to resist an unjust government – but finds them unconvincing. He quotes Barclay, 'the great champion of absolute monarchy':

'But if anyone should ask, must the people then always lay themselves open to the cruelty and rage of tyranny? Must they see their cities pillaged, and lain in ashes, their wives and children exposed to the tyrant's lust and fury, and themselves and families reduced by their king to ruin and all the miseries of want and oppression, and yet sit still? Must men alone be debarred the common privilege of opposing force with force, which nature allows so freely to all other creatures...?'

Apparently not. Locke's social contract is different from Hobbes' in being not a once-and-for-all act, but an ongoing bargain between people and sovereign. If a king 'sets himself against the body of the commonwealth, whereof he is head, and shall, with intolerable ill-usage, cruelly tyrannise over the whole, or a considerable part of the people; in this case the people have a right to resist and defend themselves...' But not to go any further. For example, not to revenge themselves, or to lose their sense of respect for the royal authority.

And as to the great question of who shall be judge of whether the government or the prince or legislature is acting contrary to the trust bestowed in them by the people? 'To this I reply, the people shall be judge...' The only further appeal lies in Heaven.

In Locke's times, taxation had proved just such a cause. 'Tis true,' Locke ruefully acknowledges, 'that governments cannot be supported without great charge', so taxes may be levied, as long as it is with the consent of the people, or their representatives. But Locke sets himself firmly against the practice advanced so catastrophically by Charles I in precipitating the Civil War, and sought still by his son, that the royal prerogative allows the monarch to tax without seeking this consent. For the 'great and chief end therefore, of men's uniting into commonwealths, and putting themselves under government, is the preservation of their property'.

The relevance and appeal of Locke's philosophy to the revolutions of the seventeenth century was his own achievement. But little more of Locke might have been heard, had it not been for one of his fellow countrymen, Thomas Paine (1737–1809), some years after his death. Through Paine, Locke's liberal individualism became something much more potent, contributing the ideals as well as the language of the two events that heralded the modern world – the French and American Revolutions.


## The Rights of Man?

Paine himself was from a rather more parochial mould than Locke, primarily concerned with practical matters, such as bridges. Born in Norfolk, the young Paine worked variously as a 'staymaker', a civil servant, a journalist and a school teacher. It was whilst working for the Excise Board in Lewes in Sussex that he became interested in politics, serving on the town council, and holding heated political discussions of Locke's ideas in the White Hart Inn. Actually, Paine once remarked rather dismissively of his debt to his political forbear, that he had 'never read any Locke, nor ever had the work in my hand', but it was certainly Locke's ideas that made the running in those political debates in the *White Hart*.

Paine soon left quiet, half-timbered Lewes for the New World, on the recommendation of Benjamin Franklin himself, whom he had met in London, and at the same time moved from talk to action. On settling in Philadelphia, Paine immediately began to set out his ideas on paper: Lockean ideas of equal rights for men and women, for African and European – and even on the fair treatment for animals. Paine was thus one of the first in America to press for the abolition of slavery. His book *The Rights of Man* is rightly considered a political classic, even overshadowing Locke's ponderous prose, whose ideas in it he so largely borrowed. But it would be the novel issue of national self-determination that made the name of Thomas Paine historically significant – the issue that John Adams, second President of the United States, once described as a dreadful 'hobgoblin', 'so frightful... that it would throw a delicate person into fits to look it in the face'.

In the seventeenth century, uprisings such as the revolt of the Netherlands against the Holy Roman Emperor in Spain, had been driven by religious differences, not by nationalism as such. Even the discontent of the American colonists was directed against unjust treatment by the English king, not against royal authority in itself. Paine's nationalistic pamphlet *Common Sense* was a spark in a tinderbox which started a fire that would eventually sweep away far more than the English claim to America.

Locke's influence again is apparent in the writings of one of Paine's contemporaries and one of the first of the feminist philosophers, Mary Wollstonecraft. Writing, as it were, in parallel with Paine, producing an anonymous *Vindication of the Rights of Man* days before Paine's work (later, in 1798, even entitling one of her books: *The Wrongs of Women*) Wollstonecraft offered a radical personal narrative, endorsing the aims of the French Revolution even as many of her immediate circle were being led to the scaffold. Another work, *A Vindication of the Rights of Women* (1792), pushed forward Locke's liberal hypothesis on women's political importance, with a wide-ranging denunciation of 'male' rationality and power, criticising Rousseau in particular. For this, Wollstonecraft earned the dislike of many prominent male intellectuals of the time, and the particular soubriquet of 'hyena in petticoats' from Horace Walpole. But it was only a journalist like Paine, not a novelist, even a radical one like Wollstonecraft, far less an academic like Locke, who would write:

Why is it that scarcely any are executed but the poor? The fact is a proof, amongst other things, of a wretchedness in their condition. Bred without morals, and cast upon the world without a prospect, they are the exposed sacrifice of vice and legal barbarity. The millions that are superfluously wasted by governments, are more than sufficient to reform these evils, and to benefit the condition of every man in a nation... It is time that nations should be rational, and not be governed like animals, for the pleasure of their riders. To read the history of kings, a man would be almost inclined to suppose that government consisted in stag-hunting, and that every nation paid a million a year to a huntsman... It has cost England almost seventy millions sterling, to maintain a family imported from abroad, of very inferior capacity to thousands in the nation... (*The Rights of Man*, 1791)

Paine had a better idea for the management of the new societies:

In the first place, three hundred representatives, fairly elected, are sufficient for all the purposes to which legislation can apply, and preferable to a larger number. They may be divided into a number of houses, or meet in one, as in France, or in any manner a constitution shall direct.

And, as representation is always considered, in free countries, 'the most honourable of all stations', the 'allowance made to it is merely to defray the expense which the representatives incur by that service, and not to it as an office' – a principle sadly lost somewhere along the line.

Paine even worked out neatly, in double entry bookkeeping form, exactly how much the government would cost, which was not to be very much. In fact, when finances are done his way, there is, happily, enough money to pay all the poor people of the country some money. This money, Paine pointed out, is no more than remission of their own taxes, from hidden taxation imposed by duties on imports and so on. Furthermore, those who cannot work deserve state support, Paine calculates, as the benefits of relieving parents of the twin burdens of paying for the very young and the very old (and the sick – all right, three burdens) enable them to cease being dependent on others, and society is restored to its natural state of being an engine for the production of prosperity.

**Key Ideas**

Locke creates a picture of the world in which 'rationality' is the ultimate authority, not God, and certainly not, as Hobbes had insisted, brute force. He insists that people all have certain fundamental 'rights' and also attempts to return the other half of the human race, the female part, to their proper, equal, place in history, the family and in government.

Locke's legacy is the first, essentially practical, even legalistic, framework and analysis of the workings of society. That is his own particular contribution to its evolution.

- Property is the key to 'civil' society, and the key to property is labour. The more you work, the more you own.
- The powers of government must be strictly limited, in particular by separating the ability to make laws from the ability to make policy.

**Key Text**

Locke's *Essay Concerning the True, Original Extent and End of Civil Government* (1690)

# Timeline: From 'Free Trade' to the Slave Trade

**1703**
Lahonton's idea of the 'noble savage' is celebrated by many 'Enlightenment' thinkers throughout Europe.

**1707**
The largest free trade area in Europe, and the most significant one in the world, is created by the Act of Union between England and Wales and Scotland.

**1710**
In London, St Paul's Cathedral is completed by Sir Christopher Wren.

**1711**
The steam engine is invented by Thomas Newcomen.

**1719**
Daniel Defoe describes the adventures of Robinson Crusoe and two years later Jonathan Swift begins writing *Gulliver's Travels*.

**1721**
Russian factories buy peasants as slave workers.

**1727**
Quakers demand the abolition of slavery, 222 years after the first shiploads of black slaves were unloaded in the newly discovered Americas.

**1747**
A 'carriage tax' is introduced in England.

**1748**
Montesquieu's *Spirit of the Law* inspires later revolutionaries.

**1765**
Publication of the *Discourse on Inequality* sets Rousseau firmly against the optimism of the times.

# 5  Jean-Jacques Rousseau: Inequality or Freedom?

*The* Discourse on Inequality *is a brilliant work. This despite being wrong on almost every factual point and in many a supposed reference. It is not science – it is art, but then, so is politics. Fortunately, the author himself declares his intentions honestly, beginning his book with magnificent disdain, 'Let us begin by putting aside the facts, as they do not affect the question.'*

Thus far, what has been remarkable is the degree of consensus over the forces that shape history and therefore society. It is there in the comforting notion of 'progress' that all the philosophers seem to share. It is there in the admiration for science, and the respect for the institutions that created social life. But as the eighteenth century drew to an end, many of its values looked increasingly tarnished. The low opinion the rulers had of the ruled, the emphasis on privilege, and the aristocratic assumption that it was better not to work than to do so, along with a new indifference to practical problems such as public health and crime, all became increasingly anomalous and insupportable. New ways of looking at the world were needed, and a young Franco-Swiss philosopher, Jean-Jacques Rousseau, offered a complete reversal of the values of the time.

Rousseau did not think anything of civilisation, nor was he impressed by the achievements of science. He instead thought primitive man had been happier and better off. And he measured people's value not by their possessions, but by the divine spark that he saw in them all, the immortal soul of Natural Man. His philosophy offers a more spiritual, romantic view of the world.

And it was anathema to many. Voltaire refused to abandon 'civilisation', to accept what he called an invitation to 'go down on all fours' saying that after 60 years or so, he had lost the habit. Dr Johnson said of Rousseau and his supporters, 'Truth is a cow that will yield them no more milk, so they have gone to milk the bull.'

But many others were entranced and inspired.

## Works

Rousseau was a thinker who had many hats. He was an expert on music, and on education; one of the key figures in the Romantic movement in the arts, and the standard bearer of the romantic tradition. But he was also an unscrupulous and selfish man who, despite the fine words of his child-centred educational philosophy, packed his own five illegitimate children off to the harsh world of the local foundling home, and refused even to see them. Rousseau was insecure too, convinced that everyone was out to get him, and considered offers of help always to be trickery. He constantly complained of being 'misrepresented' and by the end of his life was almost certainly suffering from the madness of full-blown paranoia.

At least he was sometimes able to see himself for what he was. Once, having wickedly accused a servant, a maid, of stealing something in fact he himself had taken, he admitted later, in his *Confessions*, that what he had done was actually the cowardly product of his childish resentment at being rebuffed by her.

But these confessions are also a self-indulgent work. His two most influential essays were written for others. The *Discourse on Inequality* and *The Social Contract* are dedicated to his fellow free citizens of Geneva, and to the 'Magnificent and Most Honoured Lords' who governed what was then a tiny, independent state. Not that he lived there for long, or that relations with the unappreciative burghers of Geneva were particularly good. *The Social Contract* was publicly burnt in the City Square of Geneva in 1762, along with Rousseau's idealistic work on education, *Emile*.

But things were rarely entirely straightforward for Rousseau. Born in 1712, in Geneva, his mother died just a week later from illness resulting from complications following the birth. So Rousseau had to be brought up by his father, Isaac, a watchmaker, and his aunt, and instead of going to school was educated at home. Jean-Jacques' older brother, François, did not like this arrangement, and ran away from home at the first opportunity, never to return. The younger Rousseau, however, had nothing but praise for his father, admiring him to a point little short of adoration. Unfortunately, at the age of ten, Jean-Jacques lost his father too, after the patriot unwisely challenged a gentleman to a duel, and was expelled from the city as a result. Jean-Jacques was then sent to the care of his uncle, which meant living just outside the city walls, where it was intended he would continue a rarefied 'Romanesque' education until the time came for him to be an apprentice engraver.

But before this plan could come to fruition, Rousseau rebelled, refusing what he considered to be a demeaning trade, and, using a tactic his city had demonstrated some years before to gain its independence, changed his religion, becoming the ward of the de Warens of Savoy, some benevolent Catholic aristocrats. It was here, in the library of the French family, that Rousseau drank eagerly from a deep well of subversive writing drawn from the works of the great political philosophers, Hobbes, Machiavelli and Locke amongst them.

After reading Locke, as well as after his perusal of Sir Francis Bacon, Rousseau became part of a loose grouping with a peculiar form of political analysis, known as the Encyclopaedists. The group was so-called because celebrated members, such as Montesquieu and Voltaire, had contributed articles to the huge *Encyclopédie* of 1751–66. But Rousseau never really agreed with their fundamental position, typical of the Enlightenment, which was that religion and conventional philosophy were 'all empty' and should be swept away to allow for a more logical and rational, scientific calculation of the best way to organise life on earth. In addition, the Encyclopaedists believed, as many have since (completely unlike Rousseau) that new technology would usher in a better age, if given half a chance. Science would be the salvation of all mankind – unlike the religious creeds which only ever promised salvation to a minority.

At the age of 32, Rousseau arrived in Paris where he began to move in the sort of circles he felt he belonged in – being, after all, a citizen of Geneva and, as he never tired of telling people, born free. He became secretary to another aristocratic family, found a mistress, and began to write.

His first major work was, in fact, an attack on the ideas of the Encyclopaedists, and indeed the whole basis of the Enlightenment. In the *Discourse on the Sciences and Arts*, Rousseau takes on the scientists, and says that, far from being our saviours, they are ruining the world, and that any notion of progress is an illusion even as we move further and further away from the healthy, simple and balanced lives of the past. The *Discourse on Sciences* is a conscious salute to the kind of society advocated by Plato, two millennia earlier, and both a contrast with and a challenge to the prevailing orthodoxy of his times. Notwithstanding, or probably (in France) because of that, the essay was considered a great success, and earned

Rousseau the Dijon prize. With this was also bestowed upon him, at last, a certain status as that creature the French, above all, cherish – the *philosophe*.

## On Inequality

When the Academy of Dijon requested new essays on the theme: 'What is the origin of inequality amongst men, and is it authorised by Natural Law?' Rousseau took up his quill again (attentive readers will have noted the invention of the fountain pen was only in 1782, some years after Rousseau's death), developing the idea he had sketched in the Discourse on Sciences, that man in his natural state, far from being greedy, or fearful, as described by Hobbes, is in fact in living in a peaceful, contented state, truly free. This is a freedom with three elements. The first is free will, the second is freedom from the rule of law (as there are no laws), and the third is personal freedom. It is this last that is the most important.

Rousseau says that the first people lived like animals. He says this not in any derogatory sense, merely in the sense that the original people sought only simple fulfilment of their physical needs. They would have had no need of speech, nor concepts, and certainly not property. Rousseau points out that much of the imagery in both Hobbes and Locke belongs to a property-owning society, not to the supposed 'natural state' prior to the invention of property rights. By realising this, 'we are not obliged to make a man a philosopher before we can make him a man'. The first time people would have had a sense of property (he thinks) is when they settled in one location, when they built huts to live in. Even sexual union, Rousseau notes pragmatically, as well as reflecting on his own experience, is unlikely to have implied any exclusivity, being more likely to have been just a lustful episode no sooner experienced than forgotten, remembered least of all in terms of the children. Neither the father nor the mother is likely to know whose children they might beget, he argues, assuming that paternity is the defining characteristic and neglecting the mother's very definite knowledge!

Since this primitive state is actually superior to those which followed it, Rousseau goes on to suggest that the only reason why this early society ever changed must have been as a result of some sort of disaster, perhaps one causing shortages of food or other hardship. This would have forced people to start identifying certain areas as theirs, and maybe to start living in groups. This in turn would imply increased communication, and the development of language. And there is a second dimension to these changes: people began to judge themselves by a new criterion – how others thought of them. To Rousseau, this last is a change is of the utmost significance, for it is self-consciousness that was the downfall of Adam and Eve in the Garden of Eden. And it is this self-consciousness that makes humankind permanently unhappy with its lot, and resentful or fearful of others.

Since then, most unfortunately, '... the whole progress of the human race removes man constantly further and further from his primitive state'. According to Rousseau, at this point following Hobbes, society necessarily leads people to hate each other, in accordance with their different economic interests. But Hobbes' so-called 'social contract' is, in fact, made by the rich, as a way of doing down the poor. Actually, not even the rich benefit from it, as they warp themselves and become increasingly out of touch with nature's harmony, raised needlessly above their own proper state, just as the poor are pushed below theirs. Justice instead, for Rousseau, is not, to be sure, crude equality, but rather the correct placing of individuals according to their talents and abilities – according to their merit. Unfortunately, society disrupts this balance (which is also the view put so strongly by Plato in his *Republic*). But Rousseau considers the very notion of the social contract to be flawed:

> Since we have so little knowledge of nature and such imperfect agreement about the meaning of the word 'law', it would be very difficult to concur on a good definition of natural law. All the definitions we find in books have, besides the defects of lacking uniformity, the further defect of being derived from several ideas which men do not have naturally, and the utility of which they cannot conceive until after they have emerged from the state of nature.

Rousseau offers instead just two laws, or principles, that could be said to be 'antecedent to reason'. The first is a powerful interest in self-preservation and our own well-being; the second is 'a natural aversion to seeing any other sentient being perish or suffer, especially if it is one of our own kind'.

The only time 'natural man' would hurt another is when his own well-being requires it. In saying this, Rousseau is drawing a parallel for humankind with the animals who – unlike their masters – never harm each other out of malice alone. If, in fact 'I am obliged to refrain from doing any harm to my neighbour, it is less because he is a reasonable being [i.e. one capable of reasoning] than because he is a sentient one; and a quality which is common to beast and man ought to give the former the right not to be uselessly ill-treated by the latter'.

In fact, *On Inequality* is introduced by Rousseau with the observation that the most important challenge in philosophy is the injunction posed by the Oracle at Delphi, 'Know thyself'. 'The most useful and least developed of all sciences seems to be that of Man', he writes. 'It is this ignorance of man's nature which creates such uncertainty and obscurity as to the correct definition of natural right.' So long as we have no knowledge of natural man, 'we shall wish in vain to ascertain the law which he has received from nature or that which best suits his constitution'.

And the preamble introduces the issue with the noble-sounding aim of seeking to 'defend the cause of humanity' from what at that point is only a shadowy and undefined enemy. The crime is never made entirely clear either, but by the end of the essay, 'the rich', the 'law makers' and various fellow travellers appear to have been accused, found guilty and indicted, even if not actually sentenced.

Rousseau's begins his task by distinguishing between 'two kinds of inequality'. The first is 'natural or physical inequality', consisting in differences of age, health, strength and intelligence; the second is 'moral or political' and consists of 'the different privileges that some enjoy to the prejudice of others' – things such as wealth, honour and power.

The philosophers who have examined the foundations of society have all felt it necessary to go back to the state of nature, but none of them has succeeded in getting there. Some have not hesitated to attribute to men in that state of nature the concept of just and unjust, without bothering to consider whether they must have had such a concept, or even that it would be useful to them. Others have spoken of the natural right each has to keep and defend what he owns without saying what they mean by the word own. Others again, starting out by giving the stronger, authority over the weaker, promptly introduce government, without thinking of the time that must have elapsed before the words authority and government could have had any meaning.

The philosophers who have talked ceaselessly of 'greed, oppression, desire and pride' failed to realise that they were introducing into nature ideas that only originated in society. Rousseau, at this point having in the process of outlining his thesis, veiled his references in suitably opaque language, suddenly becomes more specific: it is Hobbes that is the intellectual enemy, although others who imagine man to be a timid creature, 'always trembling and ready to run away at the least noise he hears or the smallest movement he observes', are also wrong. Although Hobbes had said that man is naturally intrepid and seeks 'only to attack and fight', only Rousseau reveals man as he truly is: the *Noble Savage*.

> Let the civilised man gather all his machines around him, and no doubt he will easily beat the savage; but if you would like to see an even more unequal match, pit the two together naked and unarmed, and you will soon see the advantages of having all ones forces constantly at one's command, of being always prepared for any eventuality, and of always being, so to speak, altogether complete in oneself.

This is the favoured notion at the heart of Rousseau's alternative philosophy. To back it up, he tells the story of the Dutch sailor and the African. The sailor, disembarking at the Cape, gives the African a sack of tobacco weighing about the same as a bucket of coal to carry. When they have walked some distance and are alone, the African asks the sailor if he knows how to run. 'Run?' answers the Dutchman, 'Of course, I can run, and very well!' 'We shall see', says the African, and making away with the tobacco disappears over the horizon almost at once. The sailor, Rousseau finishes, 'bewildered by such marvellous speed', does not think of chasing him, and never sees again either his porter or his tobacco.

This imaginary story is offered to demonstrate the superiority of the natural man over the civilised man. But what then are the supposed advantages of civilisation? Rousseau deals unceremoniously with them. They are but:

> the extreme inequality of our ways of life, the excess of idleness among some and the excess of toil among others, the ease of stimulating and gratifying our appetites and our senses, the over-elaborate foods of the rich, which inflame and overwhelm them with indigestion, the bad food of the poor, which they often go

without altogether, so that they over-eat greedily when they have the opportunity; those late nights, excesses of all kinds, immoderate transports of every passion, fatigue, exhaustion of mind, the innumerable sorrows and anxieties that people in all classes suffer, and by which the human soul is constantly tormented.

So Rousseau considered Hobbes' great mistake to have been to imagine the savage as sharing civilised man's greeds and passions. Instead, Hobbes should have realised that the state of nature was a happy one. It requires a sophisticated, rational knowledge of good and evil to make civilised man so wicked.

... let us not agree with Hobbes that man is naturally evil just because he has no idea of goodness, that he is vicious for want of any knowledge of virtue, that he always refuses to do his fellow men services which he does not believe he owes them, or that on the strength of the right he reasonably claims to things he needs, he foolishly imagines himself to be the sole proprietor of the whole universe.

In even the dark heart of the savage, there is already (what others, too, such as Adam Smith, as we shall see, claim as) the central humanising characteristic: pity, and concern for others. It is there in the savage, because it is there in the animal too. Rousseau says that horses avoid trampling living creatures for similar reasons, that no animal ever passes 'the corpse of a creature of its own species without distress', and that there are even animals which give their dead a sort of burial. The 'mournful lowing of cattle entering a slaughterhouse reveals their feelings in witnessing the horrible spectacle that confronts them'. What, Rousseau asks, are generosity, mercy and humanity but compassion applied to the weak, or to the guilty – or to the human race in general? Even if it were true, he adds, that 'pity is no more than a feeling that puts us in the place of the sufferer', it is still the natural sentiment that ultimately allows the preservation of the species. It is only the philosopher who 'puts his hands over his ears and argues a little with himself' whilst another is murdered outside his window.

(Certainly this is borne out by the events of the twentieth century. It was a sophisticated and highly rational system that devised and implemented the extermination camps, and even at the end of the century, in a series of 'hands over ears' incidents, it was the intellectuals at the top of the United Nations who approved the abandonment both of ill-omened 'safe havens' in the Balkans, as well as of almost a million Tutsi Rwandans to their deaths at the hands of carefully planned and centrally coordinated mobs and militias.)

On the other hand, savage man, Rousseau writes, would wander in the forests without work, speech, home, or war, without relationships, without either need nor fear of his fellows, concerned only for a few simple physical needs. 'A savage may well seize the fruits which another has gathered', Rousseau imagines, or he may even try to enslave another he comes upon, but he cannot stop the other slipping away into the forest to gather some more for himself once his vigilance slackens. The tragedy of human existence is that someone eventually came upon a more permanent way of exploiting their neighbour. Someone invented private property.

'The first man who, having enclosed a piece of land, thought of saying "This is mine" and found people simple enough to believe him, was the true founder of civil society', says Rousseau. Before there was property, he adds, apparently misquoting Locke (who speaks of injustice), there could be no injury.

So, men 'ceased to doze under the first tree', instead developing tools from stones and branches, and using these to till the land and create huts, developing their notions of property, from which inevitably 'quarrels and fights were born'. Soon, society required 'a language more complex than that of crows or monkeys'. And there were other consequences. The conventional, 'nuclear' family was created, producing not only (what he at least professed to consider) the desirable by-product of men and women living together in conjugal and paternal love, but also some less desirable gender differences. Notably, women becoming 'more sedentary' as they become accustomed 'to looking after the hut and children whilst men go out to seek the common sustenance'. But the men too, become rather sedentary:

> This new condition, with its solitary life... left men to enjoy a great deal of leisure, which they used to procure many sorts of commodities unknown to their fathers; and this was the yoke they imposed upon themselves, without thinking about it, and the first source of the evils they prepared for their descendants.

Not only did such commodities 'continue to soften both body and mind', but they themselves 'almost lost through habitual use their power to please', and as they had at the same time degenerated into actual needs, 'being deprived of them became much more cruel than the possession of them was sweet; and people were unhappy in losing them without being happy in possessing them'.

Thus it was that Man, who was formerly free, was diminished into subjection, slave to a multitude of 'new wants' and ambitions, notably the 'burning desire to enlarge his own fortune, not so much from real need as [from the desire] to put himself above others', as Rousseau puts it, in words with echoes today for consumer societies.

In due course, this urge to dominate becomes like blood lust. The consumers are like 'ravenous wolves which, having tasted human flesh, refuse all other nourishment'. The rich use their old slaves to subdue new ones, and dream only of subjugation and exploitation of their fellows.

Rousseau paints a mocking portrait of the rich man, seeking to protect his gains by pretending concern for his victims. 'Let us unite', says his rich man, 'to protect the weak from oppression, to ensure for each that which he owns, and create a system of justice and peace that all shall be bound to, without exception.'

Rousseau thinks his explanation of civil law is more convincing than those offered by philosophers who suppose some sort of universal social contract for, as he puts it, the poor have only one good – their freedom – and to voluntarily strip themselves of that without gaining anything in exchange would appear to be absolute folly. The rich, on the other hand, have much to gain, and consequently (he thinks) it seems reasonable to suppose the thing to have been invented by them, 'by those to whom it was useful rather than by those to whom it was injurious'. (Actually, in later writings, notably *The Social Contract*, Rousseau suggests that a way around the selfishness could be through a system of majority voting in which each individual's wishes become instead part of a 'general will', rather than reflecting directly anyone's particular desires.)

Rousseau's version of the origins of the division of labour is similarly perverse and even bizarre. Instead of the use of iron improving agriculture, he sees it as a burden on the producers of food. 'The more the number of industrial workers multiplied, the fewer hands were engaged in providing the common subsistence, without there being any fewer mouths to feed.'

Then we must consider all the unhealthy trades of modern society – labouring in mines, preparation of certain metals (such as lead) – and ironically, the migration to the cities, before we can claim society has improved people's lives. Not that Rousseau is saying we should return to 'living with the bears', a conclusion he hastens, as he says, to forestall.

By contrast, Natural Man, outside society, will not tolerate subjugation, 'as an unbroken horse paws the ground with its hooves' and rears at the approach of the bit, or animals break their heads against the 'bars of their prisons', yet civil society reduces all to slaves. And the explanation offered by such as 'Mr Locke' that the government is but like a father to us, Rousseau dismisses too, for, 'by the law of nature, the father is master of the child only for such time as his help is necessary and that beyond this stage, the two are equals, the son becoming perfectly independent of the father'. In fact, by giving up liberty, a man degrades his being.

Moving from the small picture to the larger, contemporary one, Rousseau offers a 'hands-off' state. The only way that the sovereign and the people can have a single and identical interest, so that all the movements of the civil machine tend to promote the common happiness, is for them to be one and the same. No one can be outside the law, for once they are, all the others are 'at their discretion'. Furthermore, there should be few laws, and new ones introduced only with the greatest circumspection, so that 'before the constitution could be disturbed, there would be time enough for everyone to reflect that it is above all the great antiquity of the laws that makes them sacred and inviolable'.

The *Discourse*, as we have said, is dedicated to Geneva, a city that retained its independence in the face of a Europe of much larger nation states, not by any pretensions of military power, but by playing the religious card at the appropriate and opportune time, and defecting from the other Catholic areas of Switzerland towards Protestant worship, under the protection of Lutheran Berne. This protection allowed Jean Calvin, the French theologian, time to reorganise the city state of Geneva along democratic lines, with a general assembly of all citizens (but not all adults), a Council of Two Hundred, and an executive council. Rousseau considered Calvin to be a great law-giver in the mould of the Romans. But Calvin's state was in fact not so progressive, and it quickly degenerated into the rule of the executive council – an oligarchy. Calvin himself persecuted religious dissenters, expulsion from Geneva became the norm, and executions were not out of place in the free city. Calvin never considered women to be citizens, and as time went by the majority of the men were not either.

Rousseau's view of women is no more egalitarian – at best it is romantic in an unenlightened sort of way. In *Emile*, he confines the education of the fair sex to domestic science and recommends training from an early age in habits of docility and subservience. At the time of *Discourse on Inequality*, Rousseau did not appear unduly worried by any possible defect in the democracy regarding the lack of rights for the women, writing:

> Could I forget that precious half of the commonwealth which assures the happiness of the other, and whose sweetness and prudence maintain its peace and good morals? Lovable and virtuous women of Geneva, your destiny will always be to govern ours. Happy are we so long as your chaste power, exerted solely within the marriage bond, makes itself felt only for the glory of the state and well-being of the public!

Rather than challenge the system, the self-styled radical continues to stress instead the respect due to the governing magistrates:

> The people must have respect for their leaders, for the magistrates of Geneva afford an example of moderation, of simplicity in morals, of respect for the laws, and the most sincere spirit of rec-onciliation. There is not in the universe a body of men more upright, more enlightened, more worthy of respect.

He finishes, sanctimoniously:

> Magnificent and Most Honoured lords, the worthy and revered magistrates of a free people, allow me to offer you in particular my homage and my respect. If there is in the world a rank capable of conferring glory on those who occupy it, it is undoubtedly one acquired by your talent and virtue, the rank of which you have proved yourselves worthy and to which your fellow citizens have raised you.

Rousseau adds mysteriously, to any still sceptical readers, 'Beware, above all, of ever listening to sinister interpretations and malicious rumours, the secret motives of which are often more dangerous than the actions they report.'

But despite the unsavoury undercurrents, and irrespective of the truth or otherwise of the sinister rumours, the Geneva that Rousseau had reluctantly left in his youth and which remained the backdrop to his philosophising, was a successful and contented one: business was good and taxes were moderate. There was even a social security system, and corruption was almost unknown.

The details of institutions of government are not of much interest to Rousseau once their essentially malign character has been identified. He merely adds that if law and property are the first stage in human society, and the institutions of government are the second, then the third and last stage is the transformation of legitimate into arbitrary power. Human society leads people to hate each other in proportion 'to the extent that their interests conflict'. People pretend to do each other services whilst actually trying to exploit them and do them down. 'We must attribute to the institution of property, and hence to society, murders, poisonings, highway robbery and indeed, the punishments of those crimes.' That is at the individual level. On the national scale, 'Inequality, being almost non-existent in the state of nature... becomes fixed and legitimate through the institution of property and laws.' When society has, as it inevitably will, degenerated into tyranny and all are slaves again, the circle is complete, for 'all individuals become equal again when they are nothing'. And all the time 'Civil man' torments himself constantly in search of ever more laborious occupations, working himself to death, 'renouncing life in order to achieve immortality'.

Civil society is, in fact, a society of people 'who nearly all complain and several of whom indeed deprive themselves of their existence'. This is the logic of property ownership and capitalism.

## Influence

What, then, is the legacy of Jean-Jacques Rousseau? His influence is greater than is perhaps often realised. He is one of the fathers of the peculiarly French school of philosophy which is concerned with *la conditione humaine* and, in particular, with our attempts at finding our true selves. Freedom, the French challenge us, is actually within, obtained from finding our true identity, not from having satisfied social conventions and stereotypes. It requires having the opportunity to live the kind of life we want to live.

Rousseau offers a view of social evolution in which the human animal is being moulded by its environment, deriving its attitudes and values from its surroundings. With regard to human nature, Rousseau is the optimist to Hobbes' pessimist. All people are born with the qualities that will lead them to success and happiness – given the right conditions. In *Emile*, as part of his account of bringing up a child, he makes this even more explicit, describing how the child acquires needs and feelings different from those it is born with, as an effect and result of its environment. If the child is unhappy, it is because of a fault with its surroundings, and the same is true, he thinks, for adults.

The *Discourse* itself is an essay that somehow manages to be already at least 1,000 years out of date even when it was written, in the early years of the Industrial Revolution – and surprisingly contemporary. Rousseau has not only 'put aside' the facts but seems to have 'put aside' such niceties as overall theory and logical structure. Yet *On Inequality* is still, undoubtedly, magnificent; and more than that, it contains truths about human nature which other philosophers somehow failed to see. The common people to whom it is addressed did, however, recognise them, and for that reason Rousseau's tract became one of the most influential works not only of its time, but of all time. That, surely, is the true measure of a political work.

Rousseau died in 1778, the same year as his critic Voltaire, possibly by his own hand, and certainly in sad and lonely circumstances. But as Goethe commented: 'with Voltaire an age ended, with Rousseau, a new one began'.


**Key Ideas**


Rousseau's recipe for human society can be expressed in just one word: 'Freedom'. Rousseau offers us a fairly implausible idea of what this might be, and supposes it to be in conflict and opposition to the structures of modern societies. But Rousseau's legacy is still important as a reminder of non-material values, and a more optimistic if romanticised notion of humanity. What he offers us may be largely false and often is hopelessly impractical, but it is also always an important, alternative understanding of ourselves.

- People are happy and satisfied in the 'state of nature', but the invention of property brings about competition, inequality and conflict.
- Most of the desires and wants of modern society are artificial, pointless and ultimately self-destructive.

**Key Text**

Rousseau's *Discourse on Inequality* (1753)

# Timeline: From Standardising English to Numbering Houses

## 1752
Benjamin Franklin demonstrates that lightning is, in fact, electricity.

## 1755
Samuel Johnson's book of words, the 'dictionary', standardises English.

## 1759
Voltaire publishes *Candide*, a cynical portrait of a Dr Pangloss who believes that everything is always for the best in the 'best of all possible worlds'.

## 1760
Rural Britain changes for ever under the Enclosure Acts which take away the traditional rights of commoners. This is the year conventionally taken as the beginning of the Industrial Revolution.

## 1764
Houses in London are numbered.

## 1775
The War of American Independence begins; it will end in total success for the colonists after heavy defeats of the English a few years later. The distinctive federal constitution of the United States is signed into existence at Philadelphia in 1787.

## 1776
*Wealth of Nations* published.

# 6   Adam Smith's Inquiry into the Wealth of Nations

*From Smith, we gain a new perspective on human society. Where others saw society as determined by human decisions and choices, whether altruistic, as in Plato and Locke, or selfish, as in Machiavelli and Hobbes, Smith argues that economic forces have a power all of their own, and that our political arrangements, indeed our values, are only a consequence of these subtle forces.*

The English, American and French revolutions, momentous though they seemed, were only so many puffs of smoke, the superficial, political aspects of far greater, but hidden, subterranean economic volcano that had been slowly building up pressure in the preceding centuries.

The first person to examine the significance and impersonal power of these economic forces was not, as is sometimes said, the iconoclastic revolutionary, Marx, in the nineteenth century, but the highly conventional son of a civil servant lawyer, a century earlier. It is Smith who first writes of the Industrial Revolution and predicts that, like the most fearsome lava flow, it will sweep over the industrial landscape, incinerating all the old political certainties as so much dead wood, destroying all that it touches.

As with so many political activists, Smith's childhood was uneventful enough. He was brought up alone in Kirkcaldy, on the eastern coast of Scotland, by his mother, Margaret. His father had died before he was born, although it is only for psychologists to discern any effects here. But, certainly, the maternal bond was a particularly strong and lifelong one, and the father of *laissez-faire* economics also has a caring side.

Smith proceeded smoothly from Kirkcaldy school to Glasgow and then Oxford universities, although he had a low opinion of the English institution. He describes it, disgustedly, as a place where 'the greater part of the public professors have, for these many years, given up altogether even the pretence of teaching'. When, years later, he himself became Professor of Moral Philosophy at Glasgow, he was a most scrupulous lecturer, not above putting on extra sessions of related topics that students might find interesting or useful. His 'public' lecture was given first thing each weekday, followed by seminar discussions the rest of the morning, with additional lectures in the afternoon, finally finishing off with extra tutorials for selected students. (As a perk, not a punishment, of course.) Not to mention time for the considerable amounts of extra administrative work that he found for himself. At this time, students paid the bulk of a professor's salary in the form of fees directly to the lecturer, and the story goes that when Professor Smith had to leave the university just half way through the session of 1764, the students refused to accept reimbursement of their monies, saying that 'the instruction and pleasure received' was already more than they could ever repay.

Had they known that Smith merely planned a 'grand tour' of Europe in charge of two young dandies, a privilege offered in return for acting as their chaperone, they might have changed their minds. But in any case, for Smith, the leisured life deprived of his teaching and administrative duties was so dull that, early on in the tour, at Toulouse, he wrote home that he had decided to write a book 'to pass away the time'. So it was that the best-selling work of its time, and one of the most important economic analyses of all time, *An Inquiry into the Nature and Causes of the Wealth of Nations*, came to be written.

## Work

Smith is a philosopher in the mould of Plato and Aristotle. He is prepared to deal with all types of question, all types of evidence, untrammelled by notions of sticking to a narrow discipline. He is a philosopher, but he is also a social scientist, an historian and a natural scientist too. (His *History of Astronomy* is counted very highly by historians of science.) Smith's method is to examine the research and findings of others and to make new connections, new discoveries from them. He is aware that any theory he puts forward, just as with any straightforwardly 'physical' theory, such as Newton's, remains just theory, always capable of refutation. His writing is philosophy as a way of thinking, applied to real issues and questions – not philosophy as an esoteric body of obscure knowledge, as it so often is for lesser academicians.

The *Inquiry* is also the result of another grand journey, one that had started for Smith with the question of 'justice', tackled in the process of cataloguing the history of law. On this journey, he had explored the nature of ethics in *The Moral Sentiments*, before arriving in due course at economics, which is, for Smith, the hidden set of rules that govern society. Additionally (again anticipating Marxism), he believed economic realities could be observed in the changing nature of the overt laws of the judicial system.

The geographical tour itself hinged on Paris, which Smith and his two companions found much the most agreeable part. And here Smith discovered a group of French intellectuals to discuss economics with. The French held that agriculture and mining were fundamentally the source of national wealth because they alone permitted a genuine conversion of labour into production: other processes, such as manufacturing, merely turned one sort of product into another. Smith was highly impressed by this, later describing it as 'perhaps the nearest approximation to the truth that has yet been discovered on the subject of political economy'.

When the tour eventually finished, Smith returned to the British Isles, and completed his book, aided by discussions with other intellectuals, such as Benjamin Franklin, then visiting London, and incidentally dispatching Thomas Paine to the New World to start a revolution. Indeed the *Wealth of Nations* itself was published in 1776, the year of American independence. At the time, Smith was concerned that his work might be felt to be controversial – after all, he described it ironically in a letter as a 'very violent attack... upon the whole commercial system of Great Britain' – but his worries proved to be unnecessary. The book simply became a bestseller, highly sought after and popular, with its author a correspondingly popular and increasingly wealthy man. Yet, in line with his dry reputation, Smith continued to live quietly and gave away most of his new-found riches to charity – anonymously.

So what did this bestseller reveal? In the *Inquiry*, Adam Smith writes of four stages in society: an age of hunters, one of shepherds, an agrarian age, and finally an age of commerce. Society, he says, only begins to need laws and government in the second stage. The 'Age of Shepherds' is where government commences. 'Property makes it absolutely necessary', as he puts it in one of his 'Lectures on Jurisprudence':

The wood of the forest, the grass of the field, and all the natural fruits of the earth, which, when land was in common, cost the labourer only the trouble of gathering them, come... to have an additional price fixed upon them.

Animals begin to belong to people, and shepherds, unlike hunters, are concerned with future planning as well as with the present. In seeing the need to protect property as the origin of government, and hence of society, Smith is following Locke. However, unlike Locke, he also sees the process as bearing rather unequally on the citizens: 'Civil government, so far as it is instituted for the security of property, is in reality instituted for the defence of the rich against the poor, or of those who have some property against those who have none at all.' This is a radical insight.

This is also a little like Rousseau, who had spoken of the rich man's advantage over the poor. But Smith's perspective on 'savage man' is very different. He writes, in what could be an impassioned plea for the welfare state:

Among the savage nations of hunters and fishers, every individual who is able to work, is more or less employed in useful labour, and endeavours to provide, as well as he can, the necessaries and conveniences of life, for himself, or such of his family or tribe as are either too old, or too young, or too infirm to go a hunting and fishing. Such nations are, however, so miserably poor that, from mere want, they are frequently reduced, or at least, think themselves reduced, to the necessity sometimes of directly destroying, and sometimes of abandoning their infants, their old people, and those afflicted with lingering diseases to perish with hunger, or to be devoured by wild beasts.

Smith's starting point is that the central motivation of mankind is a desire for approval by others. 'Sympathy' creates a social bond. Here, it should be explained that the ordering of the chapters in his books reflects Smith's view of the importance and explanatory role of the concepts. So, the first chapter of the *Wealth of Nations* is entitled: 'Of the Division of Labour'; the first chapter of *The Theory of Moral Sentiments*, his other major work, if rather less influential, is entitled 'Of Sympathy'. Human beings, Smith explains there, have a spontaneous tendency to observe others. From this, we turn to judging ourselves, and the moral identity of the individual develops, in this way emerging from social interaction. 'Sympathy', or 'awareness of other's feelings' (we might say 'empathy'), explains morality; the division of labour explains economics. A human being growing up in isolation, Smith thinks, will have no sense of right and wrong – nor any need for the concept:

> ... without any communication with his own species, he could no more think of his own character, of the propriety or demerit of his own sentiments and conduct, of the beauty or deformity of his own mind, than of the beauty or deformity of his own face.

In his ethics, as in his economics, Smith is scientific in intention. He is aware of the possibility of self-deception, in both studies, and curses it as the source of 'half of the disorders of human life'. If only, he wrote in the *Moral Sentiments*, we could see ourselves as others see us, 'a reformation would be unavoidable. We could not otherwise endure the sight.'

However, it is self-interest that underpins the economic system. In his most famous epigram, he says: '... it is not from the *benevolence* of the butcher, the brewer, or the baker, that we expect dinner, but from their regard to their own interest'. The individual does not intend to promote the public interest, but 'intends only his own gain, and he is in this, as in many other cases, led by an invisible hand to promote an end which was no part of his intention'.

Smith illustrates the role in economics of the division of labour by considering the increase in productivity possible by changing the process of manufacture of a pin in a pin factory. Acting alone, one man could 'scarce, with his utmost industry, make one pin a day, and certainly could not make twenty. But if the work can be divided up – 'one man draws out the wire, another straights it, a third cuts it, a fourth points it, a fifth grinds it at the top for receiving the head; to make the head requires three distinct operations; to put on is a peculiar business, to whiten the pins is another; it is even a trade in itself to put them into the paper...' – ten people, he suggests, could produce

> about twelve pounds of pins a day. There are in a pound upwards of four thousand pins of middling size. Those ten persons, therefore, could make upwards of forty-eight thousand pins a day. But if they had all wrought them separately,... they could certainly not each of them make twenty, perhaps not one pin a day.

Smith then goes on to relate this to the accumulation of capital, the increase of employment and finally the emergence of mechanisms to control the resulting tendency for wages to increase.

So great are the advantages of this industrial approach, that even the humblest member of 'a civilised country' is part of a complex system providing sophisticated goods and services.

Compared indeed, with the more extravagant luxury of the great, his accommodation must no doubt appear extremely simple and easy; and yet it may be true, perhaps, that the accommodation of a European Prince does not always so much exceed that of an industrious and frugal peasant as the accommodation of the latter exceeds that of many an African king, the absolute master of the lives, and liberties of ten thousand naked savages.

Another of the advantages of dividing up labour – specialising – is that people then think of ways of improving that specific task, improvements otherwise obscured by the complexities of the whole process. And the first chapter ends with the observation:

... if we examine, I say, all these things, and consider what a variety of labour is employed about each of them, we shall be sensible that without the assistance and co-operation of many thousands, the very meanest person in a civilised country could not be provided, even according to, what we falsely imagine, the easy and simple manner in which he is commonly accommodated.

This Panglossian vision that everything is for the best in all possible worlds, mocked acerbically by Voltaire in his novel *Candide* (where no matter what disaster befalls the main character, he insists all is serendipity), is an indispensable element of Smith's analysis. In this, he is following a tradition that can be traced back to the Stoics of ancient Greece and Mesopotamia – indeed, before them, to Eastern notions of harmony. The tendency of supply and demand to reach an equilibrium, and of the market price to reflect the underlying 'natural price' are part of this philosophy.

Smith is sometimes vilified by those who aspire (at least) to be 'do-gooders', for advocating *laissez-faire* economics – leaving things to sort themselves out without government interference. It is not so often recognised that this was because he himself certainly believed that if this were done the outcome would be not just acceptable, but (*vide* Dr Pangloss) the best possible for everyone. Free trade encourages countries to specialise in what they are good at, and forces them to give up doing what they are not. This results in more goods being produced in total (because they are produced more efficiently). The same applies on a regional level too. For example, within a state, improving road links may remove physical obstacles to trade, with the effect of making a region's special wine or woolly jumpers worth transporting to the rest of the country. (However, as poorer regions also know, the reverse is also true: large efficient companies outside the region can move in and displace even the last few small cottage industries of the local communities. The overall gains may still be at the clear expense of the small region.)

There are practical restraints on this policy, but it provides a set of clear economic targets to aim at. In domestic affairs, the state is left with a minimal role, but for Smith it is not just in defence and law and order, but also in providing many of those services that commerce will not bother with – such as building sewers or bridges and providing elementary schools. And not all enterprises are even best in private hands – Smith offers transport as an example. A privately owned road can be profitable even when poorly looked after by the unscrupulous, so it is better for the state to provide them and maintain higher standards. Conversely, canals *must* be maintained, otherwise the private owner can make no money out of them, so they can be left in private hands. As far as education goes, Smith recommends the practice current then in Scotland (and which he himself had experienced) of making teachers and professors depend upon the satisfaction of their classes for their wages. Where this link is broken, Smith warns, slackness obtains (as at Oxford).

With taxation, Smith lays down four principles. (Smith generally has something of a quaternate turn of mind.) First, taxes should be based on 'ability to pay'. Second, tax policy should be made publicly known and therefore predictable. Third, taxes should be collected with the convenience of the taxpayer in mind. Finally, this should all be done with a minimum of administration or other expense. Today we might add fifth and sixth principles of proportionality and choice: taxes should not be levied on essentials, such as food or water, nor should they be so great as to be effectively punishments for an activity, for example, smoking or drinking alcohol. Environmentalists might amend this with a seventh principle of 'encouraging sustainability' and avoiding damage to the ecology of the country.

Smith notes that the division of labour is limited by the size of the available market. In a village, the specialisation is less, in a town it is more. In the town, carpentry, joinery, cabinet-making, wood-carving are separate occupations of different skilled people; in the village, one person will do all of them. Smith is not wholly enamoured with the division process however (perhaps still recalling the specialists at Oxford), noting that a worker reduced to performing one task can become 'as stupid and ignorant as it is possible for a human creature to become'; indeed the process even threatens to reduce people to 'riot and debauchery'.

To combat this unfortunate tendency (amongst other reasons), Smith says the state should provide basic education for all the citizens. 'For a very small expense the public can facilitate, can encourage, and can even impose upon almost the whole body of the people, the necessity of acquiring those most essential parts of education.'

The size of the market does not depend simply on the number of people who live in a particular area. It depends also on the roads or other transport links in the area and on the ability of producers to get their produce to the people. Smith notes the effect cheaper transport by water was having on trade at the time, recalling that ancient civilisations developed along sea coasts and river banks, and in particular around the Mediterranean sea. (This, Smith wonders irrelevantly, in one aside, being enclosed and calm, was 'extremely favourable to the infant navigation of the world... to pass beyond the pillars of Hercules, that is, to sail out of the Straits of Gibraltar, was, in the ancient world, considered a most wonderful and dangerous exploit of navigation'.) Smith deduces that if economic growth is to be sustained, the market has to widen continually. This is one of the main reasons, he believes, to support free trade.

What are the mechanisms by which this trade can be carried out? Smith has an indefatigable interest in the detail of the beginnings of money. The exchange of goods can be carried out by barter – the butcher stockpiles some beef, the baker some loaves, and so on – but as there may be a baker who does not eat beef, or other practical shortcomings of the system, this soon gives way to exchange of goods by reference to one particular commodity, such as gold or silver (or salt, which gives us the word 'salary'), and hence to money itself. He describes at some length (one of the most popular parts of the book) the transition to coinage, a process driven by the two related problems of how to stop people from adulterating the metals, or from filing small bits off to make a little extra margin for themselves. Kings and Royal Mints themselves were past masters at this, of course, with Roman silver coins, in the dying days of the Republic, worth just one twenty-fourth of what they started out as. Smith, ever frugal himself, indignantly condemns 'the avarice and injustice of princes and sovereign states', who, 'by abusing the confidence of their subjects, have by degrees reduced the quantity of metal which had been originally contained in their coins'.

But if the value of the coin used to depend on the amount of silver in it – what gave the silver its value anyway? Smith says, 'The real price of every thing, what every thing really costs... is the toil and trouble of acquiring it.' Prices are essentially measures of the amount of labour needed to make the commodity. 'Labour, therefore, is the real measure of the exchangeable value of commodities.' Rents paid in corn, Smith notes, have held their value far better than rents paid in anything else. 'From century to century, corn is the better measure because, from century to century, equal quantities of corn will command the same quantity of labour more nearly than equal quantities of silver.'

Now, on one level, this is obviously not true. (Ask an artist – or even an author!) But let Smith have his say. He admits it is more complicated than that. It is the 'nominal value' of goods that determines whether trade is profitable – so for example, tea in China is cheap, and worth the while of the European importer to purchase it. It is therefore nominal values that regulate 'almost the whole business of common life in which price is concerned – we cannot wonder that it should have been so much more attended to than the real price'.

Smith considers there to be a 'real' value for everything, and a 'nominal' value, which is its market valuation, its price. It is the nominal value that drives the marketplace. The price someone is prepared to pay is determined by several factors. There is the 'psychological' factor of how much they want it. There is the practical consideration of the manufacturer of how much they have had to spend already to produce the goods. This will include the wages of the workers, the share due to the people who have provided the investment in the machinery and premises for the manufacture, the rent of any equipment or land, and the cost of the raw materials. Smith distinguishes the types of cost because they have different effects. The workers require recompense simply for their time and effort. This he considers to be fairly straightforward.

> The difference of natural talents in different men is, in reality, much less than we are aware of... [that] between a philosopher and a common street porter, for example, seems to arise not so much from nature as from habit, custom, and education. When they came into the world, and for the first six or eight years of their existence they were perhaps very much alike, and neither their parents nor play-fellows could perceive any remarkable differences...

If everyone had to do everything for themselves, as would be the case without the division of labour and the mechanisms for the trading or bartering of goods, people would all appear much the same too. Yet, people do in fact get paid very different amounts for jobs – and it is certainly not due to the different amount of time and effort invested. (Although largely spurious claims may be made to this effect – or about the rarity of the skills involved in certain kinds of work. Media stars, university professors, managers and chief executives are amongst today's examples of this self-serving delusion. We might add to what Smith said, the general rule that the more people are paid, the more important and unique they believe themselves to be!) Smith himself acknowledges that each factor, such as wages or rent, of the 'natural price' is in itself subject to the influence of demand in relation to supply.

However, 'Labour alone, never varying in its own value, is alone the ultimate and real standard by which the value of all commodities can at all times and places be estimated and compared. It is their real price; money is their nominal price only.' He puts it like this:

> The labour of the manufacturer fixes and realises itself in some particular subject or vendible [sellable] commodity, which lasts for some time at least after that labour is past. It is, as it were, a certain quantity of labour stocked and sorted up to be employed, if necessary, upon some other occasion.

Various examples are offered. There is the simple case of fish. Those caught from the sea involve only the labour and capital costs, those caught from rivers will also include a 'rent' charge, to the owner of the fishing rights. There is the more sophisticated case of the factory. The owner of the factory requires a return on the investment, which varies with the amount of capital invested. This is because this capital could have been simply put in a bank (where the manager could then lend it to others for a small fee) and left to grow by compound interest. Profit and interest are basically the same sort of thing – return on capital. Rent, Smith sees as different, because rent may simply be a charge imposed without any original investment, although any asset that can be rented can probably be sold too – in which case we might say to Smith that the distinction disappears. But Smith describes the landlord as one who 'loves to reap where others have sowed'. 'They are the only one of the three orders whose revenue costs them neither labour nor care, but comes to them, as it were, of its own accord, and independent of any plan or project of their own.'

So Smith's economic analysis depends on a three-fold division which seems to collapse into a two-fold one. But there is another more serious problem, too. The price of say, nails, will depend on their 'usual price', the demand for things made using nails, the demand for other things made with nails, which are competing for the supply, the availability of iron to make nails and blacksmiths to smelt them (or however they are made!) and indeed all of these things may in turn be affected by the price of nails. When the price of a 'variable' depends on itself, we have what physicists term 'feedback'. (The amount of feedback with the nails may not be very noticeable or significant, but consider the price of houses or postage stamps or shares!) Feedback makes these phenomena behave strangely. In fact, this phenomenon of 'non-linearity' is what makes the stock markets so attractive to investors. Because no one can predict anything reliably, it is always possible for someone to make a large profit by, say, speculating on the price of nails.

Smith accepts that supply and demand are 'complex' and cannot be represented by any simple (linear) relationship. Take wages, for example. The only *real* component of wages, he says, is the amount necessary to keep the worker alive, although Smith does insist that the subsistence wage is actually a bit more – that which is 'consistent with common humanity'. But in any case, in a growing economy, there may be a shortage of workers, obliging the employers to compete amongst each other for the workers, particularly by raising wages. He compares the experience of the then 'tiger' economies of Britain and America with the static economy of China, and the shrinking one of Bengal, concluding that it 'is not the actual greatness of national wealth, but its continual increase, which occasions a rise in the wages of labour'. This improvement of the 'lower ranks' is not an 'inconveniency' but a moral necessity, for no society can surely be flourishing and happy, when the greater part of the members are poor and miserable. 'It is but equity, besides, that they who feed, cloath and lodge the whole body of the people, should have such a share of the produce of their own labour as to be themselves tolerably well fed, cloathed and lodged.' But in the *absence* of economic growth, Smith predicts that wages will be forced down to the subsistence level.

Smith details the all important subject of wage levels a bit more precisely too. There are several components. There is the 'unpleasantness' factor. Unpleasant work will be avoided if the worker can subsist without doing it, and therefore the employer must raise the wage to compensate. Smith assumes all work to be basically worse than not working – 'toil and trouble', an assertion which may not be universally true (unemployment itself can be a heavy burden), but surely is a reasonable approximation. Secondly, work which requires skill or training is like work which requires an expensive machine – the cost of hiring a professional must reflect this. Smith thinks work which is irregular may attract an extra premium (although we might argue that this is clearly not the case with 'casual work' such as that epitome of low-paid work, picking harvests for farmers). Jobs requiring people to step back slightly from their own selfish interests, such as being a doctor, also need to be given additional rewards.

Smith observes that people tend to be optimistic about their chances of success in life. In a lottery, for instance, the chances of winning may be slightly less than the chance of being run over getting the lottery ticket (to embellish his example). People will tend to feel optimistic and sure that this sort of reality does not apply to them. Indeed, they may behave irrationally by buying several tickets – irrationally, since even if they bought *all* the tickets in the lottery, they would still end up with less money than they had put in. Similarly, Smith notes, people will not pay a small premium for insurance against fire, because they believe that this misfortune will not befall them anyway. For this reason, jobs involving a calculation of risk, such as being a soldier, or even taking on difficult legal cases which require winning, may not obtain the extra premium that the market should determine, if everything was worked out logically.

Smith's legacy is to explain economics in terms of the circulation of goods and materials, acted upon, as Locke, too, says, by labour. But Smith distinguishes the different characteristics of capital and income, and explains the significance of savings. He begins by observing that capital is of two types, fixed and circulating. Fixed capital is like the lathes in a factory, or the skills of their operators. Circulating capital is the profit from the selling of the products, as this profit can then be used to buy a new carriage for the factory's owner, which involves more profits for the carriage maker, and all their suppliers too. Because of this, it is circulating capital that keeps the economy going, and only certain parts of the economy produce it. Civil servants, teachers and soldiers, for example, do not produce any circulating capital, although they may be useful for other reasons. (It could be said, indeed, that they may facilitate others in the making of circulating capital, thereby increasing the amount of circulating capital.)

However, Smith does have his eye on certain activities which he considers to be essentially worthless. The labour of the 'menial servant', such as that of a footman who puts his master's coat on him each morning, he says, 'does not fix or realise itself in any particular or vendible commodity. His services generally perish in the very instant of their performance, and seldom leave any trace or value behind them...'

The same goes, Smith adds dismally, for some of the 'gravest and most important, and some of the most frivolous professions... Like the declamation of the actor, the harangue of the orator, or the tune of the musician, the work of all of them perishes in the very instant of its production.' We must leave aside speculation as to whether Smith would have considered the advent of sound and video recording technology as making these professions any the less transitory and frivolous, but indubitably the entertainments industry today is now a major source of 'circulating capital'.

Smith is actually rather against spending in general (let alone on frivolities): he sees it as usually unnecessary and inferior to saving. Money saved is available for business to borrow, creating new jobs which in turn create new goods and new profits. These new profits more than cover the initial borrowings, creating 'a perpetual fund for the maintenance of an equal number in times to come'. The urge to save, Smith thinks, is 'the desire of bettering our condition, a desire which, though generally calm and dispassionate, comes with us from the womb, and never leaves us till we go into the grave'. Yet what is saved? Just intrinsically worthless lumps of metal or promises to pay.

The *Wealth of Nations* is not just a discourse on the dismal science. It contains many profound insights into sociology, psychology and ethical behaviour. The historian H.T. Buckle said of the work: 'looking at its ultimate results, [it] is probably the most important book that has ever been written, and is certainly the most valuable contribution ever made by a single man towards establishing the principles on which government should be based'.

The book is a great work. But its greatness lies not in its originality, for little in it had not been suggested elsewhere before, and Smith, as a scrupulous scholar, would have been aware of the discussions. It is rather in the clarity and comprehensiveness of his vision.

## Influence

In the intervening centuries between Plato and Aristotle, economics appeared in philosophical and political debate only as a side issue with moral or immediately practical implications. So the scholastic philosophers commented on the ethics of charging interest, and in the seventeenth century there was a vigorous debate about the merits of foreign trade. Smith effectively carved out the whole subject as a new and separate discipline with its own questions, debates and occasionally solutions.

Marx and Engels adopted Smith's problematic theory that the value of something depended on the amount of labour put into it – the 'labour theory of value' – and then drew revolutionary conclusions about 'surplus value' and 'exploitation'. Marx also follows Smith in distinguishing 'productive' labour from 'unproductive', before going on to derive a parasitical middle class.

Smith's political influence is huge. But it might have been even greater. A major part of *The Theory of Moral Sentiments* concerning law-making and government, although laboured over for many years, was never completed to the scrupulous Scot's satisfaction and, just before he died, perhaps thinking of his friend David Hume's famous epigram about works of sophistry and illusion, he stuffed it into the fireplace and 'consigned it to the flames'.

## Key Ideas

Smith describes the 'hidden hand' of economics that guides all our actions and decisions. In fact, he makes a powerful case for leaving government, especially trading policy, to the hidden hand. Yet there is also a desire for approval by others – which can lead to conflict and upset the natural order.

- People come together naturally, because of the practical advantages: notably the efficiencies of specialisation and the division of labour as well as out of an awareness of other's needs and feelings.
- Because civil society is concerned with property rights, it inevitably discriminates against the poor in favour of the rich.

## Key Text

Adam Smith's *An Inquiry into the Nature and Causes of the Wealth of Nations* (1776)

# Timeline: From Air Travel to the First Railways

**1780**

This year marks a period of great technological advances. But the technological changes also result in great political stresses. In this year, the mundane but important invention of the fountain pen.

**1785**

The first air crossing of the English Channel – by Blanchard and Jefferies in a hot air balloon. The first successful balloon flight at all had only been two years earlier, by the Montgolfier brothers.

**1786**

The first interior (gas powered) lights for houses used – in German homes. Meanwhile, in Japan, a famine claims over a million lives.

**1788**

The first convicts are transported to Australia, where the native peoples are being brutally displaced.

**1791**

Thomas Paine writes the *Rights of Man* against a background in Europe of the Fall of the Bastille (1789) as part of the French Revolution and a clampdown generally on the freedom of its citizens. However, this is also the year a bill is introduced by William Wilberforce in the English Houses of Parliament to abolish slavery.

**1793**

Meanwhile, in the newly 'United States', a law is passed requiring escaped slaves to return to their owners. In revolutionary France, the Reign of Terror rages – one arguably less terrible effect of which is that compulsory education from the age of six is introduced.

**1795**

William Pitt introduces income tax in England as an emergency wartime measure (supposedly temporary). In France, Camacérès begins to develop the Napoleonic legal code, and, a year later, the country goes metric.

## 1800

Britain, now at the height of its Industrial Revolution, produces over a quarter of a million tonnes of iron a year and dubs itself 'Workshop of the World'. For the first half of the nineteenth century, Britain alone accounts for a quarter of the world's trade. Alessandro Volta invents a portable means of storing electricity – the battery.

## 1801

The first 'railway' begins to operate – but not for passengers. Horses haul wagons of fruit, vegetables and coal along.

## 1804

Robert Trevithick builds the first locomotive, although the first commercially useful one has to wait until ten years later and George Stephenson.

## 1805

The first factory lights enable owners to increase working hours. A year later, the half a million cotton workers of Great Britain are working under the ghostly and inadequate illumination of gas lights.

# 7 Marx and Engels: The *Communist Manifesto*

*For all Adam Smith's economic logic, the tidy march of society towards industrial nirvana was to be upset by a scandalous pamphlet, produced by two Germans whose names would become infamous. For the next 150 years, from the 1840s to the 1990s, as eagerly anticipated by the pamphlet's authors, Karl Marx and Friedrich Engels, the world appeared increasingly to split into 'two great warring camps' – a capitalist West, and a communist vanguard, centred on the Soviet Union and China.*

The *Communist Manifesto* opens with the famous promise: 'Let the ruling classes tremble at a communistic revolution. The proletarians have nothing to lose but their chains. They have a world to win!'

Alas, of course, reality was never so simple, as many failed communist societies could testify, not to mention failed 'anticommunist' dictatorships. But for a century at least, it seemed as though Marx was right and it would be a straight fight between the workers' forces calling for common ownership of 'the means of production', and an increasingly beleaguered and unpopular elite clinging to private ownership. It also seemed it must be true that certain macro-economic factors were all that created and defined societies and the lives of their citizens.

Karl Marx and Friedrich Engels wrote a great deal, of a largely rather turgid quasi-economic variety. There are not just the three voluminous parts of *Das Kapital*, but also the *Critique of Hegel's Philosophy of Right*, in which Marx and Engels declared that religion was 'the opium of the people' and the *Theses on Feuerbach* in which it is observed that 'philosophers have only interpreted the world in various ways – the point is to change it'. Not to forget the numerous essays, *On Religion, On Literature and Art, On Ireland* and so on, nor other documents such as letters and correspondence. From these last, differences of approach between the two men can be seen. Much of historical communism, in fact, followed Lenin's interpretation of

Engels, rather than Marx himself. Perhaps that is why Marx is said to have declared sadly in a letter to a friend towards the end of his life, 'All I know is that I am not a Marxist.' But in this chapter, at least, 'Marx' may be taken as a shorthand for the work of both men. Anyway, considerately for the workers of the world, their views are essentially encapsulated in just one document – the relatively short and colourful 'manifesto' for the embryonic Communist Party, written in German, printed in London and speedily translated into French in time for the insurrection in Paris of June 1848.

1848 was the 'Year of Revolutions' in Europe. Protests rocked not only Paris, but Rome, Berlin, Vienna, Prague and Budapest. The 'Paris Insurrection' in particular started, as street protests against royal interference in civil government developed, on resentment at the perceived betrayal of the principles of the 1789 revolution, which had promised not only 'liberty' but, more problematically, 'equality' as well. After troops fired on crowds it did indeed escalate into the provisional government of the Second Republic, which promptly cracked down on the protesters even more harshly than the first one had done.

The other revolutions of that year too quickly fizzled out in failure for the working class, beaten back by the bourgeoisie, as was to happen time after time again, to Marx and Engels' frustration. Nevertheless, this was the backdrop to the *Manifesto* – a chaotic period in which there seemed to be a new class of worker, facing a new type of exploitation – a situation which had, to be sure, already engendered the new political movement of 'socialism'. But neither Marx nor Engels ever had much time for socialism, which they considered a middle-class concern, respectable to the bourgeoisie where any decent doctrine should have been subversive. Communism, on the other hand, was much better: the unacceptable face of working class power, presenting a totally alien face to the capitalist class.

Marx and Engels's strategy is summarised in the *Manifesto* for the benefit of the new movement. The 'fundamental proposition' is that 'in every historical epoch' the prevailing 'mode of economic production and exchange' and 'the social organisation necessarily following from it' determine the political structures of society, along with the intellectual beliefs and ideas. That is, economics determines social life, and that decides political positions. In one of the *Manifesto*'s more memorable phrases (and one that has become part of the shared consciousness (true or false) of the modern world), Marx and Engels argue that it therefore follows that 'the whole history of mankind has been a history of class struggles, contests between exploited and exploiting, ruling and oppressed...'

This idea, as Engels ambitiously puts it in the preface to the English version of the *Manifesto*, is comparable to Darwin's theory of evolution. Marxism is the theory of the evolution of societies. It is as impersonal and its conclusions as inevitable as Darwin's biological model of the development of species.

## Context

What was the background to the *Manifesto* itself? What sort of social and economic forces shaped its authors? Marx and Engels' lifelong collaboration had begun in the early 1840s after a crackdown by the repressive Prussian government began to make life impossible for Marx, then attempting to make a career as a journalist on the *Rheinische Zeitung*. Abandoning Germany for Paris, he met Engels in 1842 and the two formed the partnership which would prove so productive, at least in literary terms. Marx, who had studied law in Bonn and philosophy and history in Berlin (receiving a doctorate in due course from the University of Jena, for his thesis on the Ancient Greek philosophers, Epicurus and Democritus), is generally credited with providing the scholarship, imagination and passion; Engels, with the philosophical rigour and practicality (as well as being the better writer). Not to mention the money. It is Engels who attempted to make Marxism into 'scientific socialism', using the 'best of' philosophy, political science and traditional socialism.

The *Communist Manifesto* is much more than an interpretation of history as a preparation for the coming of true socialism. As they said, the point was not to understand the world, but to change it. So the *Manifesto*'s emphasis is on the class struggle, and its consequent call for revolutionary action indeed led to Marx being arrested in Cologne in 1849, after the crushing of the 1848 revolutions, and tried for sedition. Although acquitted, Marx spent the rest of his life as an exile in London, supported financially by Engels' Manchester textile business. There he pored over books in the reading room of the British Museum, leaving the front-line action to others. Indeed, Marxism began to stress the inexorable changes in economic production over the role of the proletarians.

Marx, the individual, lived a rather sad and lonely life of straitened circumstances, if not true poverty, apparently deeply affected by the early deaths of four of his seven children, from malnutrition and poor living conditions. The son of a wealthy German lawyer, who had renounced his Jewish faith in order to progress in his career, he married the 'most beautiful girl in Trier', the daughter of the Baron of Westphalen, Jenny, to whom in due course it fell to pawn the family silver (marked with the crest of the Dukes of Argyll), and cope with Marx's unfaithfulness, which had produced an illegitimate child by one of their servants. In between, she had to edit and write out many of the revolutionary scripts. (How great an input Jenny Marx may have had into the *Manifesto* is unknown, but it may well have been more than is conventionally acknowledged.) All the while, Marx vowed never to allow 'bourgeois society' to make him into a 'money-making machine', and money that was given to him or otherwise came to the family was frequently expended rather ineffectually on either revolutionary projects, school fees, or just parties. In many ways, Marx's writings are a substitute for physical activity – revolutionary or otherwise. And in a way, he was a great snob, embittered by personal experience. Just before his death he observed that he was 'the best hated and most calumniated man of his time'. But the *Manifesto* dates from a more optimistic time in his life. It opens with a piece of literary braggadocio: 'A spectre is haunting Europe – the spectre of communism.' It was time, Marx and Engels contended, to 'meet this nursery tale of the spectre' with the publication of the founding principles of the Communist Party.

The key elements of this are the division of society into two groups: the bourgeoisie, who are essentially those rich people who either hire others to work for them, or simply own the factories the work goes on in; and the proletariat, being those who, 'having no means of production of their own', are forced to sell their labour in order to live.

This division is traced back through time in an effort to show that it is a 'universal truth'. 'Freeman and slave, patrician and plebeian, lord and serf, guild master and journeyman, in a word, oppressor and oppressed', stand in constant opposition to one another, always carrying out a battle, sometimes overt, sometimes covert, 'a fight that each time ended either in a revolutionary reconstitution of society at large or in the common ruin of the contending classes'.

The perennial claim of the liberals that class conflict is always only in the past, and that the world is now all 'middle class', is a sham. 'The modern bourgeois society that has sprouted from the ruins of feudal society', Marx writes, 'has not done away with class antagonism. It has but established new classes, new conditions of oppression, new forms of struggle in place of the old ones.'

In the 1850s, the *Manifesto* describes society as a whole already increasingly 'splitting up into two great hostile camps, into two great classes directly facing each other: bourgeoisie and proletariat'. (Although today, 150 years on, the proletariat, or full-time workers, often are the bourgeoisie too. But the words still strike a chord, for even as the workers are 'embourgoisiefied', there develops what contemporary Marxists have described as the new 'unworking class', of casual labourers, the unemployed, the old, the mad and the sick – together making up a new underclass.)

And, as Marx continues, when we examine the characteristics of the new industrial society, we see that the bourgeoisie has established itself as the supreme power in the modern state, running the government, turning it into 'but a committee for managing the affairs of the whole bourgeoisie'.

The bourgeoisie, wherever it has got the upper hand, has put an end to all feudal, patriarchal, idyllic relations. It has pitilessly torn asunder the motley feudal ties that bound man to his 'natural superiors', and has left remaining no other nexus between man and man than naked self-interest, than callous 'cash-payment'. It has drowned the most heavenly ecstasies of religious fervour, of chivalrous enthusiasm, of Philistine sentimentalism in the icy water of egotistical calculation. It has resolved personal worth into exchange value and, in place of the numberless indefeasible chartered freedoms, has set up that single, unconscionable freedom – free trade. In one word, for exploitation, veiled by religious and political illusions, it has substituted naked, shameless, direct, brutal exploitation.

The bourgeoisie has also stripped occupations such as medicine and the law, the church and teaching, of their 'halos', turning everyone into its paid wage labourers: the family has been reduced by the bourgeoisie into a mere money relation, Marx adds, all somewhat unexpectedly. Unexpected, for Marxists should, in a sense, favour these changes. But the *Manifesto* is sprinkled with barbed and sarcastic asides which are not intended to be wholly consistent with its central arguments. (It is almost as if a doctoral student's philosophical essay had fallen into the hands of an overzealous newspaper sub-editor – a perspective which may, in fact, not be so far from the mark.)

In industrial society, the workers themselves become mere appendages of machines, of whom only the most simple and monotonous activity is required. The 'lower strata' of the middle class, the shopkeepers and tradespeople, sink gradually into the proletariat, as the capitalists render their skills irrelevant by the might of their new methods of production.

The *Manifesto* says that industrial society requires constant change, as opposed to the tranquillity of the feudal and other epochs. 'Constant revolutionising of production, uninterrupted disturbance of social conditions, everlasting uncertainty and agitation distinguish the bourgeois epoch...', it warns, in one of its prolonged if rather tiring bouts of ironic, oxymoronic language.

Similarly, bourgeois society relies on a constantly expanding market, a claim we have already seen with Adam Smith's analysis of the creation of wealth. The industries demand raw materials from ever more obscure and remote sources, and must persuade consumers of new and exotic needs, thus creating a world market. The same applies in the intellectual sphere, with the rise of a 'world literature'. Legal systems, governments and methods of taxation must transcend any frontier. The 'most barbarian' nations are dragged into the impossible equation, with the cheap prices of commodities the 'heavy artillery' with which the bourgeoisie forces the barbarians to capitulate. All nations, on pain of extinction, are compelled to adopt the capitalist mode of production.

> Modern bourgeois society with its relations of production, of exchange, and of property, a society that has conjured up such gigantic means of production and of exchange, is like the sorcerer who is no longer able to control the powers of the nether world whom he has called up by his spells.

The insatiable forces of production even begin to threaten their bourgeois midwives, and, through continual crises, the whole of bourgeois society. But it is not only these forces that undermine the system. By creating the proletariat, the bourgeoisie has already 'forged the weapons that bring death to itself'.

At first the counter-struggle is carried out by a few individuals (polite coughs from Marx and Engels), with the labourers still 'an incoherent mass'. But with the growth of industry, the strength of the workers increases, and as it grows the workers become more conscious of this strength and their power. At the same time capitalism is forced to worsen both wages and conditions for its workers, thereby inadvertently causing the growth of workers' clubs to protect their wages. Thus are unions born. This is where the tone of the pamphlet changes, as Marx and Engels change from analysts to activists, seeing in the unions the bourgeoisie's eventual 'grave diggers'.

Hitherto, every form of society has been based, as we have already seen, on the antagonism of oppressing and oppressed classes. But in order to oppress a class certain conditions must be assured to it under which it can, at least, continue its slavish existence. The serf, in the period of serfdom, raised himself to membership in the commune, just as the petty bourgeois, under the yoke of feudal absolutism, managed to develop into a bourgeois. The modern labourer, on the contrary, instead of rising with the progress of industry, sinks deeper and deeper below the conditions of existence of his own class. He becomes a pauper, and pauperism develops more rapidly than population and wealth.

It is because the bourgeoisie is incompetent that it is unfit to govern (the *Manifesto* adds, with unusual reasonableness). Unfit, because it cannot stop its slaves sinking in poverty to such a point that it ends up feeding them. 'What the bourgeoisie therefore produces, above all, is its own grave diggers. Its fall and the victory of the proletariat are equally inevitable.'

The *Manifesto* does not propose that communists form a separate party from the proletarian movement as a whole, as they should have no interests separate and apart from the whole. Communists are only the 'most advanced and resolute' part of the working class. They understand better than the rest that the abolition of the institution of private property is essential, for property represents (as Smith puts it) stored up, or (as the *Manifesto* puts it) expropriated, labour. However, with Marx's definition, since the wage labourer only receives the bare subsistence necessary to continue working, private property necessarily represents exploitation. Or, in the famous phrase of Pierre Joseph Proudhon, Marx's contemporary and the first anarchist: 'property is theft'.

But the *Manifesto* does not believe that revolutionaries need to be prepared to enter into long arguments on economics, advising them to say instead: '... don't wrangle with us so long as you apply, to our intended abolition of bourgeois property, the standard of your bourgeois notions of freedom, culture, law, etc. Your every ideas are but the outgrowth of the conditions of your bourgeois production and bourgeois property, just as your jurisprudence is but the will of your class made into a law for all.'

Far better simply to enumerate the 'generally applicable' require-ments of communist revolution, as Marx and Engels go on to do. These are offered in pocket summary form as a series of ten or so points, simple to remember:

• Abolition of land ownership and rents
• A heavy progressive income tax
• Abolition of all inheritance rights
• Confiscation of the property of all those who no longer live in the state, or who rebel against the new government
• Centralisation of all capital and credit in a state bank
• Central state control and ownership of the means of commu-nication and transportation
• Increased state production through factories and farming; development of underused land
• 'Equal liability of all to labour'; new armies of workers, especially to work the land
• Disappearance of the distinction between town and country: population distributed evenly over the country

And, lastly:

• Free education for all in state-run schools, preparing the children for work in the new industries

In the meantime, the *Manifesto* concludes, communists should support every 'revolutionary movement against the existing social and political order, bringing to the fore, as the main issue, the property question'. This should be done, 'no matter what its degree of development at the time': by which Marx and Engels mean the political aspects rather than the economic stage prevailing. (It was left to Mao Zedong in China to make the important doctrinal changes necessary to allow communist theory to apply to pre-industrial peasant societies – the kind of societies where it actually took root to some extent, as it had done earlier in Russia.) Otherwise, the *Manifesto* presses for unionisation and makes it clear that for communists the only way forward is the 'forcible overthrow' of existing social structures. ('Let the ruling classes tremble at a communistic revolution. The proletarians have nothing to lose but their chains. They have a world to win!')

According to the authors, in this battle the communists are assured of eventual victory thanks to two things. The capitalist mode of production necessarily results in recurrent economic crises, perhaps creating wealth for a few, but increasing poverty for an ever growing working majority. At the same time, Marxism predicts, equally optimistically, that there will be 'ever growing' realisation amongst the proletarians of their exploitation – that 'law, morality and religion are... just so many bourgeois prejudices'.

Certainly, even bourgeois economists do accept that capitalism has its 'cycles', with recurrent troughs and adjustments – in bad cases, economic depressions. But, as is discussed later, in Chapter 10, on this crucial, factual claim of increasing absolute poverty, Marxism seems simply to have been wrong. Marx and Engels did not perceive the almost inexhaustible ingenuity of the capitalist system in increasing production through technical progress, and generating within itself apparently unlimited financial resources, making possible high standards of living not only for the tiny minority of mill owners, and the ever expanding ranks of the petty bourgeois, but for increasing numbers of the workers too.

Then again, some, such as one former Marxist, Andre Gorz, have suggested in recent years that the truly oppressed class of modern capitalism is not that of the workers any more – but of the 'unworkers' – the old, the unemployed and the very young (such as the 'street children of South America), who cannot work and must rely on state hand-outs or charity (or crime) for their sustenance. Even at the time that Marx and Engels were writing, this view was being expressed in Russia by Bakunin, who foresaw an uprising of the 'uncivilised', driven by their instinctive desire for equality. Bakunin predicted, in contrast to Marx, that the revolutionary instinct would be enfeebled by 'civilisation', and that violence was part of a primitive urge.

The other important claim of the pocket analysis offered by the *Manifesto*, is the so-called 'materialist conception of history', the idea that, in Engels' words, 'men must first of all eat drink, have shelter and clothing, therefore must work, before they can fight for domination, pursue politics, religion, philosophy [!], etc'. Because of this realisation, attention shifts from the activities of the leaders to the experiences of the led, from the kingly individuals of conventional history towards the social trends of economic science. By deciding that the battles of conventional political history are of little importance, Marxism instead raises to prominence another ongoing struggle, one that changes from epoch to epoch but remains essentially the same – the struggle of the exploited against their oppressors. These are essentially two classes, defined by the knowledge – consciousness – of the exploited that they *are* oppressed. (Although Marx recognises the gradations of social class, he rejected them as unimportant, as he did also the nationalistic impulse – and the motivation of racism which had produced the slavery of the nineteenth century.)

In the *Communist Manifesto*, Marx and Engels were confident that each stage of society – Asiatic, ancient, feudal and bourgeois – was both necessary, and invariable. Other, earlier, practical social experiments, such as the Diggers of sixteenth-century England, were therefore not of much interest to them. Later, this was a view which they needed to amend, to explain the possibility of revolution in peasant societies – such as Russia.

But what of the other radical, but pre-industrial, social experiments? Revolutionary politics did not start with Marx. In nineteenth-century England alone, there were many currents of radicalism to be swept along on: Jacobinism from the French revolution; Luddism from the battle of factory workers against increasing mechanisation and the unemployment associated with it; legislative battles for trade union rights and the freedom of the press, and popular campaigns for welfare and working hours protection. But for Marx and Engels, these were all so many false starts, deviant forms of socialism, and for that reason the *Manifesto* takes time to explain exactly what is wrong with each, in sequence:

- feudal socialism: merely aristocrats using sympathy for the workers to denounce the bourgeoisie
- clerical socialism: mere 'conscience-salving'
- petty-bourgeois socialism: nostalgic, unrealistic and ultimately reactionary
- 'humanist socialism': erroneously puts 'humanity' above class struggle
- bourgeois socialism: reform by do-gooders

• 'utopian socialism': which consists only of fantastical visions of the future, such as those advanced by Robert Owen and Henri Comte de Saint Simon

## Influence

What is offered by the *Communist Manifesto* is also a theory of psychological and social relationships. It involves a kind of *anomie* or alienation as a central feature of life in industrial society (to use the terms coined by the nineteenth century's new breed of 'social scientists'). The key to reforming social life, whether its problems are material or spiritual, is therefore, as Marx and Engels see it, and as Rousseau also concluded, to abolish property. With no property, there can no longer be two classes. No bourgeoisie, as they can no longer exist once they no longer have control of the 'means of production'. No proletariat, as they become effectively part owners instead with their former adversaries. With no classes, there is no longer any conflict, and there is no need either for laws or the repressive role of the state. Instead of calculations of profit, production can simply be organised for need. Marx and Engels imagine this as being not only more efficient than under capitalism, but also more rewarding for the workers involved. In place of alienation comes involvement and satisfaction.

Actually, as history has shown, these calculations of need are anything but simple, indeed they are extremely complex and difficult to make, and as the command economies of the former Soviet Union demonstrated, anything but efficient. It is *possible* to set up a bureaucracy to calculate how many two inch nails to make, and then to provide them at a set price, but there is no guarantee that the calculation will be right.

Marxist freedom is freedom from blind economic forces, replaced by the shared plans and controls of the collectively planned economy. But the shackles of the market are not so easily broken, and Marxism in practice is control by not one but two masters – the detached and unaccountable control of the bureaucracy, and still the irrepressible effects of countless individual market decisions.

But the *Manifesto* is based on several tenets, each of which are independent of the others. So, unlike religious creeds, such as Catholicism or Islam, or indeed western science, it is possible to believe parts of the *Manifesto* to be true, whilst having doubts about other elements. The first of these tenets is that all history is the history of class struggle, in a society shaped by the prevailing mode of production. The second is that these struggles inevitably result in social disorder, and that, in a capitalist society, this disorder leads to the workers seizing power. The third credo is that the final stage will represent the ultimate goal of the human spirit, and further developments will be neither necessary or possible. Accordingly, communism is the 'end of history'.

The first and second tenets look historically verifiable, but in fact aren't really, as the ambiguity of human events requires interpretation as well as investigation. (And crucially, for the second, there is no fixed 'time scale'.) The third is clearly unverifiable.

So the *Communist Manifesto* (like anarchism, the rival ideology of the times) requires of its adherents a great deal of blind faith. In this, it is more of a religious doctrine than a scientific theory. In fact, where the words of the *Manifesto* actually took root was amongst the pre-industrial societies of Africa, China and South America, and Russia itself – amongst the 'rural idiots', as Marx and Engels used to refer to people who worked on the land. And as the last years of the twentieth century showed, as the industrialisation of Russia and China proceeded under communism, it brought about the collapse of the command economy and the return of capitalism.

Of course, Marxism also took hold amongst that most bourgeois of all bourgeois groups, the university intellectuals, albeit often in a selective form, perhaps adopting the language and images of Marxist 'alienation' or 'false consciousness' to make broadly humanist points. Although Marx and Engels were passionate (at least on paper) about the conditions of the workers, they did not make any appeal in their theory to 'human rights'. They merely maintained that by the laws of economics, capitalism would collapse, producing the worker state. But Marx and Engels themselves were not humanists: they genuinely lacked feeling for their fellow human beings, not just wishing to dispense with it in their philosophical system building. Marx even insisted on changing the motto of the Communist League when he joined it in 1847 from 'All Men are Brothers' to 'Proletarians of the World Unite!', not out of creditable egalitarianism to sisters, but because he objected to the implication in the notion of universal brotherhood that it included the enemy. Instead, in the years before the tragedy of the First World War, the two revolutionaries looked forward to the last 'great war dance' of the capitalists, expecting, and hoping, that this would usher in revolution.

## Key Ideas

The *Communist Manifesto* outlines Marx and Engels's theory of society. It is an important document, a rich smorgasbord of social science, philosophy and history. Many of its asides – about globalisation, deskilling, even 'embourgoisiefication' – seem prescient and far-sighted in the light of subsequent developments, and still speak across the centuries. But it contains far less that is new, far less that is original, than it promises.

- The materialist conception of history is, as we have seen, very old, and much of Marx and Engels' writing on this and other matters is merely a reworking of other people's theories.
- The 'dialectic' itself, with its notion of two classes fighting each other, before destroying themselves to produce a new class, can be seen in non-materialist form in the philosophy of Hegel, along with a version of the evolution of history, and much of that is borrowed from Plato.

Many of the *Manifesto*'s economic 'insights' are conventional in both scope and nature. Nonetheless, Marxism has been a powerful force in shaping society, whatever the flaws and inconsistencies in its theoretical base.

Since the 1980s, with the implosion of the Soviet Union, and the conversion of even old communist societies, such as China and Cuba, into proto-capitalist economies, the legacy of the *Manifesto* is today an almost mundane one. The future may reveal Marxism as no more than an historical cul-de-sac. But, if it is, then it is at least one which did shift attention away from the 'bourgeois' agenda of nineteenth-century politics, mitigated by the charitable intentions of paternalists and liberals, towards a more holistic calculation of the respective rights and duties of rich and poor within capitalist society.

## Key Text

Karl Marx and Friedrich Engels' *Communist Manifesto* (1848)

# Timeline: From Roads Paved with Tarmac to Roads Paved with Gold

### 1806
The US Federal Government bans importation of slaves – but the law is not enforced.

### 1810
John McAdam begins a road programme in England, giving his name to the new technique of surfacing roads. The first canned food is made – but the process is very risky and prone to poisoning purchasers.

### 1811
Jane Austen writes *Sense and Sensibility*, published in the same year as protests against the gradual mechanisation of factories erupt as the Luddite riots.

### 1819
The Factory Acts in Britain forbid the employment of children under nine in cotton factories. Even with its limited scope, the law is largely ineffective, and it is not until 1838 that a general restriction on workers under nine years of age comes into force.

### 1821
James Mill publishes his 'Essay on Government', and James Faraday discovers the principles of the electric motor. Ten years later, Faraday develops the electric dynamo, which enables electricity to be produced more easily.

### 1825
The first passenger railway – the 43 kilometres of the Stockton to Darlington line – is opened.

### 1828
Peasant revolts in Russia, reacting against harsh feudal conditions, become a regular occurrence and remain so for a generation. Revolutions in the rest of Europe peak 20 years later.

### 1829
Niépce and Daguerre's photographic process results in the first true photographs. The daguerreotype, which uses silver salts, follows nine years later.

**1830**
The first person is killed by a train.

**1831**
Charles Darwin travels on *HMS Beagle* as naturalist for a survey of coral formations. Working out the implications will take him another 20 years.

**1834**
Six Dorset labourers – the Tolpuddle Martyrs – are transported to Australia for their part in an attempt to set up a Trade Union. Instead, the British devise the workhouse system to deal with the problem of unemployment and, later in the century, the first concentration camps, in South Africa.

**1836**
And it is in Britain that the government starts to record the birth, marriage and death of its citizens centrally by law, the first time this is believed to have been attempted.

**1840**
The Penny Post is introduced in London. Envelopes are invented shortly afterwards, too. But the 1840s are a period of corn and potato famines in Ireland and throughout Europe, and the railway-led boom collapses.

**1841**
At this time, the US imports 135,000 slaves a year to toil for its 17 million population (which is slightly less still than Britain's, at just over 18 million).

**1842**
The Chinese are forced to sigh the hated 'Unequal' Treaty of Nanjing, giving the European imperialist powers extensive rights in the East.

**1848**
Beginning of the Californian gold rush. This is the time of a massive increase in emigration from Europe to the New World. And John Stuart Mill's *The Principles of Political Economy* is published.

# 8   The Principles of Political Economy: J.S. Mill and the Limits of Government

*At the time Mill was writing, the new science of economics, inaugurated, at least as a popular subject, largely by Smith, was vexed by problems resulting from the country's involvement in wars against Napoleon. The recently founded Bank of England had had to default on repayments of the National Debt, new taxes were causing controversy, and inflation was upsetting economic relationships as workers found their wages buying less and less food. It was a situation that required a systematic approach: so step forward the utilitarians.*

Leafing through a copy of Joseph Priestley's pamphlet, an *Essay on Government*, Jeremy Bentham found a system for grounding the authority of the law on the principle of maximising the happiness of the greatest number. This was the essence of 'utilitarianism', and Bentham wrote about it (notably in the *Introduction to the Principles of Morals and Legislation* of 1789) when not working on his attempts to construct a large circular prison, the 'Panopticon', where everything the prisoners did could be watched.

Utilitarianism has become, as much as anything, the founding principle of western liberal democracy. After all, if everyone is equal, and they all have a vote, then the politically shrewd, if not the right, policy will be something pretty close to this method for pleasing the maximum number of people. Bentham's own aims were slightly different, however. He had only wanted to 'systemise' the study of society and found in the process that he had produced a system for evaluating both social and individual action. Only later, would John Stuart Mill, whose education was under Bentham's watchful gaze, adapt and adopt Bentham's 'felicifilic calculus' for his progressive, egalitarian vision of liberalism. Whilst Bentham was the son of a lawyer who became a 'political theorist' after his attempts to construct the Panopticon were thwarted, Mill's political interests went much wider.

Mill spent most of his life as a clerk in India House, London, with a brief spell as a Member of Parliament, particularly interested in women's rights, constitutional reform and economics. He also believed, unlike Bentham, that some forms of happiness were better than others. Which, essentially, relegated the pleasure principle to second place, behind some sort of notion of values. Mill's version of utilitarianism holds that allowing people to decide for themselves as much as possible increases the general happiness, thereby arriving at a philosophy arguing in favour of liberty of thought, speech and association.

Mill reflects his upbringing by his immersion in utilitarian theory and accepts that the greatest happiness of the greatest number is the goal of sound social policy. However, in his twenties the effects began to wear off, as Mill discovered, like Smith, the importance of the moral sentiment. And for Mill, there is the new perspective and influence of his lifelong collaborator on his great political works, Harriet Taylor.

## Work

The *Principles of Political Economy* (*with Some of the Applications to Social Philosophy*) was written in 1848, around the same time as Marx and Engels were fomenting (or attempting to foment) proletarian revolution. It is essentially an attempt to emulate Mill's illustrious Scottish predecessor, Adam Smith, in setting out the workings of the modern state. Unlike Smith, however, Mill is a poor writer and lacks both the insight and the subtlety of the Scot. Despite, or perhaps because of, his famous education at the hands of James Mill (Greek at age three, Latin at eight and Logic at thirteen), where Smith has pace and acuity, Mill has leaden prose (*vide* Book V, chapter 9, section 8, 'I proceed to the subject of Insolvency Laws...') and plodding mathematics. Take his discussion, in Book IV, of the relationship of supply and demand for example. Adam Smith, Mill complains:

> overlooked the circumstance that the fall of price, which if confined to one commodity really does lower the profits of the producer, ceases to have that effect as soon as it extends to all commodities; because, when all things have fallen, nothing has

THE PRINCIPLES OF POLITICAL ECONOMY

really fallen, except nominally; and even compared in money, the expenses of every producer have diminished as much as his returns. Unless indeed labour be the one commodity which has not fallen in money price, when all other things have; if so, what has really taken place is a rise of wages; and it is that, and not the fall of prices, which has lowered the profits of capital.

This is the point about 'feedback' in the economic system, that we saw earlier. It is an important criticism, but not well made: arguing in this rather dreary way, Mill proceeds to discuss the workings of the quintessential corn market, where he finds that the 'interest of the landlord is decidedly hostile to the introduction of agricultural improvements' and ultimately that the 'doctrine that competition of capital lowers profits by lowering prices, is incorrect in fact, as well as unsound in principle.' But the deficiency is not merely of style: Mill himself (a bit later in the work) notes that there actually is a 'tendency for profits to fall' which can only be offset by improvements in production.

Mill's strength is less in the analysis, particularly not the economic one, than in the system building, particularly the ethical one, and the idealism, where he places economic and social claims in a new framework of political rights. For example, he writes, following Smith, that only labour creates wealth, but capital is stored up labour, and may be accumulated – or even inherited – quite legitimately. Inheritance is acceptable, even when initially based on an injustice, once a few human generations have passed, as to remedy the injustice would create worse problems than leaving the situation alone. But at the same time, he says, on the other hand, the inheritance of wealth, beyond the point of achieving 'comfortable independence', should be prevented by the state intervening and confiscating assets. People who want to live more than 'comfortably' should work for it.

Mill thought that this 'Benthamite' part of his book would cause more than a little stir, and indeed hoped to become notorious for it. However, tucked away in nearly half a million other words, it attracted little interest.

Still, the whole book only took Mill just eighteen months to scratch out in manuscript form, a rate of 1,000 words a day, including a six month break to campaign for peasant rights in Ireland prompted by awareness of the desperate plight of the Irish peasants during the potato famine of the late 1840s. Since, to all intents and purposes, 'political economy' is inseparably intertwined with many other branches of social philosophy, Mill goes on to suggest a radical political and social agenda from what would otherwise be fairly uninspiring economic theorising. He wrote in a letter to a friend, 'I regard the purely abstract investigations of political economy as of very minor importance compared with great practical tensions that the progress of democracy and the spread of socialist opinions are pressing on.' It is these elements, largely confined to the end portion of Book V, which make for the most original parts of the whole work.

Mill is one of the first writers to consider themselves 'social scientists', and was firm in his conviction that the social sciences were justly related to the natural sciences, and could be pursued using similar methods. Mill, like Plato, distinguished, between the study of individuals, which would be largely psychology, and the study of collective behaviour, which would be largely economics and politics. He tried out various terms for summing up his approach, such as 'social economy', 'political economy' (which he thought might belong on its own somewhere), even 'speculative politics' but eventually returned to what he called Comte's 'convenient barbarism' – sociology. This new science was to be pursued using deduction from observations and analysis of historical trends.

Like the Enlightenment Encylopedists and many since, Mill considered himself to be living in a new age of invention and discovery, but perhaps unlike us, he was sure that the discoveries were yet in their infancy, and that 'production is the perpetual, and so far as human foresight can extend, the unlimited growth of man's power over nature.' The marvel of telegraphic communication, for example:

> The most marvellous of modern inventions, one which realises the imaginary feats of the magician, not metaphorically but literally – the electromagnetic telegraph – sprang into existence but a few years after the establishment of the scientific theory which it realises and exemplifies...

Mill goes on to say that it is impossible not to look forward to 'a succession of contrivances for economising labour and increasing its produce', as well as, more speculatively,

> a continual increase of the security of person and property. The people of every country in Europe, the most backward as well as the most advanced, are in each generation, better protected against the violence and rapacity of one another, both by a more

efficient judicature and police for the suppression of private crime, and by the decay and destruction of those mischievous privileges which enabled certain classes of the community to prey with impunity upon the rest.

As if this wasn't optimism enough already, Mill predicts that generation after generation the people will also become better protected against 'arbitrary exercise of the power of government'. Taxation will in all European countries grow 'less arbitrary and oppressive' (although a little taxation is a good thing) and wars 'and the destruction they cause' will be confined to those 'distant and outlying possessions' in which Europeans come 'into contact with savages'.

As to these latter, Mill is clearly disagreeing with Rousseau's vision of the 'noble' savage. Although, he concedes, they may individually have superior general abilities to soft, pampered, civilised man, the savage cannot match the 'greater capacity' of 'civilised human beings collectively considered'. What Rousseau saw as a disastrous loss of autonomy for man in the 'state of nature', Mill welcomes.

> In proportion as they put off the qualities of the savage, they become amenable to discipline; capable of adhering to plans concerted beforehand, and about which they may not have been consulted; of subordinating their individual caprice to a preconceived determination, and performing severally the parts allotted to them in a combined undertaking.

It is this element of 'cooperation' that is the key to modern societies. From it characteristically follows a great 'flowering of co-operatives' and joint-stock companies.

Towards the end of the *Principles*, in a section headed 'the limits of the *Laissez-faire* or Non-interference Principle', Mill proceeds to make his most distinctive contribution to political philosophy, as he turns his mind to the setting out of the limits of government. 'Whatever theory we may adopt', he writes,

> ... respecting the foundation of the social union, and under whatever political institutions we live, there is a circle around every individual human being which no government, be it that of one, of a few, or of the many, ought to be permitted to overstep... That there is, or ought to be, some space in human existence thus entrenched around, and sacred from authoritative

intrusion, no one who professes the smallest regard to human freedom or dignity will call into question: the point to be determined is, where the limit should be placed; how large a province of human life this reserved territory should include.

Mill himself marks the boundaries very clearly: 'I apprehend that this ought to include all that part which concerns only the life, whether inward or outward, of the individual, and does not affect the interests of others, or affects them only though the moral influence of example.'

Even when the activity appears to affect others, the onus of proof must lie on the defenders of legal prohibitions. For to be prevented from doing what one is inclined to, from acting according to one's own judgment of what is desirable, 'is not only always irksome, but also always tends, *pro tanto*, to starve the development of some portion of the bodily or mental faculties...'

In essence, such prohibitions partake 'in a great or small degree, of the degradation of slavery'. So, although reared as a utilitarian by men who believed in the dispassionate calculation of wants and needs, Mill ends up stating explicitly:

Scarcely any degree of utility, short of absolute necessity, will justify a prohibitory regulation, unless it can also be made to recommend itself to the general conciseness, unless persons of ordinary good intentions either believe already, or can be induced to believe, that the thing prohibited is a thing which they wish to do so.

This principle is crucial, for as self-styled democrats tend to forget, experience proves that

the depositaries of power who are mere delegates of the people, that is of a majority, are quite as ready (when they think they can count on popular support) as any organs of oligarchy to assume arbitrary power, and encroach unduly on the liberty of private life.

The public taken collectively, Mill shrewdly adds, is 'abundantly ready' to impose, not only its generally rather narrow views of its own interests, but even its abstract opinions and aesthetic tastes, as laws binding on individuals.

But there is another, pragmatic, reason to resist the attempts of the state to increase its role and power, a reason that is a consequence of the principle of the division of labour. This is that 'every additional function undertaken by the government, is a fresh occupation imposed upon a body already overcharged with duties'. It follows:

> A natural consequence is that most things are ill done; not much done at all because the government is not able to do it without delays which are fatal to its purpose; that the more troublesome and less showy of the functions undertaken are postponed or neglected, and an excuse is always ready for the neglect while the heads of the administration have their minds so fully taken up with official details, in however perfunctory a matter superintended...

The solution to this problem is quite simple – the devolution of power. Small is beautiful: 'the inconvenience would be rescued to a very manageable compass, in a country in which there was a proper distribution of functions between the central and local officers of government, and in which the central body was divided into a sufficient number of departments'.

So, by way of an example, Mill praises the creation of a British Railways Board, as he imagines it – a separate and independently functioning body carrying out a clearly delineated task for the public. If, in retrospect, such state bodies are today seen to be as effectively unresponsive and disinterested as any central government one, it is not necessarily a criticism of the underlying principle. And the approach appears to be experiencing something of a resurgence with the late twentieth century fashion for 'downsizing' and 'privatising' aspects and functions of not only central but local government. Mill's straightforward claim is that: 'the great majority of things are worse done by the intervention of government, than the individuals most interested in the matter would do them, or cause them to be done, if left to themselves'.

After all, even if the government were to be superior in intelligence and knowledge to the most intelligent and knowledgeable individual or group in society, it would still be inferior to all the individuals of the nation taken together. '*Laissez-faire* should, in short, be the general practice; every departure from it, unless required by some great good, is a certain evil.' Mill warms to his theme, observing (as many of us will recognise can be the case with social relations within the workplace or even the family!) 'that, as a general rule, the business of life is better performed when those who have an immediate interest in it are left to take their own course', uncontrolled and unhindered by either the law or 'the meddling of any public functionary'.

But there are exceptions. Mill thinks the most important is in the ability of the 'uncultivated' to judge matters of cultivation, that is to say, 'things which are chiefly useful as tending to raise the character of human beings'. Those individuals, Mill sadly notes, who 'most need to be made wiser and better, usually desire it least'. Even if they could be brought to desire it, they would be 'incapable of finding the way to it by their own light... Education, therefore, is one of those things which it is admissible in principle that a government should provide for the people.'

However, 'it is not endurable that a government should, either *de jure* or *de facto*, have complete control over the education of the people. To possess such a control, and actually exert it is to be despotic'. And he continues, without apparent irony, as noted above, but certainly with some piquancy: 'A government which can mould the opinions and sentiments of the people from their youth upwards, can do with them whatever it pleases.'

The safety valve is to allow free choice from rival educational institutions, and the right of parents to educate their own children, subject to some unspecified state supervision. Mill then considers the case of those who may suffer when a '*laissez-faire* attitude' is followed. He identifies four particular groups for concern: children, very poor people, such as those incapable of any work, women – and animals. Children, like animals, require special protection from 'the most brutal part of mankind'.

> It is by the grossest misunderstanding of the principles of liberty, that the infliction of exemplary punishments on ruffianism practised towards these defenceless creatures, has been treated as a meddling by government with things beyond its province; an interference in domestic life. The domestic life of domestic tyrants is one of the things which it is the most imperative on the law to interfere with.

The linking of women and children's protection in the Factory Acts Mill sees through as mere mischief. Whilst children are not sound judges of their own interests, 'women are as capable as men of appreciating and managing their own concerns, and the only hindrance to their doing so arises from the injustice of their present social position'. Specifically that the law makes 'everything which the wife acquires the property of her husband, while by compelling her to live with him it forces her to submit to almost any amount of moral and even physical tyranny...'

The women in the factories, Mill argues, are the only women who are not slaves or drudges. Women's rights can only be advanced by opening access to jobs, not by adding limitations. As for the poor and destitute, he sees a compelling *prima facie* case for helping. Yet, he goes on,

> in all cases of helping, there are two sets of consequences to be considered; the consequences of the assistance, and the consequences of relying on the assistance. The former are generally beneficial, but the latter, for the most part, injurious, so much so, in many cases, as greatly to outweigh the value of the benefits.

Worse still, this is most likely to be the case when the need is most extreme. 'There are few things for which it is more mischievous that people should rely on the habitual aid of others, than for the means of subsistence, and unhappily there is no lesson which they more easily learn.'

This is the 'problem' that the US wrestles with most doggedly. In the land of plenty, there are still, in the words of the song, so many in the ghetto, and the explanation is increasingly seen (by the well-off) to be that the gutters are full of those who have learnt the will-sapping habits of dependence. In the liberal democracies, welfare – 'workfare' – is designed for them instead of charity, either private or state provided.

But there is another way around the problem, one which governments have been less eager to try. Mill puts it this way:

> In so far as the subject admits of any general doctrine or maxim, it would appear to be this – that if assistance is given in such a manner that the condition of the person helped is as desirable as that of the person who succeeds in doing the same thing without help, the assistance, if capable of being previously calculated on, is mischievous: but if, while available to everybody, it leaves to every one a strong motive to do without it if he can, is then for the most part beneficial.

Subject to certain conditions, Mill holds it 'highly desirable that the certainty of subsistence should be held out by law to the destitute able-bodied, rather than that they should depend on voluntary charity'. Although Mill is not putting it quite in this form, what he is saying corresponds to the idea of the 'citizen's wage', that is to say, a minimal amount necessary to ensure subsistence, paid as of right to each citizen, leaving each with not only the duty but the practical necessity to find ways to improve their lot further through their own efforts. After all,

> In the first place, charity almost always does too much or too little; it lavishes its bounty in one place, and leaves people to starve in another. Secondly, since the state must necessarily provide subsistence for the criminal poor while undergoing punishment, not to do the same for the poor who have not offended is to give a premium on crime.

The problem is that the state must act by general rules: it cannot discriminate 'between the deserving and the undeserving indigent'. It owes 'no more than subsistence to the first, and can give no less to the last'. In words which have been well and truly forgotten, Mill warns: 'The dispensers of public relief have no business to be inquisitors.' So Mill concludes Book V of the *Principles of Political Economy*:

> I have not thought it necessary here to insist on that part of the functions of government which all admit to be indispensable, the function of prohibiting and punishing such conduct on the part of individuals in the exercise of their freedom, as is clearly injurious to other persons, whether the case be one of force, fraud, or negligence. Even in the best state which society has yet reached, it is lamentable to think how great a proportion of all the efforts and talents in the world are employed in merely neutralising one another. It is the proper end of government to reduce this wretched waste to the smallest possible amount, by taking such measures as shall cause the energies now spent by mankind in injuring one another, or in protecting themselves against injury, to be turned to the legitimate employment of the human faculties, that of compelling the powers of nature to be more and more subservient to physical and moral good.

## Influence

Mill is one of the founding figures of liberalism, now unquestionably one of the great survivors of political theory. His brand is grounded in the utilitarian ethic adopted from Jeremy Bentham, rather than on the appeal to fundamental rights of that other great liberal Englishman, John Locke. Despite different starting points, each arrives at the characteristic set of individual rights and freedoms.

Yet if liberalism offers equality before the law, at the same time it accords individuals secondary status: to that law, and the institutions and authorities embodying it. The free-market vision of society is rooted in fear, the central justification behind the state, at least in Thomas Hobbes' and John Locke's brand of 'democracy'. In Hobbes' case, fear of death or exploitation, in Locke's, and many contemporary capitalist societies, fear of loss of their material possessions (or fear of the consequences of attempting to steal other peoples goods). Liberalism does not even suggest any positive purpose for human existence; perhaps thinking individuals should find it for themselves. There is a defensiveness in Mill, too.

The French and American revolutions were epoch-making in that they seemed to correct a sense of inferiority that feudal society engendered and required, replacing it instead with something approaching a sense of dignity and common humanity. Afterwards, for the first time, the state formally recognised the importance of all its citizens, bestowing upon them important powers and rights. Whilst Thomas Hobbes, John Locke and the architects of the American Declaration of Independence held that rights were largely a means of protecting the individual from the rapacious desires of their neighbours, the rights also appeared to include more positive freedoms to create and develop, just the sort of freedoms which lay behind the economic expansion spearheaded by the Protestant entrepreneurs who created the European Industrial Revolution.

But what sort of 'freedom' is this, anyway? Mill himself writes that 'after the means of subsistence are assured, the next in strength of the personal wants of human beings is liberty'. Yet, liberalism is essentially freedom from rather than freedom to. Freedom from arbitrary laws or taxes, from being made to work against one's will, freedom from being told what to believe, and freedom from being obliged to participate in social activities that cannot be justified by being necessary for the well-being of the community. It is not freedom to work, or to live in a home, or to be healthy – as the ever widening underclasses of the consumer societies can vouch. Indeed, increasingly it is not even freedom from the first two, as it is increasingly the underclasses who pay the highest proportion of their meagre incomes in taxes (for example, on purchases of alcohol or cigarettes) or are drummed into 'work-fare' employment schemes, whilst the rich operate through tax-exempt corporations.

F. A. Hayek, in *The Road to Serfdom*, his influential book written in the aftermath of the Second World War, specifically warns that 'nothing has done so much harm to the liberal cause as the wooden insistence of some liberals on certain rough rules of thumb, above all the principles of *laissez-faire*'. Instead, he says, the correct attitude of the liberal towards society should be more like that of a good gardener towards their plants – tend them carefully and try to create the conditions in which they can flourish. Yet, any intervention by government in the operations of liberal society is to mix ideologies, to veer either towards the right or the left, towards socialism or fascism.

## Key Ideas

Mill takes the principle of maximising the general happiness and sets in a framework of individual rights and freedoms. At the same time, he claims to create the social conditions in which talent, creativity and culture can thrive. Conversely when the state interferes it:

- is invariably a worse judge of both policy and of practicality than the individual
- normally makes matters worse

The tragedy is, as Mill acknowledged, that without any limitations at all on their freedoms, people will still tend to use them simply to injure and harm one another.

## Key Text

J.S. Mill's *The Principles of Political Economy* (1848)

# Timeline: From Outbreaks of Cholera to Outbreaks of Panic in Cinemas

**1851**
One million people have died in the Irish potato famine.

**1854**
Baron Haussmann begins constructing the characteristic wide sweeps of the Parisian boulevards – for the convenience of troops and as a means of deterring rioters.

**1855**
Dr Snow's cholera map shows that the cause of an outbreak in Victorian London was the Broad Street drinking pump.

**1859**
Charles Darwin's *Origin of Species* is published, affecting the way people see social obligations as well as they way they perceive the natural world. *On Liberty*, by John Stuart Mill, is published.

**1861**
As part of a process of Russian modernisation, all serfs are made freemen.

**1862**
An early machine gun invented by Gatling fuels an arms race. In the following years Wilbrand develops TNT explosives (1863), Svend Foyn invents the harpoon gun (1864), Winchester makes the repeating rifle, and Whitehead the torpedo (1866). Finally, Nobel, in 1867, discovers the power of dynamite. After this, Nobel decides armaments have developed too far, and funds the peace prize named after himself.

**1865**
The American Civil War ends with the surrender of the Confederates. A year later, the Civil Rights Act sets slaves free.

**1870**
The British introduce (compulsory) free education for all.

**1871**

Otto von Bismarck, Prime Minister of Prussia, marches through a seething Paris as the culmination of his campaign of German unification and expansion.

**1874**

The first typewriters arrive.

**1877**

The railway strike heralds a (confrontational) new era in industrial relations for the US.

**1879**

Thomas Edison discovers that tungsten in a vacuum glows brightly for a long time, and the first electric light is created.

**1882**

Standard Oil now has 95 per cent of all refinery capacity in the US. It will not be until 1911 that the government acts to break up the monopoly.

**1884**

The Berlin Conference sets out the ground rules for the European 'scramble for Africa' that will trigger the process of turning spheres of influence into full-blown colonies.

**1889**

The Eiffel Tower opens – by far the tallest building ever built.

**1896**

The Lumière brothers introduce films to the public, including the famous 'train arriving at a station', which causes panic wherever it is shown. The first comic strip (by Rudolph Dicks) is printed in the US.

**1899**

For the first time, people are able to communicate instantaneously – the 'wireless' is used to send messages between London and Paris. The Twentieth Century has truly arrived.

# 9 Positivism and the Science of Society: Emile Durkheim and Max Weber

*Then, in the nineteenth century, knowledge became an industry. A social and public enterprise with a workforce of researchers and scholars, grouped by subject into divisions, communicating with one another by thesis and article, judging work by common standards. Knowledge was churned out in a kind of progression. It accumulated in books and libraries. It became an institution.*

A small part of the new 'knowledge institution' was given over to sociology, as the academic study of society. And the door formally opened in the year 1842 with the publication of the *Cours de Philosophie Positive*, by Auguste Comte (1798–1857). Comte was a middle-class French intellectual whom John Stuart Mill would later accuse of devising a 'despotism of society over the individual', although others would trace both the origins of sociology, and the despotism, to Jeremy Bentham's efforts to ground the authority of the law on the principle of maximising the happiness of the greatest number.

Whatever the truth of that, it is with Comte, who had been inspired by his study of medieval Catholic scholars into attempting to produce a new 'religion of humanity' and a blueprint for a new social order, that the science of society really starts.

In the *Cours*, Auguste Comte, like René Descartes and many philosophers since, starts from a position of deep admiration for both the precision and authority of the natural sciences, epitomised (at least in the public mind) by the advances in physics and chemistry. His 'positivist' idea was that the methods of natural science were the only way to understand human nature, both in individuals and collectively, and hence the only way to find out how to organise society. And Comte wanted to apply these 'scientific', quantitative methods to society itself, dissecting it to discover the laws and the principles governing it. Of these, he considered his most important discovery to be a 'Law of Human Progress' (well, it sounded important), according to which, all societies pass through three stages: the *theological*; the *metaphysical*; and the scientific or *positive*.

The defining feature of each stage is the mental attitude of the people. During the theological stage, people seek to discover the 'essential nature of things' and the ultimate cause of existence, interpreted as God. Philosophers, Comte thought, were stuck at this stage, perpetually but fruitlessly pursuing these sorts of question. Most people, however, were at the next, the metaphysical stage, which involves increasing use of abstract theory, although there is still a sense of the underlying essence of things, epitomised by broadly ethical notions of value. The final stage comes only when enough people put aside the illusions of opinion (echoes of Plato) and confine themselves to logical deduction from observed phenomena. This is the so-called scientific (or positive) stage. 'Now each of us is aware, if he looks back on his own history, that he was a theologian in his childhood, a metaphysician in his youth and a natural philosopher in his manhood', Comte rather unconvincingly declares.

The stages are also supposed to correspond to periods of human history. The first relates to the pre-historical and medieval world, whilst the metaphysical stage is compared to the sixteenth, seventeenth and eighteenth centuries, a time when monarchies and military despots gave way to political ideals such as democracy and human rights, including, most importantly for social life, property rights. The last stage in history will be a scientific, technological age, when all activity is rationally planned and moral rules have become universal.

This, at least, is Comte's vision. It is as this final stage beckons that the science of society – sociology – comes into its own, with its task both of explaining and determining social phenomena and the history of mankind.

Comte was an idealist who wrote of 'love' as the guiding principle and of bringing 'feeling, reason and activity into permanent harmony'. It was left to Emile Durkheim and Max Weber, as well as, to some extent, John Stuart Mill, to carry on the development of the science of society. Durkheim in particular attempted to show how a new social consensus could provide the values of community and social order, values that had, Durkheim felt, characterised the pre-industrial era, and could now combat the increasing disorder stemming from the rapid changes resulting from industrialisation. To do this, he adopted a *positive* methodology, that is to say, he used the methods of natural science to understand social phenomena which were taken as essentially just another part of the natural world, collecting statistical evidence on suicides, on the labour force, on religion and on education. But Durkheim, as did Weber, then built upon this logical structure a more profound, metaphysical theory of social life with an almost completely subjective underpinning morality.

## Durkheim

Emile Durkheim (1859–1917), unlike Marx, tried to achieve this new social consensus without losing the benefits of individual emancipation and freedom that technology is perennially supposed to make possible. His solution is centred around what he calls 'the collective consciousness' and the notion of 'social facts'. These last are 'ways of acting, thinking and feeling, [that are] external to the individual' – such as the customs and institutional practices, moral rules and laws of any society. Although these rules 'exist' in the minds of individuals, Durkheim says the true form can be found only when considering the behaviour of 'the whole' – that is of society itself. In this, not for the last time, he is echoing the words of Plato and Socrates 2000 years before. Like Plato, Durkheim considers society to be essentially a moral phenomenon, created within a framework of overarching eternal values. And, like Plato, he rejects individualism and introspection as assumed and proposed by thinkers such as Thomas Hobbes and Adam Smith, with their attempts to create generalities out of particulars and to build social structures out of human atoms. Instead, turning their models upside down, he makes society primary – the cause and not the effect.

Durkheim rejects Hobbes' vision of the world in the 'State of Nature', saying that

... when competition places isolated and estranged individuals in opposition, it can only separate them more. If there is a lot of space at their disposal, they will flee; if they cannot go beyond certain boundaries, they will differentiate themselves, so as to become still more independent. No case can be cited where relations of pure hostility are transformed. . .

If society were based, for example, on calculations of interest, and
social contracts, then the key social relationship would be the
economic, 'stripped of all regulation and resulting from the entirely
free initiative of the parties'. Society would simply be the situation
'where individuals exchanged the products of their labour, without
any action properly social coming to regulate this exchange'.

But Durkheim thinks this is not actually how society does
function. 'Is this the character of societies whose unity is produced
by the division of labour?' he asks rhetorically. And he continues,
answering himself: 'If this were so, we could with justice doubt their
stability. For if [self-]interest relates men, it is never for more than
some few moments.'

Taking up Hobbes' challenge (as well as adopting his language)
Durkheim goes on:

> Where interest is the only ruling force, each individual finds
> himself in a state of war with every other since nothing comes to
> mollify the egos and any truce in this eternal antagonism would
> not be of long duration. There is nothing less constant than
> interest. Today, it unites me to you: tomorrow, it will make me
> your enemy.

We have to look elsewhere for explanation of the 'organic'
solidarity of society. Durkheim concludes that since 'the greater part
of our relations with others is of a contractual nature', if it were
necessary 'each time to begin the struggles anew', only a fragile kind
of social relation could result, 'only a precarious solidarity'.
Durkheim chooses instead what he sees as Comte's 'organic'
approach, in which everything is related to a whole.

In the same way that an animal colony, for example, a beehive,
'whose members embody a continuity of tissue from one individual,
every aggregate of individuals who are in continuous contact form
a society. The division of labour can then be produced only in the
midst of pre-existing society.' Individuals must be linked through
material facts, but also by 'moral links' between them. Hence,
Durkheim concludes,

> ... the claim sometimes advanced that in the division of labour
> lies the fundamental fact of all social life is wrong. Work is not
> divided among independent and already differentiated individuals
> who by uniting and associating bring together different aptitudes.
> For it would be a miracle if differences thus born through chance

circumstance could unite so perfectly as to form a coherent whole. Far from preceding collective life, they derive from it. They can be produced only in the midst of a society, and under the pressure of social sentiments and social needs. That is what makes them essentially harmonious.

Societies are built up out of shared beliefs and sentiments, and the division of labour emerges from the structure created. Durkheim returns to Comte, to remind the reader that, in Comte's words, 'cooperation, far from having produced society, necessarily supposes, as preamble, its spontaneous existence'. What brings people together are practical forces such as living in the same land, sharing the same ancestors and gods, having the same traditions. Rousseau, Hobbes, and even the Utilitarians, are all guilty of disregarding the important social truth, that society pre-dates the individual. 'Collective life is not born from individual life, but it is, on the contrary, the second which is born from the first... Cooperation is... the primary fact of moral and social life.'

Compare human beings with animals. Animals are almost completely under the yoke of their physical environments. Human beings, however, are almost free of their environment but dependent on social causes. Animals have their societies too, but they must be very simple, restricted, and the collective life is simple and limited. With human societies, there are more individuals living together, common life is richer and more varied: 'social causes substitute themselves for organic causes. The organism is spiritualised.'

As societies become more vast, and particularly, more condensed, a psychic life of a new sort appears. Individual diversities, at first lost and confused amidst the mass of social likenesses, become disengaged, become conspicuous, and multiply. A multitude of things which used to remain outside consciences because they did not affect the collective being became objects of representations. Whereas individuals used to act only by involving one another, except in cases where their conduct was determined by physical needs, each of them becomes a source of spontaneous activity. Particular personalities become constituted, take conscience of themselves.

People exist within and depend on only three 'types of milieu': the organism, the external world, and society.

If one leaves aside the accidental variations of hereditary, – and their role in human progress is certainly not very considerable – the organism is not automatically modified; it is necessary that it be impelled by some external cause. As for the external world, since the beginning of history it has remained sensibly the same, at least if one does not take account of novelties which are of social origin. Consequently, there is only society which has changed enough to be able to explain the parallel changes in individual nature.

Thus, Durkheim introduces the new science of 'socio-psychology'. (Elsewhere he speaks of sociology too as the 'science of ethics'.) As Rousseau and Smith had pointed out in the eighteenth century, and modern economists like G. K. Galbraith have done subsequently, the role of necessity actually plays a very small part in economics – much more is explained by reference to psychology. Social facts are not the result of psychic facts, but the latter are in large part an effect of the former. Perhaps sociologists are however unfortunately in the habit of making the serious error of confusing the cause and the effect. For example, Durkheim disputes claims that in the parent–child relationship we see the logical expression of 'human sentiments inherent in every conscience', insisting that to say this is to reverse the true order of the facts. 'On the contrary, it is the social organisation of the relations of kinship which has determined the respective sentiments of parents and children.' The sentiments would have been completely different if the social structure had been different, and the proof of this (Durkheim triumphantly concludes) is that paternal love is unknown in 'a great many societies'.

Now Durkheim is happy to concede that it is a 'self-evident truth that there is nothing in social life which is not in individual consciences'. But 'everything that is found in the conscience, has come from society'. Although society 'may be nothing without individuals', each of them is much more a product of society than a creator of it.

Are there any exceptions to this? Great leaders, for example? Durkheim recalls that in Melanesia and Polynesia, for example, it is said that an influential man has *mana*, and that his influence is due to this quality. However, really, Durkheim says, it is evident there that his authority is solely due to the 'importance attributed to him by public opinion'. (Like modern-day 'media personalities', they are just 'famous for being famous'.) The special status and powers of great leaders, as imagined by Max Weber and Friedrich Nietzsche, for example, is an illusion.

And Durkheim considers our very awareness, our 'consciousness' to be not an individual but a social phenomenon. He argues that there are two types of *symbol* which create societies and cement the individual human beings into the social whole. These are collective representations, such as national flags and other shared symbols, and moral codes, such as notions of basic rights, and even unwritten, generally accepted, beliefs such as the idea that young children should be given toys to play with or that swimming in rivers should be free. Together, these written and unwritten rules create a 'collective consciousness'. This consciousness is part of the psychological make-up of each individual in society, and is also the origin of more formal moral codes. Many things follow from this interpretation. For example, stealing from your neighbour is wrong not because of the affront to the neighbour, but because of the affront to the collective consciousness itself. And Durkheim draws from this, more generally, the conclusion that self-interest, or even consideration of the interests of the majority (the goal assumed by utilitarianism), is incapable of producing moral behaviour. Instead, the 'collective consciousness' functions as a kind of watchdog for its own well-being, as well as expressing a position based on certain principles.

Durkheim goes on:

It has often been remarked that civilisation has a tendency to become more rational and more logical. The cause is now evident. That alone is rational which is universal. What baffles understanding is the particular and the concrete... the nearer the common conscience is to particular things, the more it bears their imprint, the more unintelligible it is...

That is why we look on 'primitive civilisations' as we do. In fact, they are very like our own, and operate in a similar way. But 'the more general the common conscience becomes, the greater the place it leaves to individual variations. When God is far from things and men, his action is no longer omnipresent nor ubiquitous. There is nothing fixed save abstract rules which can be freely applied in very different ways.' The collective conscience becomes more rational, and 'for this very reason, it wields less restraint over the free development of individual varieties'.

In essence, the key to social life is symbolism. It is the way that individuals communicate most effectively, and their social values are preserved and embodied in the sacred symbols. Social life

> ... in all its aspects and in every period of its history, is made possible only by a vast symbolism. The national emblems and figurative representations with which we are more especially concerned in our present study are one form of this, but there are many others. Collective sentiments can just as well become incarnate in persons or formulae, some formulae are false, while others are persons, either real or mythical, who are symbols.

Although Durkheim does not make this point, we might observe here that language itself consists essentially of symbols. But Durkheim does make a novel distinction between types of possible society. This is between 'simple' ones, where the population is small and dispersed within its limited territory, and 'complex' ones, with more members, closely packed, interacting and interdependent. The former are held together by traditions that operate uniformly on the various members, who are like little atoms – undifferentiated in themselves and interchangeable. The individuals in 'simple' societies share a powerful sense of shared purpose and function. This results in a type of social cohesion Durkheim calls 'mechanical'.

The other way of organising society, which Durkheim calls 'organic', is more complex. It involves a range of parallel institutions and traditions, with individuals falling into increasingly distinct sub-groupings, each with its own traditions and 'social norms'. Within each grouping, individuals can become specialised and fulfil a particular function in the social whole. The division of labour, which Marx sought to abolish (as creating inequality), is seen by Durkheim as a desirable aspect of this evolution.

In the simple, mechanical social structure, punishment's sole purpose and function is to defend the collective from the danger presented by a rogue element, and so is swift and severe. In the organic society, there is more of an emphasis on repairing the malfunctioning part – and so the law is likely to emphasise undoing the wrong done, and preventing further damage, rather than simply rooting out the disease. This is partly because the cohesion of organic society is fundamentally one of interdependence, so even a malfunctioning part is valued.

And there is a particular disease of complex societies, that Durkheim identifies and gives a name to, *anomie*. This is the sense of futility and alienation that leads individuals to take their lives, for example, but, also perhaps, to attack their fellow citizens. Durkheim suggests this is caused by a failure to replace the 'mechanical' cohesion of the simple society with new social bonds.

In all this, Durkheim's method for investigation was to try to find tangible instances of these admittedly immaterial social facts, through sophisticated analysis and interpretation of official statistics. These he found in fastidious trawls through collections of official statistics, population statistics, official descriptions of the nature of the workforce and professional groupings – even in the minutiae of the judicial codes. His most celebrated (for want of a better word) study is of the number of people committing suicide. For Durkheim, suicide was not just an individual activity (tragedy) but an action directly linked to and reflecting a general breakdown in social cohesion.

In *Suicide: a Study of Ideology*, Durkheim takes the discovery that self-destruction is more prevalent amongst certain religious groups (Protestants) than others (such as Catholics) to argue that this is because the 'collective consciousness' is stronger in the Catholic communities. In a modern society, *anomie* (with its associated feelings of alienation from the whole, and individual futility) is such a threat that Durkheim says the various sub-groupings in society, for example, the employees of a large multinational, or the vocational ones of professional groupings of academics, teachers, medical workers – or even politicians – need to be 'united and organised in a single body'. Taking the idea further, in the *Division of Labour*, Durkheim suggests professional groupings or unions should act almost as an extended family, taking an interest in all aspects of their members' well-being.

We can find a contemporary parallel in Japan. Since the Second World War, the Japanese *zaibatsu*, or large corporations (such as Mitsubishi), have tended to act in this quasi-paternal way, with children joining the same corporation as their parents, having been educated in one of its schools, attending one of its training colleges if necessary, and then working for it all their lives. In addition, Japanese workers will probably spend any free time or holidays at the *zaibatsu*'s leisure facilities, and any job changes will be within the organisation. In return, the corporation expects lifelong loyalty from the workers, and a sense of shared aims and aspirations. It also recognises a lifelong responsibility to provide both for its workers and their families.

The desirable aspect of all this is that workers feel very much part of a group, and gain a sense of security and shared purpose. For the *zaibatsu* this enables them to achieve high standards of industrial performance, with workers' ideas a key part of improving efficiency, and any investment in training being protected by employee loyalty. This is less likely to be the case in the west, with its notion of 'high-flyers' changing jobs and companies at will. Western companies, maximising both workforce and market 'flexibility', tend to operate on short-term investment strategies, demanding that any investment in both physical and human 'capital' show a quick return. The Japanese industrial model allows investment to be protected long enough for long-term gains to become worthwhile.

Even so, there is a downside to the approach. By substituting collective decisions for individual desires and ambitions, the pater-nalistic *zaibatsu* can contribute to an extreme cult of service like that which characterised the Japanese war machine, and today still leads, contrary to Durkheim's expectations, to many 'unsuccessful' Japanese individuals taking their own lives, feeling that they have failed to live up to the standards of the 'collective consciousness'.

## Weber

Another of Durkheim's fellow 'knowledge workers', with a more prodigious output than most, was Max Weber (1864–1920). Like Durkheim, he made a study of the different characteristics of the various Christian groupings. He too claimed to have discovered important differences between Protestants and Catholics, with impli-cations for social reality. In fact, Weber built on his own statistical analysis of Protestantism an almost existential model of society in which social science, being rooted in values, was ultimately subjective.

Weber's particular insight, set out in his best known work, *The Protestant Ethic and the Spirit of Capitalism*, was that the Industrial Revolution in Europe was linked to a rejection of traditional and elaborate Catholic religious practice, and a Protestant ideology which emphasised the virtue of a lifetime spent working hard with no greater aim than serving God. The second stage of this realisation was a view of material goods which held them to be only important in that they reflected God's approval of one's efforts. For the new breed of capitalist, Weber thought, this made the success of the entrepreneur something worth striving for. It also, conveniently, justified reducing the workers to the absolute bare minimum required for successful production.

In particular, Weber argued that the development of capitalism occurred in Holland and England because they were Protestant powers, and that the economic discoveries associated with the time flowed from this pre-existing fact, rather than vice versa – a view that harmonises with Durkheim's approach, by putting the social before the economic.

Not that Weber is necessarily in favour of this. In *The Origin of Modern Capitalism*, Weber argues that 'in the east it was essentially ritualistic considerations, including caste and clan organisations, which prevented the development of a deliberate economic policy' and thus that capitalism could only develop once the political administration – the bureaucracy – was created, as in the British parliamentary system.

And, in contrast to Durkheim, Weber again makes the individual's perception of the world the key to understanding society. *The Protestant Ethic and the Spirit of Capitalism*, his study of attitudes to work, published in the early years of the twentieth century, attempts to show how individual perceptions are tied up with economic practice. Weber's works on social science in general, such as the *Methodology of Social Sciences*, and the uncompleted *Wirtschaft und Gesellschaft* (part one eventually translated as *Social and Economic Organisation*) contain three new ideas which became highly influential. (At least, that is, in sociological circles where their obscurity was less of a handicap.)

Weber's career was largely spent in several professorial positions in respectable German universities, churning out his heavy-handed theories, although he was actually employed too, for a period, as a bureaucrat himself – as a hospital administrator during the First World War. He defines 'sociology' (in typically turgid style) as the science of the analysis of the social causes of social effects. As a science, it must be 'value free', a notion that was important for Weber and led to an intense and prolonged academic debate within Germany. Of course, Weber realised, values are often present in individual perceptions, and his investigation of the relationship of Christianity, in its Protestant form, and capitalism, exemplifies the central role values play in social life.

Paradoxically, perhaps, Weberian sociology is value laden in itself. Weber insists, almost as an axiom of his theories, that rationality is good. In fact, like the Ancient Greeks, Weber assumes that an action with a rational purpose, must be good – and that, *mutatis mutandis*, as the magician might say producing an implausible rabbit, if an action is not good, it cannot be rational. Any activity without conscious intent is mere 'behaviour'. Digestion is merely behaviour, but stealing apples is social action, Weber says. (But the distinction is not really very clear – feeling hungry is not social action, but it might be all that propels someone to steal some apples, without really thinking about it.)

The first novelty of Weberian sociology concerns the organisation of modern societies (those that Weber calls 'bureaucratic'), rationality and explanations of human behaviour; and his theory of 'ideal types', these last being a kind of theoretical model, rather than a value judgement. If the language is confusing and long-winded, to make matters worse, Weber's three ideas begin to blur into one another, and may even be fundamentally ambiguous and confused. In particular, bureaucracy and rationality are inextricably linked.

Bureaucracies, Weber thinks, naturally promote a 'rationalist' way of life, just as rationality itself is inclined to prefer government according to rules, rather than mere authority. Weber himself, as a German, was particularly influenced by the new highly organised state under Bismarck – although he was also concerned at the threats it posed to individual liberties and differences. Weber wanted to see the bureaucracy taking over the running of itself, monopolising the use of violence through the police and army, but also allowing for certain legal rights for citizens, if necessary against the state, thereby still facilitating the growth of business and capital.

The second social strategy for Weber, as for Durkheim, stems from his conviction that it is not enough to explain activity in terms of causes and mechanisms – there must be a purpose. Furthermore, Weber thinks, in society at large, the purpose is normally an economic one. There may be other types of social cause – artistic, moral, religious or environmental (closer to Durkheim's vision of the collective consciousness, for example) – but Weber sees these as kinds of rationality in themselves.

The best form of rationality is when the choice of means and ends either

- 'accord with the canons of logic, the procedures of science or of successful economic behaviour', or
- 'constitute a way of achieving certain ends, when the means chosen to achieve them accord with factual and theoretical knowledge'.

Otherwise, if the ends are motivated (contaminated) by values – religious, moral or aesthetic – or if values influence or determine the means employed, then the behaviour is 'value-rational' (which is not as good). This is typified by the case of the principled parent who refuses to borrow money and so is unable to feed the family properly.

Sometimes the ends may be decided by tradition, which is a kind of value. This is typically the key factor in history, Weber says, describing how in traditional Chinese society, if you sold your house and moved out but later became homeless, you could return to your old home and expect to be taken back in, for the new owner would not risk offending the 'spirits' by refusing to help another. Thus, Weber argues, tradition hinders economic progress. Then again, sometimes behaviour is affected by emotions and passions; this is 'affectual action', and that, too, is opposed to rational behaviour.

It is *zweckrational*, or goal-rational, behaviour which is most logical, similar perhaps also to the more simple-minded models of market economists or utilitarians. For example, if someone wishes to buy a gold watch, they may start doing overtime at work to save money for the purchase. Weber doesn't necessarily think that people actually do behave as tidily as this – the extra money of our worker may go on beer and nights out – but he thinks the notion may have some explanatory force anyway. Capitalism depends on rationality in two ways: for the movement of free and property-less workers in response to the demands of the free market; and for the freedom of those with capital to invest – such as entrepreneurs – to choose where to do so, based on maximising profit.

In the *Origin of Modern Capitalism* (1920), one of a series of lectures given at the end of his life, Weber puts it thus: 'Very different is the rational state in which alone modern capitalism can flourish – its basis is an expert officialdom and rational law.'

Weber also supposes that the extent of the goal-rational behaviour depends on the structure of the society – arguably a rather unsatisfactory element in the theory, given that each is being used to explain the other.

Actions which result from the way people feel are non-rational, as are certain sorts of actions, like that of the generous Chinese home owner, motivated solely by a sense of needing to conform to existing practice and authority – the behaviour of the extreme traditionalist.

Weber thinks that one or other of these 'ideal types' can be applied to each individual and will serve to explain their ways of behaving. So, when the individuals, with their various notions of rationality, interact, it can be predicted that they will do so in one of just two ways. They will work cooperatively with one another, either for reasons of tradition and other not wholly *zweckrational* reasons, or from a more calculated assessment of their self-interest. The former is typical of family and nationalist bonds, and the latter is found in 'associations' such as those modern industrial society may create.

So Weber aims to produce out of these various types of rationality, and the three types of society, a formal system for describing and even calculating behaviour. But his theory also has a 'normative' outcome – it acts as a standard measure and carries over to become a political recipe. Weber argues that unless society is ordered by a strong authority, rational judgments will be limited to pragmatism. He proposes instead that this authority needs to be respected, almost worshipped.

Weber, like his fellow German, Friedrich Nietzsche, has now moved onto dangerous ground. Nietzsche, as we shall see later, will end up with his 'Superman' exploiting and tyrannising the masses, but Weber still expects the structure of his society to be essentially democratic (through the system of appointments to posts and roles).

He is led to suppose both a need for the 'cultivated man', the cultivated individual who is opposed to the specialist, to staff the bureaucracy and a role for something, perhaps akin to both religion and the cult of the individual, that he calls *charisma*. Charisma is a word taken from theology, meaning to have divine grace, something supernatural bestowed upon individuals. According to Weber, society requires a charismatic figure or entity. God is the original charismatic figure, but the people, the folk, the march of history are other examples.

Later, indeed, the fascists would create Weber's ideal of the bureaucracy under the charismatic leader. And, as he had said, 'the masses submit because of their belief in the extraordinary quality of the specific person – the magical sorcerer, the prophet, the leader of hunting and booty expeditions, the warrior chieftain' – a leader not bound to 'general norms, either traditional or rational'.

Actually, Weber, unlike Durkheim, even allows these leaders to change the direction of history, making it impossible to predict (and thereby somewhat undermining the rationality of his whole intellectual edifice). Complex, and full of paradoxes, competing elements of 'social reality' are allowed to subvert the monolithic bureaucratic forces of Weberian modern society.

## Key Ideas

The 'positivist approach' can give a different, general picture of life and society. Statistical methods are the tools for those today seeking to organise, design and control societies – and their power can be seen in the increasingly sophisticated manipulation of markets by governments, media, and business, perhaps in turn all manipulated by the huge transnational corporations of the modern global economy. Rather than the idealised individuals imagined by Rousseau and some liberal theorists, social science reveals that behaviour can also be explained by seeing people as just atomic parts of the machine that is society. But, at the same time, Durkheim and Weber build on the statistical analysis of the workings of the machine to produce a more metaphysical, idealised model of reality.

- Individual morality and indeed consciousness are created from social life and the collective consciousness.
- Social life is created out of a vast symbolism.

## Key Texts

Emile Durkheim: *Social Rituals and Sacred Objects* (1912) and *Precontractual Solidarity* (1893)
Max Weber: *The Protestant Ethic and the Spirit of Capitalism* (1930)

# Timeline: The Modern Era: From Fordism to Fascism

### 1903
Henry Ford sets up an automobile company, and the first Model T cars follow five years later. The first coast-to-coast crossing of the US by car takes just 65 days. Meanwhile, in Britain, Emmeline Pankhurst sets up a Women's Social and Political Union to demand the vote.

### 1906
The Trades Disputes Act in Britain allows unions to organise strike action without being liable for damages in the civil courts, thus evening up the balance between employers and employed.

### 1907
Free meals and medical care for school children, and pensions for the retired, are introduced in Britain. The state has assumed responsibility for looking after its citizens.

### 1909
Sweden introduces votes for all adults, male and female, but campaigns by the suffragettes in Britain for the same rights are unsuccessful, and the leaders of the movement are imprisoned in 1913.

### 1915
Poison gas is used for the first time, during the First World War.

### 1916
The Battle of the Somme produces over one million casualties.

### 1917
In October, the Bolsheviks overthrow Russia's provisional government and Lenin becomes Chief Commissar.

### 1918
The revolutionary Bolshevik government in Russia nationalises all large-scale industries.

### 1919
Benito Mussolini establishes the Italian Fascists. Out of the ruins of the First World War have emerged two great ideological forces – fascism and communism.

# 10 Behold the Man! The Deceptive Appeal of Power: Hegel, Nietzsche and the Fascists

*Fascism is essentially the doctrine that elevates that part of the human psyche concerned with control over others – power – to a creed. As such, it is different from other political philosophies only in degree. Communism and fascism blur into each other, and in a way National Socialism is, like liberalism, only claiming 'the centre ground'. Conservatism, socialism and even liberalism are none of them immune from the siren call of the fascist ideology, with its deceptive egotistical promise of fulfilment.*

It seems unfair to associate any one philosophical tradition, let alone any one country, with fascism, yet that is what has happened with Germany, a country which has brought so many cultural and scientific gifts to the world, yet whose name has become historically synonymous with world war and the politics of fascism. In fact, it *is* unfair, not least because fascism is actually an Italian ideology, echoed in Spain, paralleled in Japan; and Hitler himself was an Austrian. Indeed others, such as Karl Popper in the twentieth century, often concentrating more on the superficial aspects than on the philosophical underpinnings, have seen Plato as the original fascist, with the *Republic* providing a paradigm of totalitarianism. But this would be a misreading – both of Plato, and of the fascist ideology. Rarely has a creed been so swiftly and totally severed from its intellectual base.

Fascism, as an ideology, is not particularly repugnant. It is idealistic and, if its practical incarnations are appalling, it is always open to its adherents to say, as the supporters of communism do of the experiment of the Soviet Union, that 'true' fascism has not yet been seen. Nazism bears the same sort of relationship to fascism, as Stalinism does to communism, that is to say, an historical rather than a logical one. Nor does fascism have much to do with the present-day holders of the name, who are motivated by a mixture of hatreds and resentments – racism, homophobia, xenophobia – which really do not add up to any kind of political philosophy, other than a shared emphasis on conflict and 'recognition'.

For the political theorist, then, conflict and the desire for recognition are the hallmarks of both fascism, the concept of the state, and Nazism, the practical incarnation, and both are to be found paradigmatically in German thought, starting with the writings of Hegel. That philosophy professor's dream of a Prussian state run along strictly logical and rational lines does indeed share some characteristics with Plato's, as does his emphasis on the 'universe of mind' existing somewhere apart from the 'universe of nature'. Unlike Plato, though, Hegel mixed together the two universes, creating, in a very real sense, both fascism and communism out of the ensuing storm.

# Hegel

Facism's high water mark is the 1930s, and that is why this chapter is placed where it is here. But its roots are much earlier, with Georg Wilhelm Hegel in the early nineteenth century (1770–1831). Hegel, like so many political theorists, starts with the history of the world.

Drawing heavily on eastern philosophy for many of his ideas, he begins his history with a critical survey of Indian, Persian and Chinese thinkers, claiming that, in those societies, only the ruler himself had any freedom to think rationally, and that therefore their philosophers were suspect. Only in ancient Greece, according to Hegel, could individuals begin to be rational, albeit still carrying too much intellectual baggage from their religious and social traditions.

But it is not until the Protestant Reformation, which allowed each individual the ability to 'find their own salvation', that a 'glorious mental dawn' occurs. It is then that 'the consciousness of freedom' which is the driving force of history, makes possible the first truly rational communities, such as that, Hegel suggests, exemplified by the Prussian monarchy of his own time. (A system proving its rationality by providing his professorial salary and position, as Schopenhauer later scoff.)

Hegel's new rational society aims to combine both individual desires: for wealth, for power, for justice, with the social values of the community – a kind of early 'third way' politics. But Hegel's solution also involves reclassifying all desires that are not compatible with the requirements of the social whole as 'irrational', hence not what the individual really wants. Instead, the collective will, the *Geist* (similar, it would seem, to Durkheim's later 'collective consciousness' – though Durkheim's creation does not need any physical form, and Hegel's does) is given complete power and authority. This is what makes Hegel the founding father of the two totalitarian doctrines: fascism and communism.

Lying behind this totalitarian concept of society is a view of the universe not as a collection of fundamental particles, whether atoms or souls, but as a whole, an organic unity. 'The True is the Whole', Hegel writes in *The Phenomenology of Spirit*. It is an illusion to think of anything as separate from anything else, and, in as much as we do so, our thinking is flawed. Actually, even 'the whole', which replaces all these imagined separate objects, is not essentially one substance, but many, just as an organism, such as the human body, is made up of different parts with their own characteristics and functions. Even that most basic distinction – between space and time – results in us misguidedly splitting up the world and thereby losing touch with reality. (This is also what Einstein was concerned to announce in his theories of the 'space–time continuum' and relativity.) Hegel calls reality – this 'whole' – 'The Absolute', and it is his contention that all that is true of the world can be formally deduced from consideration of the Absolute using logic.

The Absolute is also rather like God (a rather austere kind of God, like Aristotle's). A quote, from Hegel's lectures on the *Philosophy of History*, gives the flavour:

> That this *Idea* or *Reason is the True*, the *Eternal*, the absolutely *powerful* essence; that it reveals itself in the world, and that in that world nothing else is revealed but this and its honour and glory – is the thesis which, as we have said, has been proved in philosophy, and is here regarded as demonstrated.

Typically, logic is valued by philosophers as helping people to avoid asserting anything that is self-contradictory, and this type of approach has had a profound influence on Anglo-American philosophy up to the present day, when its limitations (particularly in consideration of political and ethical matters) are better recognised.

But Hegel's notion of logic is different from the usual one. For example, consider a statement like 'the universe is spherical'. For Hegel, this is 'self-contradictory'. It is self-contradictory because the universe is supposed to be infinite, and something cannot be infinite if it is bounded. However, unless the universe is bounded, then it cannot be said to be spherical or indeed to have any shape at all. (While he thought all this certain, mathematicians would disagree.) This approach illustrates the *dialectic*. The dialectic is a process – here one of reasoning, but it could equally well be of political or economic systems, as it was famously later taken by Marx – which proceeds from one view, the thesis, to pose another opposing view – the antithesis. These then combine to produce a synthesis, dissolving the original view, and destroying themselves. However, the synthesis now becomes the new thesis, which in turn is found to be unsatisfactory, so that the process repeats itself.

In the *Science of Logic*, Hegel begins by considering the notion of 'being' as in the proposition 'the Absolute is Pure Being'. But Pure Being without any qualities is nothing, so the Absolute is also not-being or Nothing – the thesis has evoked its own contradiction. The synthesis of this contradiction – the two notions of Pure Being and Nothing – is *Becoming*. (This again is a notion which Hegel has lifted from eastern philosophy.) And again, the synthesis in turn is still unsatisfactory, so the process continues. Each stage of the dialectic contains elements of the previous stages, so that by the end of the process everything is included, and it is this 'everything' that is the Absolute.

The progress of abstract categories in the *Logic* is paralleled, Hegel believes, by the progress of societies. History shows us one form of social organisation gives place to another, always shuffling forwards towards a kind of 'social-absolute'. Again, none of this is particularly original to Hegel, elements are there in both oriental and Greek philosophy, and Hegel was aware of this.

What is more original is that for Hegel, the origin of society is in the first *conflict* between two humans, a 'bloody battle' with each seeking to make the other recognise them as master, and accept the role of 'slave'. (We may suppose that the apparently relevant conflict between male and female, resulting in the subordination of the latter, is less significant. It is not part of Hegel's analysis anyway.) In Hegelianism, it is the fear of death that forces part of mankind to submit to the other, and society is perpetually thereafter divided into the two classes: of slaves and masters. It is not material need that propels one class to oppress the other – it is a conflict borne solely out of the peculiarly human lust for power over one another. The French Revolution, Hegel thought, was the slaves revolting. But, unlike, say, Thomas Hobbes, he approves of the motivation calling it the 'desire for recognition'. For many, this risks death, but that is indeed the way towards 'freedom'.

In fact, Hegel modestly claimed his *Phenomenology of Mind* as achieving the final stage in humanity's evolution, by making mankind fully conscious of true freedom. But it *was* still a strange form of freedom – the freedom of following the laws of a monarch or totalitarian state – with Hegel firmly opposed to 'anti-freedom', which was being able to do what you like. It could be said here that Hegel is merely espousing the liberal notion of freedom under the 'Rule of Law' – allowing maximum choice, subject to the rule of law – but in fact, Hegel does want to go further than this, and replace many of the humanising qualities of liberalism with such things as the 'German Spirit' and the purifying process of war. He writes:

The history of the world is the discipline of the uncontrolled natural will, bringing it into obedience to a universal principle and conferring subjective freedom... The German Spirit is the spirit of the new world. Its aim is the realisation of absolute truth as the unlimited self determination of freedom – that freedom which has its own absolute form as its purpose.

Individuals, for Hegel, have little intrinsic worth, because value resides only in the whole. He identifies Christianity as both the most socially significant religion, and the worst one, because it embodies the political structures of liberal democracy. Christianity suggests that all people are equal, in that they each have a soul of equal worth, and that they are free, in that they are able to choose to live according to the law of God. But Hegel thinks that, because it says that God created Man, rather than Man creating God, and because it only offers equality in heaven, Christianity is a slave ideology.

Hegel goes on to imply that liberal democracy is also a 'slave ideology' as it offers universal recognition of people's importance, by elevating the Christian edict to 'treat your neighbour as yourself' to a practical legal and political stance.

Hegel evoked strong reactions even at the time. One of his most bitter opponents, Schopenhauer, a contemporary, was devoutly opposed to him, ever since he himself had rashly chosen to deliver an inaugural lecture at a time when the celebrated Professor Hegel, then at the peak of his career, was also pontificating in the building. Schopenhauer so bitterly resented the small audience that attended his own talk, that he vowed never to lecture again.

'The emblem at the head of Hegelian university philosophy', he wrote pithily later, should be a 'cuttlefish creating a cloud of obscurity around itself so that no one sees what it is, with the legend, *mea caligne tutus* (fortified by my own obscurity)'.

## Hegel's Influence

But Hegel was a very dangerous kind of cuttlefish, not just one that squirts ink around itself defensively, but one with sharp teeth. On the one hand his *Volkgeist* ('spirit of the people') philosophy led to Marx and Engels – the neo-Hegelians – adapting the notion of the dialectic and writing the *Communist Manifesto*; on the other hand it contributed to Mussolini and Gentile (another neo-Hegelian) writing the *Dottrina del fascismo*. Both doctrines adopt the Hegelian notion of individual self-consciousness being embodied in the state. Both manifestos led to the untold sufferings of millions of ordinary and extraordinary people, victims of ideologues with Hegelian notions of 'the march of history', and contempt for the sufferings of individuals in the face of it. Both fascism and communism elevated to practical policy an abstract philosophy that would have been better left to go musty in the common rooms and library of Berlin University.

Indeed, as Hegel's writing was, even by the standards of German philosophy, particularly dry and indigestible, inaccessible to ordinary readers and unlikely to have had any repercussions in the world outside academia, that is most likely what would have happened had it not been for the much more exciting writings of Schopenhauer himself, and later Nietzsche, both of whom owed Hegel more of an intellectual debt than they liked to admit.

What is Schopenhauer's role in this story? Let us go back to Germany in 1788 when Arthur Schopenhauer was born – so called by his parents to facilitate a career in business ('Arthur' is a name in several European languages). He went to boarding school in Wimbledon, London, where he developed what one biographer, Christopher Jannaway, describes as 'rather a lonely streak'. Schopenhauer writes at one point that, in his view, 'company is a fire at which man warms himself at a distance'. He came to conclude that five out of six people are worthy only of contempt.

At university, Schopenhauer studied medicine, but became interested in philosophy, in particular, Plato, Kant and the ancient Hindu *Upanishads* – a poetical work proclaiming the essential unity of all existence. Together these were the three ingredients of Schopenhauer's proto-existentialist (for want of a real word) work: *The World as Will and Representation*.

> The vanity of existence is revealed in the whole form existence assumes: in the infiniteness of time and space contrasted with the finiteness of the individual in both; in the fleeing present as the sole form in which actuality exists; in the contingency and relativity of all things; in continual becoming without being; in continual desire without satisfaction; in the continual frustration in which life consists. (*On the Vanity of Existence*)

Schopenhauer's main idea, developed early, was that beyond the everyday world of experience is a better world in which the human mind pierces appearance to perceive reality. There is *Vorstellung* (representation) and *Wille* (will), which is, he argues, what the world is, in itself. Schopenhauer represents another side of the German spirit, a more subtle, profound and, in places, compassionate one. And whatever the philosophers at Jena may have thought, he did have one admirer. One who combined both traditions, and became the prophet of the philosophy of power.

### Ecce Homo

Friedrich Nietzsche's first reading of Schopenhauer's *The World as Will and Representation* was a revelation, which he adapted to his own, recognisably fascistic, ends. Born in the 'Decade of Revolutions', in 1844 (in the Prussian town of Röcken) Nietzsche sees human beings, and indeed all of life, as engaged in a struggle, a struggle to increase their power. As to alternative theories, for example that of Mill and the utilitarians, he puts it succinctly in *Twilight of the Idols*, 'Man does not strive after happiness, only the Englishman does that.'

Nietzsche was a philosopher poet who wrote of Supermen and battles, of 'the will to power', and of magnificent destinies. Yet Nietzsche, the historical man, was a rather less dashing figure, physically unattractive and prone to ill health, headaches and chronic short sight, along with intestinal problems, all together ensuring that he knew little of those two great human pleasures: good food and sleep. It seems likely that he knew little of the third pleasure, either, as there was little romance in his life, despite a claimed 'voracious sexual appetite' and his eventually contracting syphilis. At least, that was what Freud alleged, saying he had contacted it in a Genoese male brothel, explaining Nietzsche's obsession with his own ego as homosexual and narcissistic. (Nietzsche himself did describe a visit to a brothel which took place in 1865, but claimed to have come away without touching anything 'but a piano', from which he would have been most unlucky to have contacted syphilis.) His own self-diagnosis blames, rather feebly, the weather for making him a 'narrow, withdrawn, grumpy specialist' instead of a significant, brave 'spirit'. Then again, he says that his sickness 'liberated me slowly', by forcing him to give up his teaching and books, and instead to break his habits, and above all, to 'put an end to all bookwormishness'.

At the age of 40, at which point many accept their middle-aged lot, Nietzsche declared himself to be the 'first immoralist' ('proud to possess this word which sets me off against the whole of humanity'), and announced his intention to 'revalue' all values, starting with the unmasking of Christianity (a task already, as we have seen, undertaken by Hegel) before finishing up by, literally, making 'good' 'bad'. Nietzsche, prescribes his own version of morality – the anti-morality. Where conventional teaching, epitomised by Christianity, but also so strongly advanced by Socrates, would have it that people should be good, and through being good will come happiness, Nietzsche argues that this 'slave morality' is born out of guilt, weakness and resentment. Good is only a shadow form of the absence of this resentment, whereas in 'master morality', good is primary, being equivalent to 'nobility' and 'strength', and bad is the derived form, 'low' and 'common', the failure to achieve this. But his task was attempted too late and was never completed. Instead *Ecce Homo*, 'Behold the Man', a semi-blasphemous title in itself, has to stand as his definitive work, for in the spring of 1889 he descended into a twilight world of his own, never emerging from madness.

Dying, certainly unloved, and, no doubt more importantly in his own terms, unnoticed, at the relatively early age of 56, Nietzsche cuts in many ways a tragic furrow in history, the opposite of what he would have wanted. The end of *Ecce Homo* is supposed to be an ode to his own excellence, but it is more nearly an anthem to the later German fascist creed.

> The concept 'God' invented as the antithetical concept in life – everything harmful, noxious, slanderous, the whole mortal enmity against life brought into one terrible unity! The concept 'the Beyond', 'real world' invented so as to deprive of value the only world which exists – so as to leave over no goal, no reason, no task for our earthly reality! The concept 'soul', 'spirit', finally even 'immortal soul', invented so as to despise the body, so as to make it sick – 'holy' – so as to bring all to all the things in life which deserve serious attention, the question of nutriment, residence, cleanliness, weather, a horrifying frivolity!... Finally, it is the most fateful, in the concept of the *good* man common cause made with everything weak, sick, ill-constituted, suffering from itself, all that *which ought to perish* – the law of *selection* crossed, an ideal made of opposition to the proud and well-constituted, to the affirmative man, to the man certain of the future and guaranteeing the future.

It is here that the Nazi policies of eugenics and race found their voice, sitting comfortably alongside Hegel's earlier attempts to recommend the breeding of Prussian characteristics. The fact that Nietzsche's terminal illness was brought on by the sight of a coachman beating his horse in a cruel manner, a spectacle prompting the first immoralist to intervene out of – of all things! – pity, is one of the small ironies of history.

But why did Nietzsche hate Christianity so? Nietzsche's father had been a Lutheran minister, and his mother was the daughter of another. The things are likely connected. Again, his father went mad eventually, and so did Nietzsche, from 1889. Perhaps it is the incipient sense of insanity that makes his writings so distinctive. After his father's death, the young Nietzsche was brought up in Naumburg by his mother, her sisters and, from his father's side, his grandmother and two of her sisters. The experience did not agree with him. Alongside his dislike of the meek, forgiving, caring Christian, Nietzsche's philosophy is characterised by a deep contempt for womankind. The other half of the species are seen as incapable of 'greatness', and his writing is sprinkled liberally with snide references often of no particular relevance to the philosophical issues under discussion.

Who knows? Perhaps I am the first psychologist of the eternal-womanly. They all love me – an old story: excepting the *abortive* women, the 'emancipated' who lack the stuff for children. Happily, I am not prepared to be torn to pieces: the complete woman tears to pieces when she loves... I know these amiable *maenads*... Ah, what a dangerous, creeping, subterranean little beast of prey it is! And so pleasant with it!... A little woman chasing after her revenge would over-run fate itself. The woman is unspeakably more wicked than the man, also cleverer; goodness in a woman is already a form of *degeneration*...

Strangely enough, despite Freud's theory, Nietzsche spent much time happily with both his sister Elisabeth, who later wrote up his notes, and thereby earned the blame of subsequent philosophers for everything 'bad' in his philosophy and the credit for nothing meretricious; as well as with his mother; and indeed wooing 'Lou', with whom he posed in a photograph with a cart, Lou holding a whip, and Nietzsche and friend acting as the horses. Some might look for evidence of sexual confusions in the fact that the young Nietzsche had been sent (like Schopenhauer) to a respectable German boarding school at an impressionable age. It was there that he immediately stood out by writing a precocious essay in praise of Hölderlin, a then uncelebrated German poet whose work also had the mark of insanity. This scarcely reassured his teachers, who already (wrongly) considered the young Nietzsche to be physically suspect by virtue of his father's illness, but Nietzsche eventually did go to university where he studied Theology and Philosophy. His eccentric style impressed others so much that at the scandalously young age of 24 he was made a professor without ever so much as having had to write a 'serious' essay. Leipzig conferred a doctorate without thesis or examination, and Nietzsche was free thereafter to concentrate on his bizarre but original work.

Typical of this was what emerged after Nietzsche looked at ancient Greek society. Instead of idolising it as a cultured and rational theatre, source of enlightened ideas and virtues, as other philosophers did, under Nietzsche it becomes a dreadful place, full of the screams and sounds of drunken excess from Dionysian orgies, culminating eventually in (magnificent) tragedy, full of unspeakable horror. Nietzsche liked the idea of such orgies. Developing his theme in *Of the Use and Disadvantage of History for Life* (1874), he wrote (as already noted) that the goal of humanity is not in some supposed general strategy or process, such as the maximisation of happiness, but is rather in the activities of its 'highest specimens'. These are men who 'transcend history', and are bound by no laws other than that of their own pleasure. 'The man who would not belong in the mass needs only to cease being comfortable with himself; he should follow his conscience which shouts at him: "Be yourself!" You are not really all you do, think, and desire now' (*Schopenhauer as Educator*, 1874).

However, the freedom to be yourself is curtailed by what Nietzsche sees as an overriding, almost biological (genetic?) urge – the will to power. In many of his writings, he tries to explain behaviour as power seeking, and even suggests that this is the motivation of the rest of nature too, including plants and rocks.

The roots of this theory of conflict can be seen in Nietzsche's early interest in the ancient Greeks, where life was indeed a series of contests: for the physically strong, in athletics or fighting; for musicians and poets in competitions; and, of course, for philosophers, such as Socrates, in debates. In Nietzsche's eyes, Socrates was, in fact, a very powerful man, although there is an element of definition-bending here, for in his usual sense, Socrates was also weak and indeed was imprisoned and executed by his enemies. In any case, Nietzsche reserves his approval for Heraclitus, the aristocrat from Ephesus with the nickname 'the Dark', whom he allows as a fellow believer in the importance of destruction: '... destruction, the decisive element in Dionysian philosophy, affirmation of antithesis and war, *becoming* with a radical rejection even of the concept of "*being*"...' (And still the Hegelian influence too!)

Like Hegel, Nietzsche applies his theory of power to history, and makes some illuminating new interpretations, all based on power psychology. The Superman – *Übermensch* – (sometimes implausibly translated as the 'Overman', which sounds like a sort of waterproof shoe) is for Nietzsche the logical outcome of his theory, an individual enjoying his (and it must be *his*) power to the full, untrammelled by notions of justice or pity. In 1884, Nietzsche wrote, in *Der Wille zur Macht*, 'One must learn from war to associate death with the interests for which one fights – that makes us proud; [and to] learn to sacrifice many and to take one's cause seriously enough not to spare human lives.'

## Nietzsche's Influence

Hitler read Nietzsche avidly, seeing in the philosopher some sort of fellow spirit, and Nietzsche's philosophy was adopted and quoted by the Nazis as in some sense embodying Nazi values. It is the discussion of the 'master/slave' relationship that is of most historical resonance. But many of Nietzsche's rhetorical flourishes, such as the despising of the weak, the sick and the handicapped, also fed easily and conveniently into the policies of the Nazi state – even if, as was indubitably also the case, Nietzsche himself had no time for theories of racial supremacy and actually admired the Jews for having crucified the Christian prophet. In fact, Nietzsche even rails regularly against his fellow countrymen: 'As far as Germany extends, it ruins culture... the Germans are incapable of any conception of Greatness...'; 'the Germans have no idea whatever how common they are; but that is the superlative of commonness – they are not even ashamed of being German...'.

The Nazi propagandists got around this apparent contradiction by explaining that his writing was merely a criticism of Germany before the Third Reich. And Nietzsche's anti-morality certainly elevated war to the status of being an end in itself. 'Among the decisive precon-ditions for a Dionysian task is the hardness of the hammer, joy even in destruction.' In the concluding chapter of *Ecce Homo*, 'Why I Am Destiny', Nietzsche says in a passage which appears to both gleefully and uncannily anticipate the Holocaust: 'I know my fate. One day, there will be associated with my name the recollection of something frightful – of a crisis like no other before on earth, of the profoundest collision of conscience, of a decision evoked against everything that until then had been believed in, demanded, sanctified. I am not a man, I am dynamite.'

Perhaps Nietzsche's writings were twisted and distorted through the lens of his sister, the only source for his actual writings (and certainly herself later active with the Nazis). Whether or not this is true, the writings have their own life. Hitler certainly saw himself as a kind of 'philosophical despot and artist tyrant' as imagined by the philosopher. In one of his works, Nietzsche explains how such despots will

... mould men as an artist would... to achieve that universal energy of greatness, to mould the future man by breeding and, at the same time, by destroying millions of bungled humans, we will not be deterred by the suffering we create, the equal of which has never been seen!

Nietzsche's writings are not really terribly good literature – but the philosophers think they are. And they are not really terribly good philosophy – but the literary critics think they are. Both are impressed by his rejection of 'rationality' (Socrates' 'great mistake') and by his 'deliberate contradictions'. In this way, he has been able to retain a largely undeserved reputation for profundity and originality.

Philosophically, Nietzsche's point is that there is no meaning to life except that which individuals can create for themselves. As fascism is largely about the state, not the individual, seeking to subsume the individual need for 'recognition' into the pomp, power and ceremony of the state, the two theories are in some ways at opposite logical poles. Yet, in both theories, the only way out of this futility and meaninglessness for the individual is through action and creation – and the purest form of these is through the exercise of power. In practice, the Nazi state offered individuals a chance to have power over others, and to enjoy it, untrammelled, as Nietzsche said, by 'notions of justice or pity'.

Nietzsche's legacy is not so much a philosophical justification for anti-morality, as a philosophical precedent for it. He offers legitimacy to those seeking to explain why fundamental offences against common morality are not important. The chain of ideas that led from Hegel through Schopenhauer to Nietzsche was now ready to be taken to its fateful conclusion by the new political ideologues.

## Italian Fascism

Fascism, although widely bandied about as a term for any regime that people disapprove of, is correctly identified as the ideology of the Italian fascists in the first half of the twentieth century under Benito Mussolini. And Mussolini actually started his career as a socialist, gradually developing extreme syndicalist notions centred around an all-powerful state. The manifesto of his party can be said to be *La dottrina del fascismo* written by Mussolini and the former liberal, Giovanni Gentile, a respected 'neo-Hegelian' philosopher.

These days, the term fascism is most closely associated with Adolf Hitler, who admired Mussolini and adopted the doctrine as the ideology of the German National Socialists. For that reason alone, fascism must be treated as a serious historical theory. But in a sense, Hitler's Nazis were barely 'fascists' – in the same way that they were barely 'socialists', national or otherwise. Mussolini and Gentile's doctrine was rather more subtle and persuasive.

Gentile gave fascism an idealistic and spiritual aspect. Where liberalism and socialism sought to benefit each individual, fascism sought to benefit the nation. As President Kennedy put it once, people were not to ask what the state could do for them, but only ask what they could do for the state. The well-being of the nation provided a high moral purpose for each individual, a purpose that took precedence over the squabbles of workers and unions on the one hand, and of capitalists and libertarians on the other. The original fascists felt that the philosophies both of socialism and of individualism served only to divide the nation and weaken it. Hence, instead of trade unions and private enterprise, fascists created a single unifying force, capable of ensuring that companies and workers alike worked in the interests of the state. This force was to be the fascist party, united behind a charismatic leader. The fascists created Weber's ideal of the bureaucracy under the charismatic leader.

But Gentile's language in describing the benefits of this approach went further too. Fascism, he wrote, echoing Hegel, would restore the patriotic morality of 'service, sacrifice and indeed death'.

Fascism was not just an economic theory, or a quasi-legal structure of rights, but much more – a way to live and a way to attain fulfilment. It was not enough to do what the fascist government said – the fascist citizen also had to *want* to do it, and to believe in doing it. That is why one of the most potent images of the fascist state is of massive parades lined with enthusiastically waving crowds.

Mussolini added to this his own notion of fascism as an 'action theory' – and the highest form of action was violence. Echoing Nietzsche, it was only through violence that individual fascists could truly fulfil themselves and it was only through wars that the fascist state could maintain its ideological purity. When Mussolini used violence to seize power in Italy in 1922, the process was part of the new way of governing – not just a necessary prerequisite. In many people's eyes, the courage of the fascists in fighting for power conferred nobility on the movement and cleansed it of the impurities of the shambling democratic state.

Like Hitler, but certainly not like Nietzsche, Mussolini also stressed nationalism. For Mussolini, Bismarck was a great figure, who had succeeded in binding together the various elements of Germany into a powerful nation, and he also admired Machiavelli for what he saw as Machiavelli's endorsement of power, especially military power – ignoring or missing the earlier Italian's emphasis on justice.

However, Mussolini's nationalism should not be confused with the German brand, which identified nationality with 'race'. Crucially, for Mussolini, it was the role of the state to create a people out of what in reality would be a mix of very different races. It was the failure of Hitler to understand this that led German fascism to the most grotesque irony of bureaucratic rules and structures, all aiming to make logical a doctrine of racial purity created out of irrational hatred and prejudice. Mussolini himself, the father of fascism, even wrote at one point explicitly that *a people is not a race*, instead it is a group united by an idea perpetuating itself. In this way, if Marx was not a 'Marxist', as he complained, certainly Mussolini was not a 'fascist'. However, he was not a very strong leader either, and steadily over the period of the Second World War, Italian fascism too adopted the anti-Semitic policies of the Nazis, even if these were never implemented with any enthusiasm by the Italians, despite increasing German pressure for action as the Nazi officers gradually took control of the region.

Likewise, although Mussolini built up a fairly efficient party machine, and installed party members in key jobs, it was left to Hitler on the right, and Stalin on the left, to really create the conditions of fear and total control that the fascist philosophy suggested. Mussolini banned strikes and nationalised key industries, but Italy's economic performance remained stuck at the same levels. The claim that Mussolini at least 'made the trains run on time' is probably the greatest thing that can be said of that fascist society, and this claim is largely apocryphal.

For, indeed, Italy proved infertile soil for its new seed. The most extreme symbol of Italian fascism – the Abyssinian exploit, in which the Italian army annexed their former colony – was barely achieved, shocking though it was as an example of a sophisticated modern army attacking simple villagers with planes and bombs. (Nowadays, such wickedness is a commonplace. Even the most liberal democrats scarcely hesitate to order the use of such force.) It was also evident to all that the fascists had little more than self-aggrandisement and defiance of the League of Nations as their aims.

The Italian people had as much appreciation of grand displays as anyone, but they also had a well-developed distrust and cynicism about the motives of their leaders, and the fascists were no exception. Unlike the German SS, the Italian army was made up of conscripts who were disinclined to fight for a political party, and perhaps also reluctant to abandon their humanity for an ideology. Ordinary Italians largely refused to go down the path of atrocity that others were to explore so eagerly.

## Key Ideas

For fascism,

- all life is a striving after *power*, with human beings important only as the means to the ends of the exercise of this power;
- the state should be organised rationally, with individuals complying with and fitting in to its requirements.

In some ways, Nietzsche had a rather naïve notion of the power of an individual, whereas Mussolini and Gentile were essentially investing power in the state, under, of course, a charismatic leader. In the aftermath of the horrors of the Second World War, there is little explicit political appetite for the Hegelian doctrine of unfettered state power, although many regimes contain elements of the philosophy in practice. It seems, too, that the Weberian cult of the charismatic national leader has run its course.

Adam Smith too thought liberalism and the free market could offer people a route to satisfy their desire for 'recognition', through the accumulation of material goods. These are not 'necessities of nature', but 'superfluities'. As Smith puts it in *The Moral Sentiments*, 'The rich man glories in his riches, because he feels they naturally draw upon him the attention of the world... the poor man, on the contrary, is ashamed of his poverty.'

If we recall, with Smith, that 'wealth, as Mr Hobbes says, is power', and that money is power in tangible, exchangeable form, then there are parallels between the more radical doctrines of materialism and fascism. It can be argued that the philosophical appeal of life as the pursuit of power goes deeper than just an historical stage, apparently now passed through.

## Key Text

Nietzsche's *Ecce Homo* (1908)

# Timeline: From the Great Depression to the New Economics

## 1920
Ghandi starts a campaign of civil disobedience against the British in India.

## 1921
In China, a Communist Party is founded. In the US, the Ku Klux Klan are increasingly violent – and can expect a quarter of a million supporters to attend their 'conclaves'.

## 1922
Stalin becomes Secretary General of the Russian Communist Party and sets up the OGPU – forerunner of the KGB, Russia's secret police. The Italian fascists march on Rome and King Emmanuel III invites Mussolini to become Prime Minister.

## 1923
Adolf Hitler similarly attempts a putsch in Bavaria, but is unsuccessful and is imprisoned.

## 1924
Lenin dies and is succeeded by Stalin who establishes a personal dictatorship. In Italy, the fascists are successful in the elections and, from 1925, also establish a dictatorship.

## 1925
Experimental television pictures are transmitted by John Logie Baird in Britain.

## 1927
The Shanghai massacres of communists by the Nationalist government take place in China. Chiang Kai Shek rules as a dictator.

## 1929
The Wall Street Crash. The World economy plunges into depression. From Glasgow, unemployed marchers make their way to London.

**1930**
The Nazis are now the second largest party in the German parliament.

**1931**
Collapse of 3,000 German banks as unemployment rises to nearly 6 million.

**1932**
Fascist parties are founded in Britain and Spain. The Nazis are now the largest party in the German parliament. Aldous Huxley's *Brave New World* is published. The slump reaches its nadir in the US, there is a 'Great Hunger March' in London, and in India the British put Gandhi in prison.

**1933**
The Nazis use their new powers to set up a one-party state. Concentration camps are opened for enemies of the party. When the German President, Hindenberg, dies the following year, Adolf Hitler becomes sole leader – Fuehrer – of Germany. The 'Long March' begins in China, saving Mao's peasant army, ready one day to defeat Japanese fascism.

**1935**
Nazis start systematically targeting Jews.The Italians invade an independent country, Abyssinia, demonstrating the impotence of the League of Nations.

**1936**
Germany, Italy and Japan reach strategic agreements.

**1938**
First anti-Semitic laws in Italy. Germany annexes Austria.

**1939**
Spain joins the fascist community. Germany annexes Czechoslovakia, and then Poland, precipitating the Second World War.

**1941**
Germany sets up the first extermination camps.

1942

Two technological breakthroughs in the US – the first nuclear reactor and the first 'modern' computer.

1944

The Bretton Woods Conference creates two international institutions, the International Monetary Fund and the World Bank, to determine the shape of the post-war world.

1945

Violent end to Italian, German and finally Japanese fascist movements. Perhaps 35 million people have died in the fighting (most of them on the Eastern Front), and at least another 10 million have been murdered in the concentration camps. In China, a new People's Republic is being set up under Chairman Mao.

# 11 Mao's Little Red Book

*The most popular political pamphlet of them all is Mao's little Red Book. It has been helped by being more or less compulsory for millions of people. And not only to buy, but to read and memorise. But, in fact, it is quite a good read: short, pithy and to the point. For more than two generations, the effects and implications of this pocket-sized collection of Mao's philosophising shaped the world's most populous nation. But Maoism's influence goes far beyond China's borders.*

The Chinese Marxists under Mao had two primary goals: to save China from the foreign enemies who had overrun it, and to make the country strong and rich in the future. Not particularly original, both of these were to be achieved through programmes of technological modernisation and public education. Being essentially pragmatic in outlook, they selected from any of the range of Marxist and Chinese philosophies those elements that they felt could be used most effectively in the pursuit of these aims. Maoism became a mixture of Marx and Engels' writings, Lenin and Trotsky's subsequent interpretations, and the two distinctive Chinese philosophies of Confucianism and Taoism.

In Confucianism, the primary function of government, apart from details such as raising taxes, is education. All officials, from the emperor and the mandarins down, have a sacred duty of educating the masses, particularly in a moral sense. Li Dazhao, one of the early Chinese communists, influenced the development of Marxism in China away from historical determinism, by allowing countries to 'telescope' their progress from an agrarian society to communism, by education, that is through a consciousness of the class struggle. This doctrine was also incorporated into Maoism as the policy of 'permanent revolution'.

Another element in Confucianism is the desire to create a 'one-minded' society. So also Maoism. The people should all think the same on any important matter. Mao himself included egalitarianism as such a 'one-minded' goal. The challenge of this orthodoxy by Liu Shaoqu contributed to the destructive conflict of the Cultural

Revolution, Mao's flailing attempt to reassert his philosophical dominance and political supremacy. Following Mao's death in 1976, and Deng Xioping's succession, egalitarianism was abandoned in place of something closer to the western conservative notion of 'trickle-down' – some people must get rich first, creating wealth that later benefits the others.

In the West, surprisingly few consider Maoism a distinct philosophy and fewer still have looked at what the Little Red Book actually said. But the story of human society in many ways begins in China, so let us finish it there too.

**The Red Book**

Strictly speaking, the book is entitled *Quotations from Chairman Mao Tse-Tung* (nowadays usually spelt 'Zedong'). However, as even in party circles in China itself no one actually uses this unwieldy title – it is mostly just called 'the Red Book' - I have used either this or the affectionate sounding soubriquet 'little Red Book' instead. Though in China itself, it should be noted, the book inspired a great deal more than just affection. For many years it had almost the status of a bible or holy book, carried around for reference at all times, and even touched for good fortune, or for protection at moments of strife.

The little Red Book starts with Marxism, or, at least, with what is perceived to be 'the science of dialectical materialism' behind the varied and inconsistent writings of Marx and Engels. It speaks in revolutionary phrases, short statements designed to be learnt and recited (and for decades in all China's schools and colleges and work places they were). And the Red Book starts, as does the Chinese state, as do all good Marxists, with the Communist Party. It proclaims straight away, with no concessions to the browsing reader:

> If there is to be revolution, there must be a revolutionary party. Without a revolutionary party, without a party built on the Marxist-Leninist revolutionary theory and in the Marxist-Leninist revolutionary style, it is impossible to lead the working class and the broad masses of the people to defeat imperialism and its running dogs.

Without the Chinese communists as its mainstay, China could never achieve independence or liberation, or industrialisation and the modernisation of her agriculture, the Red Book warns. Written originally just as the Second World War came to an end in April 1945, this opening section is intended to link the revolution to economic progress, and appeal to the patriotism of a people who had recently suffered so greatly and so brutally under the Japanese invaders (and before them, the western ones). Nonetheless, the Red Book recognises that it will be 'an arduous task' to ensure a better life for the several hundred million people of China and to build up an 'economically and culturally backward country' into a prosperous and powerful one with a high level of culture. So it is, like both Confucius and Plato 3,000 years before, that Mao starts with education. And, Mao thinks, there is one good thing about China:

> Apart from their other characteristics, the outstanding thing about China's 600 million people is that they are 'poor and blank'. This may seem a bad thing, but in reality it is a good thing. Poverty gives rise to the desire for change, the desire for action and the desire for revolution. On a blank sheet of paper free from any mark, the freshest and most beautiful characters can be written, the freshest and most beautiful pictures can be painted.

Education here means 'Marxist education'. But what is Marxist education? The key is 'revolutionary theory', combined with knowledge of history and a 'profound grasp of the practical movement'. Together, these are *rectification* – a 24-carat Marxist word – which means the whole Party studying Marxism. Rectification is 'putting yourself right', and practising self-criticism, to ensure that political action and social policy remains correct. In order to shoulder the task of constructing the new communist society competently and work better alongside 'all non-Party people who are actuated by high ideals and determined to institute reforms', communists need to conduct 'rectification movements', both now and in the future, and constantly rid themselves of wrong thinking.

So the 'Cultural Revolution' of the 1950s was not entirely an anomaly. Maoism, again like Platonism and Confucianism, was always obsessed with protecting the republic and maintaining the purity of the revolution in the face of the manifest tendency for material contamination and dilution. If Plato worried about the influence of bad poetry, and wanted only approved plays performed, in Red China education revolved only around the approved political poetry of party slogans such as: 'What is work? Work is struggle'; 'There are difficulties and problems for us to overcome and solve. We go there to work and struggle to overcome these difficulties'; and 'A good comrade is one who is more eager to go where the difficulties are greater.'

Or around uplifting political stories such as the ancient fable of 'The Foolish Old Man Who Removed the Mountains'. This tells of a greybeard who lived in northern China long, long ago. His house faced south and beyond his doorway stood the two great peaks, Taihang and Wangwu, obstructing the way. He called his sons, and hoe in hand they began to dig up these mountains with great determination. Another greybeard, known as the Wise Old Man, saw them and said derisively, 'How silly of you to do this! It is quite impossible for you few to dig up those two huge mountains.' At this, the Foolish Old Man replies, 'When I die, my sons will carry on; when they die, there will be my grandsons, and then their sons and grandsons, and so on to infinity. High as they are, the mountains cannot grow any higher and with every bit we dig, they will be that much lower. Why can't we clear them away?' Having refuted the Wise Old Man's wrong view (the story goes on), the Foolish One carried on digging every day, unshaken in his conviction. God was moved by this, and sent down two angels, who carried the mountains away on their backs. The moral is (teacher would add) that today, two big mountains lie like a dead weight on the Chinese people. One is imperialism, the other is feudalism.

So, revolutionary theory and history are straightforward to teach. But what of the 'practical movement'? Mao's two most famous essays 'On Practice' and 'On Contradiction', both from 1937, are concerned with this. Both reflect the guerrilla roots of Maoism – the strategy is a democratic one of building up support in the countryside ready to overthrow the Japanese. But the policy also reflects a theoretical belief about the nature of knowledge. Knowledge starts with sense-perception, is distilled into ideas and theory, and then tested through practice. Essentially, the 'practical movement' is learning through experience, through experiment even. As the Red Book goes on, 'Only through the practice of the people, that is, through experience, can we verify whether a policy is correct or wrong and determine to what extent it is correct or wrong.'

The Red Book emphasises the need for party workers to indulge in this sort of 'investigation and study', rather than end up behaving like 'a blindfolded man catching sparrows', or 'a blind man groping for fish' – or even to 'indulge in verbiage' and rest content with a 'smattering of knowledge'. Better instead that everyone engaged in practical work investigate conditions at the lower levels. 'No investigation, no right to speak.' Although there are many people who will 'the moment they alight from the official carriage' make a hullabaloo, spout opinions, criticise this and condemn that, in fact, 'ten out of ten of them will meet with failure'. For such views or criticisms, not being based on thorough investigation, are 'nothing but ignorant twaddle'. Countless times, Mao recalls, the Party suffered at the hands of these imperial envoys, who rushed here, there and everywhere. Stalin was right to say that 'theory becomes purposeless if it is not connected with revolutionary practice'. For, to 'investigate a problem is indeed to solve it', the Red Book advises.

'The only way to know conditions is to make social investigations, to investigate the conditions of each social class in real life.' The best method is to concentrate on a few cities and villages according to a plan, designed from the fundamental viewpoint of Marxism, i.e. the method of class analysis, and make a number of thorough investigations. (Which have some of the same aspects as today's citizens' panels in the United States.)

> A fact-finding meeting need not be large; from three to five or seven or eight people is enough. Ample time must be allowed and an outline for the investigation must be prepared; furthermore, one must personally ask questions, take notes and have discussions with those at the meeting. One certainly cannot make an investigation, or do it well, without zeal, a determination to direct one's eyes downward and a thirst for knowledge, and without shedding the ugly mantle of pretentiousness and becoming a willing pupil.

This applies equally to any political system concentrating power. With victory, certain moods may grow within the rulers, such as:

... arrogance, the airs of a self-styled hero, inertia and unwillingness to make progress, love of pleasure and distaste for continued hard living. With victory, the people will be grateful to us and the bourgeoisie will come forward to flatter us. It has been proved that the enemy cannot conquer us by force of arms. However, the flattery of the bourgeoisie may conquer the weak-willed in our ranks. There may be some Communists, who were not conquered by enemies with guns and were worthy of the name of heroes for standing up to these enemies, but who cannot withstand sugar-coated bullets.

Mao first of all applied this sort of 'rectification' in the revolutionary army, where he stressed it was important that democracy should be put into effect, starting with the abolition of the feudal practices of bullying and beating as well as by having officers and men 'share weal and woe'. Once this had been done, unity would be achieved between officers and men, the combat effectiveness of the army greatly increased, and there would be no doubt of 'our ability to sustain the long, cruel war'.

The Red Book spells out explicitly to any Marxists who might doubt the need to consult and win consent.

In China the army needs democracy as much as the people do. Democracy in our army is an important weapon for undermining the feudal mercenary army. Apart from the role played by the Party, the reason why the Red Army has been able to carry on in spite of such poor material conditions and such frequent engagements is its practice of democracy. The officers do not beat the men; officers and men receive equal treatment, soldiers are free to hold meetings and to speak out; trivial formalities have been done away with; and the accounts are open for all to inspect.

So democracy was taken very seriously in pre-revolutionary China, more so, in some respects, than in western democracies. 'Our duty is to hold ourselves responsible to the people. Every word, every act and every policy must conform to the people's interests, and if mistakes occur, they must be corrected – that is what being responsible to the people means.' What of the smaller concerns of the people? 'We should pay close attention to the well-being of the masses, from the problems of land and labour to those of fuel, rice, cooking oil and salt.' For all such problems concerning 'the well-being of the masses' are to be placed on the agenda. 'We should discuss them, adopt and carry out decisions and check up on the results. We should help the masses to realise that we represent their interests, that our lives are intimately bound up with theirs.' Certainly, later, communists should help people to proceed from these things to an understanding of the higher tasks, the tasks of the revolutionary war, spreading the revolution and so on, but communists should also pay attention to detail. In short, Mao recognises that education and democracy are inseparable.

What though of freedom? Social science is one of the key weapons in the fight for mankind's freedom.

For the purpose of attaining freedom in society, man must use social science to understand and change society and carry out social revolution. It is man's social being that determines his thinking. Once the correct ideas characteristic of the advanced class are grasped by the masses, these ideas turn into a material force which changes society and changes the world.

Such, Mao adds, is the Marxist theory of knowledge.

At first, knowledge is perceptual. The leap to conceptual knowledge, that is to ideas, occurs when sufficient perceptual knowledge is accumulated. This is one process in cognition. It is the first stage in the whole process of cognition, the stage leading from objective matter to subjective consciousness, from existence to ideas. Whether or not one's consciousness or ideas (including theories, policies, plans or measures) do correctly reflect the laws of the objective external world is not yet proved at this stage, in which it is not yet possible to ascertain whether they are correct or not. Then comes the second stage in the process of cognition, the stage leading from consciousness back to matter, from ideas back to existence, in which the knowledge gained in the first stage is applied in social practice to ascertain whether the theories, policies, plans or measures meet with the anticipated success. Generally speaking, those that succeed are correct and those that fail are incorrect.

The Red Book recommends the same procedure for both ideas and the practical work of the Party, in both cases leadership is necessarily 'from the masses, to the masses'. This means: take the ideas of the masses (scattered and unsystematic ideas) and 'concentrate them' (that is, through study turn them into concentrated and systematic ideas), then go back to the masses and propagate and explain these ideas 'until the masses embrace them as their own, hold fast to them and translate them into action'. Finally, remember to test the correctness of the ideas in practice. Then once again concentrate ideas from the masses and once again go to the masses so that the ideas are persevered in and carried through. 'And so on, over and over again in an endless spiral, with the ideas becoming more correct, more vital and richer each time.' This is truly the science of society.

In remarks reflecting the Chinese doctrine of means and equilibrium, 'A Single Spark Can Start a Prairie Fire' (5 January 1930), Mao expands on the theory of knowledge in philosophical language, more than a little reminiscent of John Locke.

> The fundamental cause of the development of a thing is not external but internal; it lies in the contradictoriness within the thing. There is internal contradiction in every single thing, hence its motion and development. Contradictoriness within a thing is the fundamental cause of its development, while its interrelations and interactions with other things are secondary causes...

The little Red Book goes on, now in more metaphysical mode:

> Marxist philosophy holds that the law of the unity of opposites is the fundamental law of the universe. This law operates universally, whether in the natural world, in human society, or in man's thinking. Between the opposites in a contradiction there is at once unity and struggle, and it is this that impels things to move and change. Contradictions exist everywhere, but they differ in accordance with the different nature of different things. In any given phenomenon or thing, the unity of opposites is conditional, temporary and transitory, and hence relative, whereas the struggle of opposites is absolute.

The unity of opposites is important for Marxist politics because it solves the blindfold-man-collecting-sparrows problem. We recall:

> Only those who are subjective, one-sided and superficial in their approach to problems will smugly issue orders or directives the moment they arrive on the scene, without considering the

circumstances, without viewing things in their totality (their history and their present state as a whole) and without getting to the essence of things (their nature and the internal relations between one thing and another).

Such people are bound to trip and fall. One-sidedness means thinking in terms of absolutes, that is, a metaphysical approach to problems. For communists, in the appraisal of their work, it is one-sided to regard everything either as all positive or as all negative. Recognising this 'fundamental aspect' should bring humility (even in a one-party system).

... To regard everything as positive is to see only the good and not the bad, and to tolerate only praise and no criticism. To talk as though our work is good in every respect is at variance with the facts. It is not true that everything is good; there are still short-comings and mistakes. But neither is it true that everything is bad, and that, too, is at variance with the facts. Here analysis is necessary. To negate everything is to think, without having made any analysis, that nothing has been done well and that the great work of socialist construction, the great struggle in which hundreds of millions of people are participating, is a complete mess with nothing in it worth commending. Although there is a difference between the many people who hold such views and those who are hostile to the socialist system, these views are very mistaken and harmful and can only dishearten people.

We must not be like the 'frog in the well'. In a speech at the Chinese Communist Party's National Conference on Propaganda Work (12 March 1957), Mao had declared that:

In approaching a problem a Marxist should see the whole as well as the parts. A frog in a well says, 'The sky is no bigger than the mouth of the well.' That is untrue, for the sky is not just the size of the mouth of the well. If it said, 'A part of the sky is the size of the mouth of a well' that would be true, for it tallies with the facts.

Such 'holism' even brings Mao to muddy the holy water of Marxist materialism:

While we recognise that in the general development of history the material determines the mental and social being determines social consciousness, we also – and indeed must – recognise the reaction of mental on material things, of social consciousness on social being and of the superstructure on the economic base.

Of course, Mao hastens to add, this does not go against materialism; on the contrary, 'it avoids mechanical materialism and firmly upholds dialectical materialism'. But the justification offered in the Red Book for this 'two causes – single effect', approach is unconvincing:

If in any process there are a number of contradictions, one of them must be the principal contradiction playing the leading and decisive role, while the rest occupy a secondary and subordinate position... The nature of a thing is determined mainly by the principal aspect of a contradiction, the aspect which has gained the dominant position.

Worse still, from the point of view of scientific cause and effect, 'the situation is not static; the principal and the non-principal aspects of a contradiction transform themselves into each other and the nature of the thing changes accordingly'.

However, the Party can and will lay down the general line and general policy of the Chinese revolution as well as various specific lines for work and specific policies. Indeed, Mao warns, while many comrades remember the Party's specific lines for work and specific policies, 'they often forget its general line and general policy' (which is now, it would seem, assumed to be fairly static after all). By doing so, they risk becoming 'blind, half-baked, muddle-headed revolutionaries', vacillating now to the left and now to the right, with their work suffering.

So the Red Book tells communists that, if they remember nothing else, they should always remember one key truth: it was the class struggles of the peasants, the peasant uprisings and peasant wars that were the engine driving historical development in Chinese feudal society. 'Classes struggle, some classes triumph, others are eliminated. Such is history, such is the history of civilisation for thousands of years.'

And inspirational messages for revolutionaries from talks given by Mao are given, under headings like: 'People of the World, Unite and

Defeat the US Aggressors and All Their Lackeys'; pledging support for oppressed groups abroad, notably the American blacks.

It is up to us to organise the people. As for the reactionaries in China, it is up to us to organise the people to overthrow them. Everything reactionary is the same; if you don't hit it, it won't fall. It is like sweeping the floor; where the broom does not reach, the dust never vanishes of itself.

In Mao's immortal words:

A revolution is not a dinner party, or writing an essay, or painting a picture, or doing embroidery; it cannot be so refined, so leisurely and gentle, so temperate, kind, courteous, restrained and magnanimous. A revolution is an insurrection, an act of violence by which one class overthrows another.

In theory, it is easy to identify the enemy: whoever sides with the revolutionary people is a revolutionary, and whoever sides with imperialism, feudalism and bureaucrat-capitalism is a counter-revolutionary and an enemy. They are all those in league with imperialism – the warlords, the bureaucrats, the comprador class, 'the big landlord class' and the reactionary intellectuals. Arrayed against, there is only the industrial proletariat (although alongside it is the whole of the semi-proletariat and the petty bourgeoisie). But as for 'the vacillating middle bourgeoisie', they are one day a friend, the next an enemy: communists must be constantly on their guard lest they be allowed to create confusion within the ranks.

But, in practice, often it is hard to tell who is who, who is your friend and who is your enemy. Even amongst 'the whites in the United States it is only the reactionary ruling circles who oppress the black people'. The ruling classes there can 'in no way represent the workers, farmers, revolutionary intellectuals and other enlightened persons who comprise the overwhelming majority of the white people'. So for this reason, in general, polarisation is a good thing, helping to pinpoint the enemy. After all, 'Imperialists and domestic reactionaries will certainly not take their defeat lying down and they will struggle to the last ditch, and even after there is peace and order throughout the country, 'they will still engage in sabotage and create disturbances in various ways and will try every day and every minute to stage a comeback'.

In a speech in the Red Book dating back to the early years of the revolution, Mao surveys Red China and sees socialist transformation completed in the system of ownership, and the 'large-scale, turbulent class struggles of the masses' in the main come to an end, but he sees too 'remnants of the overthrown landlord and comprador classes', a bourgeoisie still hanging on, and the 'remolding of the petty bourgeoisie' only just started. In short, the class struggle is by no means over. But then, in its various forms, the struggle – 'between the proletariat and the bourgeoisie, between the different political forces, and the struggle in the ideological field between the proletariat and the bourgeoisie' – is always bound to be 'long and tortuous'. The proletariat seeks to transform the world according to its own world outlook, and so does the bourgeoisie. Realistically, then, Mao predicts 'bourgeois and petty-bourgeois ideology', anti-Marxist ideology, will continue to exist for a long time. There needs to be a strategy to deal with the pernicious effects of what Mao calls 'liberalism', and others, even in his own Party, call 'humanism'.

> Liberalism is extremely harmful in a revolutionary collective. It is a corrosive which eats away unity, undermines cohesion, causes apathy and creates dissension. It robs the revolutionary ranks of compact organisation and strict discipline, prevents policies from being carried through and alienates the Party organisations from the masses which the Party leads. It is an extremely bad tendency.

People who are liberals in China look upon the principles of Marxism as abstract dogma. They approve of Marxism, but are not prepared to practice it or to practice it in full; they are not prepared to replace their liberalism by Marxism. These people have their Marxism, but they have their liberalism as well – they talk Marxism but practice liberalism; they apply Marxism to others but liberalism to themselves. 'They keep both kinds of goods in stock and find a use for each.'

One of the problems with these liberals is their version of 'freedom' and 'democracy'. Isn't Maoism democratic enough? The Red Book acknowledges that it denies some freedoms, but allows others.

> Within the ranks of the people, we cannot do without freedom, nor can we do without discipline; we cannot do without democracy, nor can we do without centralism. This unity of

democracy and centralism, of freedom and discipline, constitutes our democratic centralism. Under this system, the people enjoy broad democracy and freedom, but at the same time they have to keep within the bounds of socialist discipline.

For party members, this freedom has a particular form:

(1)  the individual is subordinate to the organisation;
(2)  the minority is subordinate to the majority;
(3)  the lower level is subordinate to the higher level; and
(4)  the entire membership is subordinate to the Central Committee.

In fact, the Party is a hierarchy, just as Confucius recommended. Non-members are either completely free or completely subordinate, depending on your point of view.

At no time and in no circumstances should a Communist place his personal interests first; he should subordinate them to the interests of the nation and of the masses. Hence, selfishness, slacking, corruption, seeking the limelight, and so on, are most contemptible, while selflessness, working with all one's energy, whole-hearted devotion to public duty, and quiet hard work will command respect.

(You can see why capitalism became more popular.)

Communists should set an example. Indeed, 'We Communists are like seeds and the people are like the soil. Wherever we go, we must unite with the people, take root and blossom among them...' Communists must listen attentively to the views of people outside the Party and let them have their say. If what they say is right, they ought to welcome it, and learn from the people. If it is wrong, 'we should let them finish what they are saying and then patiently explain things to them'.

Still on the horticultural theme, Mao goes on: 'All erroneous ideas, all poisonous weeds, all ghosts and monsters, must be subjected to criticism; in no circumstances should they be allowed to spread unchecked.' But the criticism should be fully reasoned, analytical and convincing, and 'not rough, bureaucratic, metaphysical or dogmatic'.

Communists can however rely on the fact that, as Marx had demonstrated (on paper) a century before, their victory 'is an objective law independent of man's will'. Even if the reactionaries try to hold back the 'wheel of history', sooner or later revolution will take place and it will triumph. It is a simple matter of the operation of economic forces. After all, the changeover from individual to socialist, collective ownership in agriculture and handicrafts and from capitalist to socialist ownership in private industry and commerce is 'bound to bring about a tremendous liberation of the productive forces'. (Collectivisation in particular actually caused massive famines in China, as it had in the Soviet Union beforehand.) But land reform was politically essential; it was the key to all other reforms. 'The political authority of the landlords is the backbone of all the other systems of authority. With that overturned, the clan authority, the religious authority and the authority of the husband all begin to totter...' Mao here is explicitly linking economic progress to women's emancipation. In fact, Maoism was always extremely progressive with regard to women whom Mao described as 'holding up half the sky':

A man in China is usually subjected to the domination of three systems of authority [political authority, clan authority and religious authority]... As for women, in addition to being dominated by these three systems of authority, they are also dominated by the men (the authority of the husband). These four authorities – political, clan, religious and masculine – are the embodiment of the whole feudal-patriarchal system and ideology, and are the four thick ropes binding the Chinese people, particularly the peasants.

As to the authority of the husband, this has always been weaker among the poor peasants because, out of economic necessity, their womenfolk have to do more manual labour than the women of the richer classes and therefore have more say and greater power of decision in family matters.

With the increasing bankruptcy of the rural economy in recent years, the basis for men's domination over women has already been undermined. With the rise of the peasant movement, the women in many places have now begun to organise rural women's associations; the opportunity has come for them to lift up their heads, and the authority of the husband is getting shakier every day. In a word, the whole feudal-patriarchal system and ideology is tottering with the growth of the peasants' power.

It makes economic sense to embrace equality of the sexes, Mao points out. 'China's women are a vast reserve of labour power. This reserve should be tapped in the struggle to build a great socialist society.' And men and women 'must receive equal pay for equal work in production.'

In the west, there is a popular perception that the conventional patriarchal family is the defining model of the family, and hence of the state too. Yet it is not necessarily so. Plato, as we have seen, thought children should be brought up collectively, and should not even know who their father was, whilst Rousseau specifically argued against the nuclear family as reducing individual freedom and encouraging laziness. In contemporary western societies, there is great concern at the breakdown of 'the family' (actually just the nuclear family: there is little concern at the earlier breakdown of the extended networks of relatives and in-laws) and its often problematic replacement by the one-parent family.

But the world's most populous nation has successfully experimented with the weakening of the paternal authority, without weakening social cohesion. In fact, Mao thought the two things were opposed in a communist state. And there are other models for bringing up children. In China, the Mosuo people, at Luya Lake, on the plateau between Sichuan and Yunnan, have long had the system of 'partnership marriage' which lasts from as little as one night to perhaps ten years, with the woman's family bringing up any children, and the father having no particular rights, even to share the home.

Mao made enormous social changes to the traditional Chinese social pattern (albeit with exceptions) but the old patriarchal model outlived him. Today, many Chinese women, particularly in the rural areas, are still second-class citizens with limited autonomy and economic rights (as are many western women, let alone those in Middle Eastern and developing countries). Some Marxists would say this was inevitable in attempting to make political changes prior to the economic changes. So how successful was Mao in changing the economic structures?

Mao recognised that even after both the country-wide victory of the Chinese revolution and the solution of the land problem, two basic 'contradictions' would still exist in China, threatening to undermine the revolution. The first would be the 'internal contradiction', that is, between the working class and the bourgeoisie. The second would be the external one, that is, between China and the 'imperialist' countries. As far as the internal contradiction goes, Mao, like Plato (and the Soviet Union) was unrelenting towards anyone identified as a class enemy – or 'liberal'. A totalitarian regime using censorship to control thought patterns is advocated enthusiastically, in the interests of the well-being of the state as a whole.

Our state is a people's democratic dictatorship led by the working class and based on the worker–peasant alliance. What is this dictatorship for? Its first function is to suppress the reactionary classes and elements and those exploiters in our country who resist the socialist revolution, to suppress those who try to wreck our socialist construction, or in other words, to resolve the internal contradictions between ourselves and the enemy. For instance, to arrest, try and sentence certain counter-revolutionaries, and to deprive landlords and bureaucrat-capitalists of their right to vote and their freedom of speech for a specified period of time – all this comes within the scope of our dictatorship.

To maintain public order and safeguard the interests of the people, it is likewise necessary to exercise dictatorship over embezzlers, swindlers, arsonists, murderers, criminal gangs and other scoundrels who seriously disrupt public order. But the second function of the dictatorship is to protect the country from 'subversion' and possible aggression by external enemies, to resolve the 'external contradiction'. The aim of this dictatorship is 'to protect all our people so that they can devote themselves to peaceful labour and build China into a socialist country with a modern industry, agriculture, science and culture'.

But post-Mao, China is flirting with competition, entrepreneurship and profit, all of which it tries to include in the definition of 'socialism'. Yet the question remains whether this is possible or whether in fact the forces of the 'free market' once unleashed will bring the whole edifice of socialism crashing down. As the third millennium – China's fifth millennium – begins, voices are increasingly predicting the end of the Maoist experiment, and that Chinese communism will merge seamlessly into western-style capitalism. But such predictions were being made even at the communist state's founding. This is why the Red Book warns that if

... the landlords, rich peasants, counter-revolutionaries, bad elements and monsters were all allowed to crawl out, while our cadres were to shut their eyes to all this... were to collaborate with the enemy and were corrupted, divided and demoralised by him, if our cadres were thus pulled out or the enemy were able to sneak in,... then it would not take long, perhaps only several years or a decade, or several decades at most, before a counter-revolutionary restoration on a national scale inevitably occurred, the Marxist-Leninist party would undoubtedly become a revisionist party or a fascist party, and the whole of China would change its colour.

To forestall this, the 'people's democratic dictatorship', from its inception, must use two methods. Towards internal enemies, it must use the method of dictatorship, that is, 'for as long a period of time as is necessary', they cannot take part in political activities and are compelled 'to obey the law of the People's Government and to engage in labour and, through labour, transform themselves into new men'. Towards the rest of the people, on the other hand, it uses not compulsion but 'democracy', that is, political activities and persuasion through education. Of course, there is a contradiction here (the people are both the enemy and the partners), resolved, it would appear, potentially by the whim of the rulers.

Mao argues that in order to be able to carry on their production and studies effectively and to arrange their lives properly, the people *want* their government and those in charge of production and of cultural and educational organisations to issue 'appropriate orders of an obligatory nature'. It is common sense that the maintenance of public order would be impossible without such administrative regulations. Administrative orders and the method of persuasion and education complement each other in resolving contradictions among the people. Yet, 'even administrative regulations for the maintenance of public order must be accompanied by persuasion and education, for in many cases regulations alone will not work'.

## Culture

Maoism emphasises culture. This is something central to Chinese society, not peripheral, optional, bolted on, as it sometimes appears to be to western politicians. So, Mao saw art and literature, as much as news or political opinions, as needing to fit into the social model. The Red Book explains:

> in the world today all culture, all literature and art belong to definite classes and are geared to definite political lines. There is in fact no such thing as art for art's sake, art that stands above classes or art that is detached from or independent of politics. Proletarian literature and art are part of the whole proletarian revolutionary cause; they are, as Lenin said, cogs and wheels in the whole revolutionary machine.

The literary and art workers must gradually move their feet over to the side of the workers, peasants and soldiers, to the side of the proletariat, through the process of going into their very midst and into the thick of practical struggles and through the process of studying Marxism and society. 'Only in this way can we have a literature and art that are truly for the workers, peasants and soldiers, a truly proletarian literature and art.'

The aim is to

> ensure that literature and art fit well into the whole revolutionary machine as a component part, that they operate as powerful weapons for uniting and educating the people and for attacking and destroying the enemy, and that they help the people fight the enemy with one heart and one mind.

There is a political criterion and there is an artistic criterion, and they are related.

> Politics cannot be equated with art, nor can a general world outlook be equated with a method of artistic creation and criticism. We deny not only that there is an abstract and absolutely unchangeable political criterion, but also that there is an abstract and absolutely unchangeable artistic criterion; each class in every class society has its own political and artistic criteria. But all classes in all class societies invariably put the political criterion first and the artistic criterion second.

In another well-known passage, Mao outlines the cultural policy:

What we demand is the unity of politics and art, the unity of content and form, the unity of revolutionary political content and the highest possible perfection of artistic form. Works of art which lack artistic quality have no force, however progressive they are politically. Therefore, we oppose both the tendency to produce works of art with a wrong political viewpoint and the tendency towards the 'poster and slogan style' which is correct in political viewpoint but lacking in artistic power. On questions of literature and art we must carry on a struggle on two fronts... Letting a hundred flowers blossom and a hundred schools of thought contend is the policy for promoting the progress of the arts and sciences and a flourishing socialist culture in our land.

Different forms and styles in art should develop freely and different schools in science should be allowed to 'contend' freely. Mao even warns that it will be harmful to the growth of art and science if administrative measures are used to impose one particular style of art or school of thought and to ban another. Questions of right and wrong in the arts and science should instead be settled through free discussion in artistic and scientific circles and through practical work in these fields. They should not be settled in summary fashion. Indeed, 'An army without culture is a dull-witted army, and a dull-witted army cannot defeat the enemy.'

This brings us to the Red Army. Orthodox Marxist theory made the army the chief component of state power. Whoever wants to seize and retain state power needed to have a strong army. In Plato's *Republic*, the auxiliaries or army took very much second place in the social hierarchy to the policy group – the Guardians, or philosophers. In China, the army continues to be held in higher esteem even than the party. In part, this is because the army is also 'the Guardian'. In part it is because it is, like Plato's auxiliaries, kept to a clearly defined role and (ideally) encroaches neither on the material interests of the people, nor on the political interests of the Party, whilst playing a role in both. During the building of the new People's Republic, the army led the way in 'socialist production' and agriculture, eagerly shouldering additional burdens.

And the army 'must cherish the people and never encroach upon their interests' ; the army must respect the government and the Party and never 'assert independence'. This is the principle that made the use of tanks and bullets against the pro-democracy student demonstrations in Tiananmen Square in 1989 so traumatic for the Chinese nation. After all, the richest source of power to wage war lies in the masses of the people. It was mainly because of the unorganised state of the Chinese masses that Japan dared to bully China, the Red Book says. When this defect was remedied, then the Japanese aggressor, 'like a mad bull crashing into a ring of flames', was surrounded by hundreds of millions of Chinese people standing upright, 'the mere sound of their voices' struck terror into him, and he was burned to death'.

History shows that wars are divided into two kinds, just and unjust. All wars that are progressive are just, and all wars that impede progress are unjust. We Communists oppose all unjust wars that impede progress, but we do not oppose progressive, just wars. Not only do we Communists not oppose just wars, we actively participate in them.

War, 'the highest form of struggle for resolving contradictions', is needed when they have developed to a certain stage. Whether between classes, nations, states, or political groups, this war has existed ever since the emergence of private property and of classes (as Hobbes put it too). In one of Mao's celebrated aphorisms, 'every Communist must grasp the truth, "Political power grows out of the barrel of a gun".' As for unjust wars, the First World War, in which both sides fought for imperialist interests, was one: Communists therefore firmly opposed that war. Revolutionary war, on the other hand, is an antitoxin which 'not only eliminates the enemy's poison but also purges us of our own filth'. Every just, revolutionary war is endowed with tremendous power, which can transform many things or clear the way for their transformation. This is because although weapons are an important factor in war, the decisive one is people. The contest of strength is not only a contest of military and economic power, but also a contest of human power and morale.

Even the atom bomb is a 'paper tiger', one which the US reactionaries use to scare people. 'It looks terrible, but in fact it isn't. Of course, the atom bomb is a weapon of mass slaughter, but the outcome of a war is decided by the people, not by one or two new types of weapon.' Perhaps this is why the US drew back at the last minute from using the bomb in Korea, against the Chinese.

Maoists advocate not so much the 'omnipotence of war' as the omnipotence of revolutionary war. War itself is a 'monster of mutual slaughter among men', and would eventually be eliminated by the progress of human society. But there is only one way to eliminate it surely: more war. By opposing counter-revolutionary war with revolutionary war, counter-revolutionary class war with revolutionary class war... then, 'when human society advances to the point where classes and states are eliminated, there will be no more wars, counter-revolutionary or revolutionary, unjust or just; that will be the era of perpetual peace for mankind'.

In practical terms, this view of war as evil, as opposed to the fascist and 'romantic' notions of war as 'joy in destruction', the purest form of action, means communists must 'endeavour to establish normal diplomatic relations, on the basis of mutual respect for territorial integrity and sovereignty and of equality and mutual benefit, with all countries willing to live together with us in peace'.

People all over the world are now discussing whether or not a third world war will break out. On this question, too, we must be mentally prepared and do some analysis. We stand firmly for peace and against war. But if the imperialists insist on unleashing another war, we should not be afraid of it. The First World War was followed by the birth of the Soviet Union with a population of 200 million. The Second World War was followed by the emergence of the socialist camp with a combined population of 900 million. If the imperialists insist on launching a third world war, it is certain that several hundred million more will turn to socialism, and then there will not be much room left on earth for the imperialists.

But aggressive military power is not necessary. One day it is also likely that the 'whole structure of imperialism will utterly collapse'. It is inevitable as all reactionaries, like their bombs, are 'paper tigers'. In appearance they are terrifying, but in reality they are not so powerful. 'From a long-term point of view, it is not the reactionaries but the people who are really powerful.' And (says Mao, borrowing from an older Chinese philosophical tradition, of yin and yang and the dynamic balance and interplay of opposing forces): 'Just as there is not a single thing in the world without a dual nature (this is the law of the unity of opposites), so imperialism and all reactionaries have a dual nature – they are real tigers and paper tigers at the same time.'

In past history, before they won state power and for some time afterwards, the slave-owning class, the feudal landlord class and the bourgeoisie were vigorous, revolutionary and progressive; they were real tigers. But over time, as their opposites – the slave class, the peasant class and the proletariat – grew in strength, struggled against them and became more and more formidable, these ruling classes changed step by step into the reverse. They changed into reactionaries, into backward people, into paper tigers. And eventually they, in turn, were overthrown, by the people.

The 'reactionary, backward, decaying classes' retain this dual nature even in their 'last life-and-death struggles against the people'. On the one hand, they were real tigers; they ate people, ate people by the millions and tens of millions. Destroying the rule of imperialism, feudalism and bureaucrat-capitalism in China took the people more than a hundred years and cost them tens of millions of lives before the victory in 1949. These were indeed fearsome, living tigers, iron tigers, real tigers. 'But in the end they changed into paper tigers, dead tigers, bean-curd tigers.'

And (in the aftermath of the Second World War) Mao offers some advice to the US Satan on the limitations of military power. 'US imperialism invaded China's territory of Taiwan and has occupied it for the past nine years. A short while ago it sent its armed forces to invade and occupy Lebanon. The United States has set up hundreds of military bases in many countries all over the world.' But Taiwan, the Lebanon and all the other military bases of the United States on foreign soil are:

> ... just so many nooses round the neck of US imperialist tiger. The nooses have been fashioned by the Americans themselves and by nobody else, and it is they themselves who have put these nooses round their own necks, offering the ends of the ropes to the Chinese people, the peoples of the Arab countries and all the peoples of the world who love peace and oppose aggression. The longer the US aggressors remain in those places, the tighter the nooses round their necks will become.

For imperialism cannot last long as it always does evil things. 'It persists in grooming and supporting reactionaries in all countries who are against the people, it has forcibly seized many colonies and semi-colonies and many military bases, and it threatens the peace with atomic war.' Thus, forced by imperialism to do so, the vast majority of the people of the world either are rising up or will soon rise up in struggle against it.

Essentially, by riding roughshod over everything, the US has made itself the enemy of the people of the world and has increasingly isolated itself. Certainly, revolutionaries will never be cowed by the atom bombs and hydrogen bombs in the hands of the US imperialists. 'The raging tide of the people of the world against the US aggressors is irresistible.'

What of the future? When Mao looked ahead to the turn of the millennium, in 1956, he saw an industrial utopia and a new powerful China.

It is only forty-five years since the Revolution of 1911, but the face of China has completely changed. In another forty-five years, that is, in the year 2001, or the beginning of the twenty-first century, China will have undergone an even greater change. She will have become a powerful socialist industrial country. And that is as it should be. China is a land with an area of 9,600,000 square kilometres and a population of 600 million people, and she ought to have made a greater contribution to humanity. Her contribution over a long period has been far too small.

Yet the Chinese *should* be modest – not only now, but 45 years hence as well. 'We should always be modest. In our international relations, we Chinese people should get rid of great-nation chauvinism resolutely, thoroughly, wholly and completely.'

China still follows the 'modest' policy. It is deeply engrained in Chinese values, not just since Mao. 'We must never adopt an arrogant attitude of great-power chauvinism and become conceited because of the victory of our revolution and certain achievements in our construction.' Every nation, big or small, has its strong and weak points. Every individual must be modest, for each may 'have many good qualities and have rendered great service', but yet each must always remember not to become conceited.

To what extent Mao himself managed to do this is debatable, but certainly for many of the early years he maintained a virtuous model of simplicity and abstinence. He was famous for only having clothes with patches, and when clothes could no longer be patched, for cutting them up to make patches themselves.

In a review of economic policy worthy of Adam Smith, 'Building our Country through Diligence and Frugality', the little Red Book advises: 'Diligence and thrift should be practised in running factories, shops and all state-owned, co-operative and other enterprises. The principle of diligence and frugality should be observed in everything. It is one of the basic principles of socialist economics.'

For, indeed, as Mao foresaw, it would take 'several decades' to make China prosperous. The road to communism is and was an uphill and bumpy one, to use a metaphor which Mao comprehensively exhausts. The way is complicated too, by tempting-looking alternative turnings. Even during the first years of the People's Republic, Mao observed a 'falling off in ideological and political work among students and intellectuals', and some unhealthy tendencies appearing in society. 'Some people seem to think that there is no longer any need to concern themselves with politics or with the future of the motherland and the ideals of mankind.'

Towards the end of the Red Book, Mao sighs that 'it seems as if Marxism, once all the rage, is currently not so much in fashion'. His solution then was that communists needed to redouble their ideological and political work. Both students and intellectuals would have to study harder. In addition to their specialised subjects, they would have to progress ideologically and politically, through studying Marxism, current events and politics. For not 'to have a correct political orientation is like having no soul'.

There is only one way forward. What Maoism has to offer to the young people, in particular, is a tempting recipe entitled:

Self-Reliance and Arduous Struggle

**Influence**

Mao Zedong, for all his later obsessions, delusions, later excesses and cruelties, left a legacy of commitment to the rights of the rural poor and to women, and set new minimum standards for education and health across the 'developing' world. By addressing himself to the uneducated, agrarian poor, Mao also changed the perception of class struggle and society in both communist and non-communist societies. And certainly, without Maoism, the Japanese fascist party would have remained transcendent in Asia, whatever reverses in Europe the fascists might have suffered.

## Key Ideas

Mao declares that 'the history of mankind is one of continuous development from the realm of necessity to the realm of freedom'. This is an old story, seen in Marx and Hegel, and earlier philosophers. But Mao changes the emphasis significantly. The process is never-ending, as in any society in which classes exist, class struggle is inevitable. Even in the long-awaited classless society, the struggle 'between the new and the old and between truth and falsehood' will never end. In the 'fields of struggle for production and scientific experiment' progress is continuous and nature undergoes constant change, yet things never remain at the same level.

- Education and democracy are inseparable.
- Nothing is all positive or all negative.

Where western theorists see a linear progression, with single causes leading to single effects, Mao sees complexity and relationships: the eastern conception of the great interplay of positive and negative, yin and yang, added to a western notion of simple cause and effect. Maoism hints at a 'third way' between communism and capitalism, which is what the Chinese government today is still seeking to explore. On their success or failure hinges more than the Chinese political system.

## Key Text

Mao's Red Book (1945)

# Timeline: From Atom Bombs to the Triumph of Capitalism

**1945**

The 'Enola Gay', the affectionately named US Air Force bomber, drops 'Little Boy' on Hiroshima, bringing about the largest single mass killing in human history – and the unconditional surrender of the Japanese.

**1948**

The UN adopts the Declaration of Human Rights. The World Health Organisation is set up. NATO is founded to defend the West. COMECON is set up by the USSR and Eastern European satellite states.

**1949**

Mao finally drives the rump of the Nationalist armies, led by Chiang Kai Shek, off the mainland to Taiwan and announces the new People's Republic.

**1950**

The Korean war starts, to end in US humiliation, mainly due to China's support for the Koreans.

**1952**

The first contraceptive pills are produced. This heralds a time of social and sexual liberalisation.

**1954**

The US Supreme Court rules that racial segregation in schools is unconstitutional. A year later, the black inhabitants of Montgomery boycott the segregated city buses, winning further concessions.

**1955**

The Warsaw Pact is established to replace COMECON, in the year of the death of Stalin. For four decades the world will be divided between two distinct blocs of influence.

**1957**

The European Common Market is established, but the United Kingdom is not part of it, busy instead detonating its own H-bomb on Christmas Island. The Russian sputnik alarms the US into a 'Space Race'.

### 1958
Mao's 'Great Leap Forward' proves disastrous as agrarian reform leads to famine. Ten years later the Cultural Revolution, an equally disastrous 'back to basics' campaign results in anarchy and random murder.

### 1959
Fidel Castro overthrows the Batista government in Cuba and sets about reforming the sugar plantations. Two years later a US invasion at the Bay of Pigs is a fiasco, but John F. Kennedy manages to win the showdown of the missile crisis the following year.

### 1961
Yuri Gagarin becomes the first man in space.

### 1969
Neil Armstrong is the first man on the moon. Buzz Aldrin is the second. The Soviet Union is not even in sight. The west has won the race – and not just for the moon.

# 12   The End of History?

*Is society proceeding slowly but surely towards a final Utopia – or towards an equally final cataclysm? Or are we following only a random and unpredictable process of change? Could slavery, mass famine, even human sacrifice, be part of the future as well as the past?*

*Most of the political philosophers seem to discern a pattern to history, and usually a positive one, generally putting great store by the apparently consistent and cumulative effects of technology. After all, once invented, few things are uninvented, at least, few things which find a profitable market. Yet, if political society is about the well-being of the people, the progress seems to be less clear. The poverty and despair of past epochs seem to change form, never to disappear. Indeed, Rousseau's noble savage may well have been a happier fellow than today's suburban clockwatcher or mortgaged wage-slave, let alone the unemployed or imprisoned.*

It is true, if rather politically suspect, to say that in material terms there has been some kind of steady progression, if not progress, in the quality of human lives. Even in the eighteenth century, Adam Smith marvelled at the standard of living of the typical European worker, as compared to the propertyless serfs and villeins of earlier times. How much more so should we marvel at the access to goods and indeed services – health, education – that pass almost unremarked today. This is the justification for political society in the liberal democracies that have spread over the globe. Yet the material progress is uneven, and access to it remains largely determined by birth. The wealth gap between the richest and the poorest nations is increasing.

In the twenty years after 1960 the richest fifth of the world's societies increased their share of the overall cake from 70 per cent to 82 per cent. For the poorest 50 or so countries (with a fifth of the world's population) that left just 1.5 per cent of world income.

Now that is not to fault liberalism, necessarily. The argument for free markets is that wealth does eventually 'trickle down'. But to say that most people are materially far better off is really only to say that science has improved manufacturing, and that manufacturing has been improved by science. And that is not to say very much. What of the people? Surrounded, yes, by the products of the material revolution, but too often bitter, resentful, depressed, or in despair? Angry, sick or just mad? Given the easily plumbed depths of human misery, has the march of progress such an implacable logic, after all?

Western systems of liberal democracy depend upon shared values and shared notions of rights – to education, to basic heath care, to take industrial action, and so on. Ultimately, politics is really a branch of 'applied ethics', and political systems must account for themselves in moral terms. Consider the case against liberal democracy.

## The Liberal Record Sheet

Liberalism depends on certain values and principles.

Take the European Convention on Human Rights (not to be confused with initiatives originating with the European Union). These include positive rights to:

- life, liberty and security of the person
- a fair trial, and access to justice
- respect for private and family life, home and correspondence
- freedom of thought, conscience and religion
- free expression, including the freedom of the press
- freedom of assembly and association, including the right to join a trade union
- marry and found a family
- peaceful enjoyment of possessions
- education
- free elections by secret ballot

together with negative rights not to:

- suffer torture, inhuman or degrading treatment
- be forced into slavery, servitude or bonded labour
- be prosecuted under retrospective criminal law

This, in many ways, is the fruit of 2,000 years of political thought, not so much struggling, either by individuals or classes, as 'fluttering' by philosophers. But how effective have the social democracies been in achieving these aims? Has, in fact, the liberal 'experiment' been any more successful than the failed communist and fascist ones?

Most of the political theorists, from Plato on, identify education as the key to moulding society, so let us start there. In most liberal democracies, theoretically, access is free and equal. Indeed, huge sums are poured into educating the most recalcitrant pupils – who may have to be physically forced to attend schools and even prevented from attacking their teachers whilst there! A remarkable reversal from previous times when education was so hard to obtain and so highly respected.

Yet it is not so strange. The children in the schools are not actually all equal in the melting pot. Nor is it just an unequal distribution of knowledge that obtains. In liberal democracies, the education system is working in a way that both prolongs and parallels the existing divisions in society.

In the cradle of liberalism, the United Kingdom, two types of education go on side by side: free universal state provision, and fee-paying private schools. Around twice as much money is available (per head) for the children in the fee-paying schools, who tend to do significantly better in exams – although this may equally well be explained by better management or motivation or discipline. (Children in private schools can be thrown out.) For whatever reason, of 8.5 million UK children, the 7 per cent who go to fee-paying schools go on to take half of the university places at the elite colleges of Oxford and Cambridge, and to make up 80 per cent of judges; 80 per cent of the generals; 55 per cent of top doctors – even eight out of eleven of the country's national newspaper editors.

In the political system, the contrast between the effortless progression of the few and the slow crawl of the rest is even more apparent. Between 1900 and 1985, three quarters of all government ministers went to either Oxford or Cambridge, the vast majority having first been to private schools. Indeed, three quarters of the century's Prime Ministers went to Oxford alone! At the turn of the new millennium, a supposedly radical reforming 'New Labour' administration was made up of one third from the two universities, under an Oxford-educated Prime Minister, who went on to appoint

new 'reforming' peers to the House of Lords – whose major characteristic turned out to be also having been at Oxbridge.

So, in the UK, although each child has an equal right to go to
university, those with poor parents still somehow fail to get there. In
fact, at the top end of incomes, those parents who pay for their
children to go to private schools, increase their offspring's chances
of an Oxbridge education by a factor of ten. And from there, in due
course, of proceeding to those often completely unrelated 'top jobs',
such as political office, 'cultural' posts in the media and the arts –
not to mention business directorships.

Now there is no miraculous process of selection that ensures
admission to the elite universities of liberal democracies – Harvard
and Princeton in the US, the 'Ecoles' in France, Oxford and
Cambridge in Britain. Nor is there anything terribly useful or special
about what goes on once you are there. The age-old problem that
stumped the Chinese mandarins – of how to devise a test for
'cultivation' which cannot be got around by those who have learnt
how to do the test – has become institutionalised and legitimised
through paper qualifications, as an acceptable form of transfer of
wealth, power and privilege.

## Equality

In all liberal democracies, despite Mill's warnings, power is still
largely inherited. You even have what is at best the absurdity, and
at worst the obscenity of 'political families', like the Bushes and ill-
fated Kennedys in the United States, or the surprisingly enduring
tradition in the United Kingdom of political constituencies being
handed on. There are the media families, where the showbiz
personality of one generation is the son or daughter of another, or
the celebrated author whose parents are also cultural icons. Not to
forget of course the commonplace but not at all 'liberal' passing on
of ever more gigantic industrial and commercial empires, some of
them the size of small nations (the inheritance aspect that Mill
himself specifically condemned as unjustifiable).

Amongst capitalist entrepreneurs, as surveys such as a popular
United Kingdom newspaper's 'Rich List' reflect, it is still those who
start off with serious money who make serious money.

In terms of equality, there are few formal areas of discrimination.
In 1999, of the UK's 26 million workers paying income tax to the

government, almost half were women. Yet, typically they are paid around 15 per cent less than their male counterparts. The International Labour Organisation calculates that two thirds of women's work is unpaid – and that on top of this, women work one sixth harder than men. Similarly, within the world's oldest National Health Service, in Britain, in the treatment of diseases such as heart disease and cancer, a significantly higher chance of successful treatment attaches itself to the affluent classes.

In terms of access to education and health, a national level of uniform provision, as in nearly all western democracies, now exists, part of the post-Second World War 'consensus' (following the housing and welfare provisions of President Roosevelt's 'New Deal' in the 1930s). But yet, so do the inequalities.

In the 25 years since the first man on the moon, global life expectancy did indeed rise – from 53 to 62 years, and infant mortality rates fell, from 110 per thousand children born, to 73 per thousand – even as sub-Saharan Africa defied the trend, suffering dramatically deteriorating conditions. But behind the overall and real improvement is a corresponding reality of the continuing direct relationship between health and wealth. In the richest countries life expectancy is now 78 years, in the poorest, 43 years – and the gap is widening. Then within countries there are equivalent contrasts: between the affluence of the new 'middle classes' in countries like Brazil (where some 120 million people live in poverty, out of a total population of 153 million), Venezuela – even South Africa and Ethiopa. In all these 'underdeveloped' countries there are millions living lives comparable to those in the richest northern 'advanced economies', and, equally, even in the richest countries a large 'underclass' remains in the shadow of unprecedented material prosperity. These are underclasses living in conditions of poverty, sickness – even of massacres – that seem completely incompatible with the veneer of modern sophistication. As a result, at the start of the third millennium there are now more people in the world than ever before – it is estimated at 100 million – who are actually disabled as a result of extreme poverty or avoidable disease. Not for them the opportunities of *laissez-faire*.

### Discrimination

Liberalism above all says all people are equal in the eyes of the law. Yet only in 1957 did the US Civil Rights Act move to enforce desegregation outlawing 'separate but equal' facilities for non-white Americans. Nor did the Act truly herald a new approach to this disease of society. In 1992, American blacks were still three times more likely to be living in poverty as their white fellow citizens. Average income for a non-white family was under two thirds that of the whites. A similar story can be read in countries with long-established liberal democracies such as Australia, Canada and New Zealand, although happily in recent years the situation is beginning to be, at least, addressed.

In liberal democratic Israel, apartheid lives on as Palestinians are formally denied basic rights, such as rights to work, to travel and even to live in certain areas. Liberal democracy does not seem to preclude torture, state assassination of opponents, wholesale destruction of homes and property of Israel's underclass. In Northern Ireland a complex web of discrimination against Catholics has only just begun to be untangled. In much of the world, from wealthy Switzerland to westernised states like Saudi Arabia, women are denied basic voting rights and economic rights to work, to health care and education.

## The Human Spirit

This brings us back to our original discussion of society. Plato insists that an essential part of the human spirit is a sense of justice. If we feel that we – or our friends – are being treated unjustly, then we feel anger. If we feel we have done this injustice to ourselves, we feel ashamed. And when we feel that our worth has been correctly assessed by others, we feel pride.

This, the desire for justice, recognition and fair treatment, may be what ultimately drives the individual, and in turn the collection of individuals that is society – not material well-being. That is why, in Plato's *Republic*, *thymos* or 'spiritedness' is given careful considera-tion, with Plato seeing this spirit as likely to 'boil over' – at perceived injustice, if nothing else. The spirit is there too in the passion for glory of Machiavelli's Princes, and in grossest form in the fascist ideology and the picture of the 'beast with red cheeks' painted by Nietzsche. Communism and fascism promised their citizens the world if they would forgo their individualism, and yet yielded only spiralling destruction and despotism. Between them is only free-market capitalism, with its political accompaniment – liberalism. But can liberal, capitalist society satisfy this demand for individual recognition and justice?

Francis Fukuyama, an analyst for the United States government by profession, thought it could. He even counted up the number of democracies for his *fin de siècle* book *The End of History* (1998), and thought he could discern a satisfactory pattern as, in the declining years of the twentieth century, as he puts it, apparently impregnable dictatorships of right and left foundered and sunk virtually without trace. 'Over the last two decades,' he notes, 'from the Soviet Union to the Middle East and Asia, strong governments have been falling over like dominoes.' Even though they have not, in all cases, given way to stable liberal democracies (he goes on), the number of these has steadily grown until liberalism has become indisputably the dominant, and the dominating, form of government of the world.

Fukuyama even tabulates the rise of liberalism in a helpful chart, showing how the three democracies of 1790 (France, the newly United States and the cantons of Switzerland) grew to 25 by the end of the second decade of the twentieth century, and 36 by 1960, distributed largely amongst Europe and her former colonies. Although the numbers then actually slipped during the 1970s, with a fashion for military dictatorships in the southern hemisphere, as well as in Greece and Portugal, by 1990 there were, Fukuyama proudly noted, 61 'liberal democracies' worldwide.

The number might have been even higher, had it not been for the illiberal tendency of the American system to subvert and topple social democratic governments as and when they emerged, particularly in neighbouring South America. There, as George Kennan, the head of the US State Department policy staff put it, in a foreign policy discussion document (PPS 23, 1948):

We have 50 per cent of the world's wealth, but only 6.3 per cent of its population... In this situation, we cannot fail to be the object of envy and resentment. Our real task in the coming period is to devise a pattern of relationships which will permit us to maintain this position of disparity without positive detriment to our national security. To do so we will have to dispense with all sentimentality and day-dreaming; and our attention will have to be concentrated on our immediate national objectives. We need not deceive ourselves that we can afford today the luxury of altruism and world-benefaction... We should cease to talk about vague and ... unreal objectives such as human rights, the raising of living standards, and domocratisation. (Quoted in *The Compassionate Revolution*, David Edwards, pp. 30–1)

That of course, was just planning-speak – designed to be uncomfortable – controversial even. Yet the reality that emerged in the post-war period was not of the 'exporting' of liberalism, but of the exporting of state terror.

- 50,000 civilian deaths in El Salvador during the 1980s
- 200,000 in Guatemala, after Democratic President, Jacobo Arbenz, rashly upset the (US-owned) United Fruit Co., and was toppled in a CIA coup
- the lost generations of Argentina, Nicaragua, Colombia, Chile, Mexico, Haiti and elsewhere

(We might also note that in 1993, 5 per cent of the world's population lived under military regimes (autocracy), 30 per cent under one-party rule (oligarchies) and 65 per cent in multi-party states (democracies).)

At the same time, free trade and competitive markets spread across the globe, resulting in what Fukuyama describes as 'unprecedented levels of material prosperity, both in industrially developed countries and in countries that had been at the close of World War II, part of the impoverished Third World'.

Only in one part of the world, the Middle East, did liberalism fail to take root. There instead, according to Fukuyama's analysis anyway, oil provided states with an alternative and very straightforward system for generating wealth, and political structures instead range from old fashioned oligarchies to the strange variant of communism practised by the Libyans.

Fukuyama has no doubt as to what is the driving force of the 'liberalisation' process. Like many of the other eschatologists – would-be diviners of historical patterns – he discerns the primary cause to be 'modern science', distinguished by its 'rationality' and adherence to sound principles of proof, as well as the multitude of technological developments, inventions and consumer durable goodies.

Another reason to discern a pattern to social development and suppose 'the end of History' (Fukuyama always spells it with a capital 'H') is the way that, thanks to this, everything seems to be the same these days. Transnational firms make it possible, if not desirable, to buy the same products in any corner of the world, to wear the same clothes, to read the same books, to watch the same TV programmes.

Chances are you can even watch them in a common language – English (not the world's most widely spoken 'first' language, but the world's most important 'second language'). It is hardly surprising that the homogenisation of all aspects of culture also produces political homogenisation – and vice versa. And the same interplay is there between the political and economic.

So Fukuyama inverts Marx, to suggest that the 'logic of modern natural science' actually leads to capitalism rather than socialism as its final stage. But then Fukuyama also differs from Marx in retaining the element of 'the human spirit' that the communists wished to exclude.

Marxists recognised the dignity and importance of individuals only when taken as a whole, as a society, condemning exploitation of the weak by the strong, even in the context of actual material improvement. Hegel thought that the human animal does differ from others in having not only material desires, but also social requirements – to be appreciated or 'recognised' as having a certain worth or dignity – but that these should be subsumed in the new rational state. From another perspective, liberalism creates a weak society of grasping individuals, interested only in the satisfaction of their desires, the achievement of a comfortable, bourgeois lifestyle, lacking any sense of pride or dignity, living either a life of ultimately meaningless self-indulgence – or resenting the absence of such. If there is a fundamental contradiction in liberalism it is that, on the one hand, it celebrates individualism, whilst, on the other, it appeals to public spiritedness, self-sacrifice and consideration for others. But although it is true that under capitalism we may rely on the self-interest of the butcher, baker and candlestick maker for the prompt delivery of meat, bread and candles, we cannot, for example, rely on that self-interest to stop them tipping their rubbish in the local brook or stream. Nor can we rely on it to stop the burning down of the world's remaining forests and the destruction of species. (Which is why the greatest challenge to the legitimacy of capitalism now is posed by the environmental movement.)

## The Communist Experiment

From the end of the 1920s to at least the mid-1950s, if not later, the Soviet economy outperformed the American one. This was in part because, during the Great Depression, the US economy had collapsed by a third of GDP, but communism, as late as the 1960s, still seemed to have achieved an astonishingly fast transformation: from a feudal system to a modern society capable of 'putting a man into space'. Even as the control economies of the Soviet republics, of North Korea, of Cuba, slipped further and further behind their capitalist neighbours, up to the moment the Berlin Wall came down, communism was still the political system that claimed the future. Yet communism failed in underestimating the importance of the individual – both as consumer and as producer. It would have needed – and completely failed to create – the 'communist' citizen who would work for others and expect nothing in return. As Hayek put it in *The Road to Serfdom*, to lose economic control is to lose political power. The consumer is actually very powerful economically even in the centralised state, and central planning of the economy is control by the state: individual freedom requires market economics.

Stalin's goal of turning the Soviet Union into a kind of massive factory, churning out iron and steel, coal and chemicals, proved not to be enough, because capitalism had all this, plus technological innovation and the increasing sophistication of its 'white collar' work, 'information' and 'post-industrial' technologies. Even as Lenin penned his pamphlet *Imperialism: The Highest Stage of Capitalism* (in the year that the First World War broke out in Europe), it was already clear that capitalism was working – at least to the extent, as Lenin put it, of 'buying time for itself'.

The least successful aspect of the communist economics was the attempt to regulate prices rationally. In the Soviet Union this Sisyphean task was charged to *Goskomsten*, a committee responsible for setting a quarter of a million 'key' prices each year. East Germany, right up to the bitter end in 1989, steadily produced notoriously bad versions of products, such as its own highly polluting motor car, that it could have imported much more cheaply from its capitalist neighbours – less the pollution and without the engineering defects. Hayek argued that the complexity of the modern market makes free market competition the only way to manage the economy, the only way that consumption and production can be brought into some sort of balance. And the other side of state price controls is that they oblige the state to attempt to control the wages of its workers. Indeed, the Cultural Revolution in China in the 1960s and 1970s can be seen as an attack on over-mighty workers, those whose skills were in demand. The hierarchical organisation of modern factories, creating elite groups of managers, white collar workers and specialists of all kinds, inevitably undermines attempts to create a homogeneous mass of equal and undifferentiated workers. The price for reversing the process of the division of labour is lower productivity and an economy that lags ever further behind.

The last hope for the Leninist doctrine was that the death of capitalism would come, not at the hands of the workers, but from the global 'class struggle' between a wealthy First World, and an exploited and hungry Third World. As last-ditch Marxists readily noted, the self-styled 'free-market' liberals were inclined to protect their markets from manufactured products from the developing world, only allowing it to supply them with cheap raw materials (including, occasionally, and grudgingly, labour, such as the Caribbean railwaymen recruited for the London Underground in the 1950s, or the Filipino women employed (at Filipino rates) for childcare by middle-class families in the United States).

However, the ability of equally poor countries such as South Korea, Hong Kong, Singapore and Thailand, the so-called 'Asian Tiger' economies, to move from dependency to become successful high-tech manufacturing nations, belies the simplicities of these predictions of their inevitable impoverishment too. And whilst the conditions of many of the workers in the 'sweatshops' of Asia may continue to be a hidden aspect of apparently westernised industries, the statistics for income distribution in the emerging economies show them actually spreading their wealth more evenly than many of their western role models.

Over Christmas and the New Year of 1989, the East German communist state finally gave in to the popular demand for the right to cross the border into West Germany, and the Berlin Wall came crashing down. The house-of-cards collapse of Warsaw Pact states followed, less by force than by a kind of collective social decision based on the inability of the state to maintain its legitimacy in the eyes of its people or even in the eyes of its own bureaucratic and security apparatus. However, elsewhere, in the rest of the world, communism hung on a bit longer. In Africa, supposedly strict Marxist states such as Ethiopia, Angola and Sudan, seemed determined that nothing less than complete economic collapse and impoverishment would persuade their ruling elites to give way.

In *The End of History*, Fukuyama writes:

> ... if we are now at a point where we cannot imagine a world substantially different from our own, in which there is no apparent

or obvious way in which the future will represent a fundamental improvement over our current order, then we must also take into consideration the possibility that History itself might be at an end.

Fukuyama's position is that, in fact, America has already found the way to humanity's elusive final Utopia. There is a clear pattern to history, just as Hegel claimed. The German philosopher, as we saw earlier, described the march of history as a 'dialectical process' of different forms of human society coming into conflict, destroying each other, and producing in the process, a higher stage. Society is supposed by Hegel to have proceeded through the stages of subsistence agriculture, monarchy, aristocracy and, finally, indus-trialisation, to arrive at the free-market, capitalist, liberal state we recognise in the west and dub 'democracy'. (Marx, on the other hand, saw the economic relationships as the key.) Fukuyama sticks to Hegel's view of 'pride' as the driving force. But, one way or another, Fukuyama, like Hegel and Marx before him, considers *this* to be the final stage – hence 'the end of history'. But how sure can he be? After all, whereas Fukuyama is commenting from the standpoint of seeing several intended-to-be-final forms of society apparently give way to liberalism (the collapse of fascism in the 1940s, the collapse of communism in the 1980s), Hegel had been equally sure and yet was writing before these two doctrines had ever been systemised, let alone had their bitter day.

## The Poverty of Historicism

And not everyone is comfortable even with the speculation. One such, Karl Popper, dedicated his influential 1957 book, *The Poverty of Historicism*, to 'the countless men and women of all creeds or nations or races who fell victims to the fascist and communist belief in Inexorable Laws of Historical Destiny'. Popper considered such attempts to be the result of misguided efforts to apply the techniques of science to society, instead of merely noting the effects of certain historical changes in social policy, in the manner of Machiavelli, Rousseau, and many others. (Although, a year earlier, we may snipe, Popper himself had not been above speculating in lectures about the implications of 'new problems brought into being by the fact that the problem of mass unemployment has largely been solved' – along, he imagined, with religious and racial discrimination.)

Popper warns against an 'unholy' alliance between the 'social engineers' and the 'historicists'. Both work from a kind of Utopian blueprint, a blueprint that claims to cover all aspects of society. And the king of the social engineers is undoubtedly Plato and all his followers. Popper, being an Austrian, and writing in the aftermath of the Nazi *Anschluss* of his country, is particularly aware of the tendency of democracies to slide towards totalitarianism. This, he thinks, can be explained by the idealism of the Platonists – by advocating the rule of the wise, the just or simply the best they invite tyranny. In *The Poverty of Historicism*, he argues that an 'open society' concentrates on constructing neutral institutions instead, allowing for the peaceful displacement of any political grouping which becomes too attached to power.

As to the historicists, Popper considers it simply not possible for us to 'observe or describe a whole piece of the world, or a whole piece of nature'. In fact, not even the smallest whole piece may be so described, since all description is necessarily selective. It may even be said that 'wholes... can never be the object of any activity, scientific or otherwise'. As John Stuart Mill put it, one problem with deconstructing history using rules is that the task is so complex that it cannot 'possibly be computed by human faculties'.

Even Comte's notion of dynamic laws of succession is dismissed by Popper, who says that even if the wind shakes a tree and an apple falls to the ground, we still cannot simply postulate one law to explain what has happened. We need much more: an explanation of wind pressure, tension and elasticity in the branch, gravity itself, and so on. Although there may be *trends*, such as population figures can exhibit, a trend or tendency should not be confused with a law. 'Trends do exist but their persistence depends on certain specific initial conditions (which in turn may sometimes be trends).' The historicists overlook this, and operate with trends as if they were in fact laws, for example, believing in the inexorability of *progress*.

It is possible to interpret 'history' as the history of class struggle, or of the struggles of races for supremacy, or as the history of religious ideas, or as the history of struggle between the 'open' and the 'closed' society, or as the history of scientific and industrial progress. All of these are more or less interesting points of view, and *as such* are perfectly unobjectionable. But historicists do not present them as such; they do not see that there is necessarily a plurality of interpretations which are fundamentally on the same level for both... Instead they present them as doctrines or theories... And if they actually find that their point of view is fertile, and that many facts can be ordered and interpreted in its light, then they mistake this for a confirmation, or even for a proof, of their doctrine.

The notion of a science of society entirely overlooks the subjectivity of knowledge, Popper objects. Even in the natural sciences, knowledge is a social and public construct affected by the partiality and self-interest of the individuals making up the scientific community. Add in the social prejudices and class bias of social scientists, and it is clear that the historicists are making more of their studies than can rightly be claimed for any kind of study. Their 'divination of hidden purposes', in Popper's phrase, is the worst kind of science. In words seemingly written for Fukuyama 40 years later, *The Poverty of Historicism* concludes:

> Modern historicists, however, seem to be unaware of the antiquity of their doctrine. They believe – and what else could their deification of modernism permit? – that their own brand of historicism is the latest and boldest achievement of the human mind, an achievement so staggeringly novel that only a few people are sufficiently advanced to grasp it.

The historicists believe they have unravelled one of the oldest problems of speculative metaphysics, the problem our study started with, identified by Heraclitus and Parmenides – the problem of change. They believe their advance is due to their living in a uniquely important period of history – one in which change has accelerated, revealing for the first time the revolutionary truth. But the reality is that the more everything changes, the more everything remains the same.

# References and Sources for Further Reading

*As political philosophy is a broad discipline, with connections to psychology, social studies, community studies, history of ideas, economics and so on, any reading list is extremely limiting. However, the following may serve as starting suggestions.*

## General

Brenda Almond, *Exploring Ethics*, Blackwell, Oxford, 1998

R. Beiner, *What's the Matter with Liberalism?* University of California Press, Berkeley, 1990

Trevor Blackwell and Jeremy Seabrook, *The Revolt Against Change: Towards a Conserving Radicalism*, Vintage, London, 1993

Tom Burden, *Social Policy and Welfare*, Pluto Press, London, 1998

David Edwards, *The Compassionate Revolution*, Green Books, Totnes, 1998

Robert Eccleshall and others, *Political Ideologies: An Introduction*, Routledge, London, 1994

Francis Fukuyama, *The End of History*, Penguin, London, 1993

A. Gutmann, *Liberal Equality*, Cambridge University Press, Cambridge, 1980

F. A. Hayek, *The Constitution of Liberty*, Routledge, London, 1960

Karl Mannheim, *Ideology and Utopia: an Introduction to the Sociology of Knowledge*, Routledge, London, 1952

Robert Nozick, *Anarchy, State and Utopia*, Blackwell, Oxford, 1990

Karl Popper, *The Open Society and its Enemies*, Routledge, London, 1945 (fifth edition 1966)

Karl Popper, *The Poverty of Historicism*, Routledge, London, 1991 (first published 1957)

John Rawls, *A Theory of Justice*, Harvard University Press, Cambridge, Mass., 1971

J.L. Talmon, *The Origins of Totalitarian Democracy*, Mercury Books, London, 1961

John Thompson, *Studies in the Theory of Ideology*, Polity Press, Cambridge, 1984

## Plato

Most of the quotes are easily found in any version of Plato's *Republic*. I have used *The Republic of Plato*, translated by Francis MacDonald Cornford, Oxford University Press, 1941; other translators adopt different styles for the dialogues, and the *Collected Works of Plato* (various editions) is probably the best source for any study of Plato's philosophy. All editions adopt the same system of book and paragraph numbers, to indicate the precise location of discussion, using a traditional system.

For an account of Democritus and early Greek philosophy, see, for example, Jonathan Barnes, *Early Greek Philosophy*, Penguin, 1987, especially from page 277.

The discussion of 'justice' is illustrated with quotations directly from Plato's *Republic*. See, in particular: Book II, 373, where a theory as to the origins of society is put forward; Book VIII, 543; Book VII, 337; Book II, 377, 378; Book III, 417, where the 'training' of the Guardians is described; Book III, 410, where 'temperance' is extolled; and Book IV, 422.

On the 'deviant' states and their consequences, see, for example: Book VIII, 546, 547 and 550.

For Aristotle's differing account of the essential nature of the state, see: the *Politics*, 9, 1280, Book III, and the *Nicomachean Ethics*, 1189, Book IV. Finally, the thoughts of Socrates in prison can be tracked down in the account of *The Last Days of Socrates*, edited by Hugh Tredennick in the Penguin Classics series (1972).

*Further Reading on Plato and Aristotle*

Plato (390–347 BC), *Plato Complete Works,* edited by J. M. Cooper, Hackett, Indianapolis, 1997 (also available in separate editions)

G. Grube, *Plato's Thought*, Athlone Press, London, 1980, and J. L. Ackrill, *Aristotle the Philosopher*, Oxford University Press, 1981 (both have accessible introductions)

## Machiavelli

Machiavelli's works have always been popular, both as literature, and as sociological and philosophical and political studies. There are again many translations, drawn largely from a version translated by Father Leslie Walker from Guido Mazzoni and Mario Casella's *Tutte le opere storiche e letterarie di Niccolò Machiavelli*, G. Barbera, Florence, 1929.

The page numbers below refer to these popular editions: the *Discourses*, edited by Bernard Crick, Pelican, 1970 and Machiavelli's *The Prince*: Text and Commentary by Jean-Pierre Barricelli, Barrons Educational Series, New York, 1975.

For the note on Machiavelli's reason for writing books, see *The Prince*, page 29; on the nature of power, see page 102 of *The Prince*; on Catholicism and the state's relations with the Church, page 103. The infamous 'means justifies the ends' passage is on page 107; on the origins of society on pages 106–7; on justice, page 368; on the need for elections, pages 527, 388; on the need for pragmatism in politics, page 496 of *The Prince* and page 121 of the *Discourses*; on the conflicting interests of Prince and people, page 276 of the *Discourses*; on the gullibility of the masses, page 239; on the need to please 'the mob', pages 112, 114, 268 and 477; and on the value of democracy, pages 116, 132, 280 and 347.

*Further Reading on Machiavelli*

S. de Grazia, *Machiavelli in Hell*, Princeton University Press, Princeton, NJ, 1989

## Hobbes

Hobbes' *Leviathan* (original text 1651) is little read but frequently referred to. As a result, like *The Prince*, it is often misquoted.

The references in the text can be seen in any standard text, but I have used: *Hobbes' Leviathan*, edited by C. B. MacPherson, Pelican, London, 1968.

For Hobbes 'mechanistic' view, see page 81, page 119, pages 29–30. The 'motions' leading to 'motivations' is discussed at page 150, including the well-known quote on the 'general inclination of mankind' at page 161 and the motivation of fear at page 163. (The 'origin of speech', crucial to social life, is discussed on pages 101–2, and 105–6.)

The 'war' of 'every man against every man' is around pages 185–6, and the nature of justice is discussed at pages 188 as well as at page 199 and 223. Hobbes' view that people are all more or less the same is at page 184, and the 'false belief' the founders of the common-wealth must implant is suggested on page 177.

The 'laws of nature' are introduced on page 188, and the 'contract' itself on page 192. Man's antisocial character is discussed around pages 227–8 and 234 , where the 'Leviathan' is offered as a solution.

Technical and practical problems with the social contract are noted on and around pages 239–40, 269, 270, 328 and 348.

*Further Reading on Hobbes*

R. Peters, *Hobbes*, Penguin, Harmondsworth, 1956
D. Baumgold, *Hobbes' Political Theory*, Cambridge University Press, 1988

## Locke

The quotes are from John Locke: *The True, Original Extent and End of Civil Government*, originally published in 1651. Page references where given are to the Penguin Everyman edition, *Two Treatises of Government*, edited by Mark Goldie, revised edition, 1993.

Locke's discussion of the 'State of Nature' is from the Second Treatise, and can be found especially at page 61, and the 'Law of Self-preservation' can be found at page 149, as well as on page 6; the importance of 'reason' in liberty is described on page 63.

Locke's vision of the thirsty man and the right to quench his thirst is on page 33 with the view of nature as conveniently there to be 'developed' is pursued from pages 39–40.

Locke's view of social security is produced in the Treatise on Civil Government, Part I, see pages 42 and 95–6 in particular.

The 'Common Weal' is praised on pages 89, 92, 124 and 131, whilst what to do if this is not the motivation is considered on pages 233 and 241.

The Thomas Paine quotations are as indicated in the text. Readers may also be interested to see Mary Wollstonecraft's *Mary and the Wrongs of Woman* (1798) for a semi-autobiographical critique of

A good general work is *Marx: A Clear Guide*, by Edward Reiss (Pluto Press, London, 1997).

A good general work on Engels is from the Past Masters Series, *Engels*, by Terrell Carver (Oxford University Press, 1981).

Chuschichi Tsuzuki's *Life of Eleanor Marx, 1855–1898* (Clarendon Press, Oxford, 1967), *The Unhappy Marriage of Marxism and Feminism*, edited by Lydia Sargent (Pluto Press, London, 1981), and Hilary Rose's *Love, Power and Gender* (Polity Press, Cambridge, 1994) give a different perspective.

*Selected Writings in Sociology and Social Philosophy (Marx)*, edited by Tom Bottomore and Maximilien Rubel (Penguin, Harmondsworth, 1963), gives the sociological perspective.

Finally, interesting and historically important is Vladimir Ilyich Lenin, *What is to be Done?*, International Publishers, New York, 1969.

## Mill

Mill's writings are easily available in many editions. I have used the Penguin edition of Books V and VI.

The discussion of profits falling is on page 77, and of prices on page 88; the 'marvellous' inventions of the time are praised on page 57. The limits of utility are noted on page 307, and of government itself from around 308–11. *Laissez-faire* is examined on page 314, and education is praised on page 318. Women's rights appear on page 324, and the limits of charity conclude Book V on page 335.

*Further Reading on Mill, Utilitarianism and Rights*

Jeremy Bentham, *An Introduction to the Principles of Morals and Legislation*, Athlone Press, London, 1970 (first published 1789)

J. Waldron, *Nonsense Upon Stilts: Bentham, Burke and Marx on the Rights of Man*, Methuen, London, 1987

William Godwin, *An Enquiry Concerning Political Justice*, Penguin, Harmondsworth, 1976 (first published 1884)

## The Science of Society

The quotations in Chapter 9 are from a number of works, and are as indicated in the main text.

*Further Reading on Durkheim and Social Science*

Emile Durkheim, *Rules of Sociological Method* (Chicago University Press, 1893) is the attempt to justify social science.

Emile Durkheim's views on symbolism and society can be best seen in *Social Rituals and Sacred Objects* (1912), and his explanation of the social nature of the individual in *Precontractual Solidarity* (1893), both reprinted in *Four Sociological Traditions*, edited by Randall Collins (Oxford University Press, 1985/1994).

K. Thompson, *Emile Durkheim*, Tavistock, New York, 1982: an introduction and overview.

R.H. Tawney: *Religion and the Rise of Capitalism* (Penguin, 1926) on Max Weber: a scholarly if rather stodgy account of Weber's theory that traces medieval theories of social ethics through to an examination of the historical evidence for the relationship of capitalism and puritanism.

Max Weber's long-winded theorising is, in fact, summed up in just one work, the *General Economic History*, a series of lectures delivered late in his life, which, although less celebrated than *The Protestant Ethic and the Spirit of Capitalism*, is a much clearer account.

A very readable account of the role of mass marketing in manipulating the purchasing decisions of individuals can be found in J.K. Galbraith's classic work *The Affluent Society* (Penguin, 1999).

## From Absolutism to Fascism

The Nietzsche quotes are from *Ecce Homo*, translated by R.J. Hollingdale (Penguin, London, 1979).

Nietzsche on 'the soul', and God can be found on pages 133–4; on women, on pages 75–6; and on the joy of war, on pages 81 and 111.

Nietzsche attack the Germans for being common on pages 58 and 124. He describes himself as dynamite on page 126, and the 'ecstasy of inspiration' on page 103.

A clear and readable account of Schopenhauer is to be found in Christopher Jannaway, *Schopenhauer*, Past Masters Series, Oxford University Press, 1994.

See Benito Mussolini, *The Doctrine of Fascism* (in Michael Oakeshott editor), *Social and Economic Doctrines of Contemporary*

*Europe*, second edition, New York, 1943) for more on the original fascist vision.

If you want to try some Hegel, a reasonable precaution is NOT to read any of the original works, but to stick to a secondary text, such as Peter Singer's *Hegel* (Oxford, 1983). After all, no one agrees on what Hegel was really saying, so you may as well read an interesting adaptation – as Fukuyama's is.

*Further Reading on Hegel and Nietzsche*

G.W.F. Hegel, *Elements of the Philosophy of Right*, Cambridge University Press, Cambridge, 1991 (first published 1821)

R. Schact, *Nietzsche*, Routledge, London, 1985. A comprehensive survey of Nietzsche's philosophy.


## Maoism

The quotes are all from the little Red Book, the text of which is available on the Internet, but otherwise only with difficulty in the west.

The book itself, however, is a collection of speeches and essays. In China, there are shops selling just Chairman Mao's thoughts, but here we must be content with a few web sites (see below). Once there, try looking at:

'Revolutionary Forces of the World Unite, Fight Against Imperialist Aggression!' (November 1948) from the Selected Works; and 'On Coalition Government' (24 April 1945) from Selected Works, Volume II.

The 'muddleheaded revolutionaries' can be found in a speech 'At the Conference of Cadres in the Shansi-Suiyuan Liberated Area', 1 April 1948.

The reality of class struggle is explained in 'Cast Away Illusions, Prepare for Struggle'; and in a speech at the 'Meeting of the Supreme Soviet of the USSR in Celebration of the 40th Anniversary of the Great October Socialist Revolution' (6 November 1957).

The poisonous weeds of free speech are pulled up in a speech at the 'Communist Party's National Conference on Propaganda Work', 12 March 1957.

Democracy as a way of settling disputes is advanced in 'On the Correct Handling of Contradictions among the People', 1957.

The 'dual nature' of everything, and the 'paper tigers' of imperialist America are described in a 'Talk with the American Correspondent, Anna Louise Strong' in August 1946, whilst the importance of winning the battle for minds is stressed again in 'On Protracted War', May 1938.

The (Marxist) history of mankind is described in 'Premier Chou Enlai's Report on the Work of the Government to the First Session of the Third People's Congress of the People's Republic of China' (now that's something like a title), whilst 'On practice', July 1937, sets out Marxist doctrine generally.

The 'frog in the well' is found in 'On Contradiction', August 1937, and the 'blindfolded man catching sparrows' in 'Rural Surveys', March and April 1941.

Lastly, the dinner party quote comes from an early 'Analysis of the Classes in Society', in 1926.

*Further Reading on Chinese Marxism*

A. Dirlik, *The Origins of Chinese Marxism*, Oxford University Press, New York, 1989

S. Schram, *The Political Thought of Mao Tse-tung*, Praeger, New York, 1963

# Some Internet Sources

### Plato

'Exploring Plato's Dialogues – A Virtual Learning Environment on
the World-Wide Web'
including the text of the *Republic* at:
http://plato.evansville.edu/texts/jowett/republic.htm

### Thomas Hobbes

The full text of *Leviathan*, some further suggested links, an essay on
the context and also a brief exposé (all courtesy of Steven Kreis at
Virginia Tech) are at:
http://www.pagesz.net/~stevek/intellect/hobbes.html
text at:
http://www.vt.edu/vt98/academics/books/hobbes/leviathan

### John Locke

There is a basic version of the Locke text at:
http://sunsite.berkeley.edu/~emorgan/texts/philosophy/1600–1 699/
locke-second-117.txt

### Jean-Jacques Rousseau

Some readers will enjoy seeing Rousseau in French
*Du Contrat Social, Ou Principes du Droit Politique*, at:
http://un2sg4.unige.ch/athena/rousseau/jjr_cont.html

## Marx and Engels

The *Communist Manifesto* and Marxism can be found at:
http://www.hartford-hwp.com/cp-usa/manifesto.html
– courtesy of the Communist Party USA.


## Adam Smith

The *Wealth of Nations* is now kept by Princeton at:
http://www.pei-asia.com/THEORY/SMITH.HTM


## Science of Society

Some ideas and further links of sociological interest are at:
http://www.ac.wwu.edu/~stephan/Sociology/302/comte/comte.html
and:
http://www.abacon.com/sociology/soclinks/sclass.html


## J. S. Mill

The writings of Mill and Bentham on Utilitarianism are at:
http://www.utm.edu/research/iep/text/bentham/benthpri.htm
and:
http://www.utm.edu/research/iep/text/mill/liberty/liberty.htm


## Absolutism

Excerpts from Nietzsche can be read at:
http://www.pagesz.net/~stevek/intellect/niet-res.html


## Mao Zedong

The little Red Book is at:
http://art-bin.com/art/omaotoc.html/intellect/niet-res.html
along with the friendly advice to 'study Chairman Mao's writings,
follow his teachings, and act according to his instructions'.

# Index